DEBATES ON
EVALUATION

DEBATES ON EVALUATION

by
Marvin C. Alkin

with contributions by
Michael Quinn Patton
Carol H. Weiss

with additional participation by
Ross Conner
Ernest House
Michael H. Kean
Jean King
Susan Klein
Alex Law
Milbrey W. McLaughlin

SAGE PUBLICATIONS
The International Professional Publishers
Newbury Park   London   New Delhi

For information address:

SAGE Publications, Inc.
2111 West Hillcrest Drive
Newbury Park, California 91320

SAGE Publications Ltd.
28 Banner Street
London EC1Y 8QE
England

SAGE Publications India Pvt. Ltd.
M-32 Market
Greater Kailash I
New Delhi 110 048 India

Printed in the United States of America

Library of Congress Cataloging-in-Publication Data

Debates on evaluation / [edited by] Marvin C. Alkin : with chapters by
    Michael Q. Patton, Carol H. Weiss.
        p.   cm.
    Includes bibliographical references.
    ISBN 0-8039-3523-4. — ISBN 0-8039-3524-2 (pbk.)
    1. Evaluation research (Social action programs)—Utilization-
-Congresses.   I. Alkin, Marvin C.   II. Patton, Michael Quinn.
III. Weiss, Carol H.
    H62.D35   1990
    361.6'1'072—dc20   90-8278
                                                                            CIP

FIRST PRINTING, 1990

Sage Production Editor: Susan McElroy

Contents

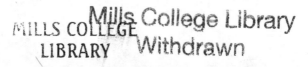

Part III. Evaluation Theory Distinctions: Further Debate

Part IV. Politics and Ethics

Preface

This is a most unusual book. We sensed it; we sensed its possibilities during our conversations in Malibu while looking out the enormous bay windows at the sand and Pacific Ocean stretched just footsteps away. The manuscript's potential was further confirmed to me when the secretary typing the manuscript commented, "You know, this is the most interesting thing I've ever typed. It's not like working on a book—I have the feeling of being right at the meeting." And that is the character that I have attempted to preserve. While some materials have been edited slightly and others deleted, the freshness of the interchange, the side remarks, frivolity, and—most of all—the sincere probing for understanding remain.

"The Event" took place when a group of ten distinguished evaluation professionals gathered together at the UCLA Malibu Conference Facility (a former Norton Simon residence) for three days of informal discussion focused on the topic of evaluation utilization. The purpose of the meeting was to synthesize positions on the current status of evaluation utilization: research, implications for practice, and potential new directions. Like many creative events, the meeting expanded to be far, far more. The frank, informal discussions, within an extremely cordial context, probed the very nature of alternative conceptions of program evaluation. As we addressed issue after issue, differences arose that were largely based on participants' views on the nature of evaluation. As we explored reasons for different interpretations and picked at subtle nuances in interpretations or positions, the depth of understanding of alternative evaluation paradigms came to be perceived. The paradigm debate is exemplified particularly by the interchanges between Carol Weiss and Mike Patton—with various individuals generally subscribing to one or the other of their views and other participants maintaining more of an eclectic position.

Organization of the Book

This book presents the unusual opportunity for readers to come to know an important group of evaluation professionals and to begin to understand them and their viewpoints more fully. What follows is an edited transcript of the actual interchange at the daily sessions. In the editing I have eliminated some cross talk and redundancies, and I have done some minimal "smoothing" of verbal statements. An effort has been made to retain the freshness of the actual conversation so that the reader might have the feeling of being part of an actual discussion.

The discussion has been rearranged so as to allow related topics to be in closer proximity to each other. (An index to the order of the original manuscript is to be found in the Appendix.) Although the discussion was guided by general questions, I must note that it was unstructured in nature and there still exists a certain amount of overlap between sections. The book is divided into four parts. Part I consists of those comments most closely related to the general topic of evaluation utilization. Part II provides more general insights into differences in evaluation theoretic positions of participants. The evaluation paradigm debate of Part II served as a precursor for subsequent articles by Carol Weiss and Michael Patton, which are presented in Part III. Various comments and interchanges dealing with political and ethical issues associated with evaluation—including misuse of evaluation findings—are presented in Part IV. There is a brief review at the end of each major part of the book.

An added feature of the book is the abundant number of "postscripts." I wanted the conference participants to have the opportunity to present further reflections or amplifications of comments made at the meeting. These amplifications take several forms. In some instances, participants felt the necessity of providing clarifying remarks on the meaning of comments made at the meeting. In other instances, participants, sparked by the text, perceived nuances not apparent during the rapid interchange of the meeting. Finally, where references were made to individuals or to books, personal or bibliographical elaboration has been provided within the notes. Additional notes have been contributed by my colleague Fred Ellett, Jr., who has read the entire manuscript and reacted from the position of a knowledgeable evaluation philosopher who did not participate in the meetings. Likewise, Michael Hendricks has also read the manuscript and provided comments from the point of view of an evaluation practitioner.

I have resisted earlier requests from the funding sponsor of the conference to prepare a summary of the meeting and its findings. Instead, I firmly believe that the results are not a synthesis about evaluation or evaluation utilization, but instead what is presented is a penetrating dialogue among reasoning theoreticians and practitioners about the nature of evaluation. There are some conclusions and areas of agreement, but more interesting and informative are the points of contention between participants and the resulting "debate." I have found the dialogue to be rich in insights and to provide a unique perspective into the rationale and thinking process of evaluators. I hope that you agree.

Acknowledgments

There are always a number of people whose important contributions must be acknowledged. The participants in the Malibu seminar have helped to create a unique manuscript by their lively discussion and willingness to express their views openly, freely—and unvarnished. The external commentators have added to our insights by their postscripts. James Burry and Joan Ruskus assisted in the conduct of the Malibu meeting. Gretchen Guiton assisted in the analysis and restructuring of the discussion material. Jana Noel was responsible for the formatting and most of the word processing. Bea Kass transcribed the original transcript of the meeting.

The seminar was sponsored by the National Institute of Education under the auspices of the Center for the Study of Evaluation. My thanks to Eva Baker and Joan Herman of CSE.

I am sincerely grateful to C. Deborah Laughton of Sage Publications, who shared my excitement about the freshness of the manuscript and simply wouldn't let me drop the project when others were frightened off by the format. She has been a source of great encouragement in the preparation of the book. My thanks also to Sara Miller McCune, publisher of Sage Publications, with whom I have had a long-time positive working relationship. She has been at the forefront of recognizing evaluation as a field and aiding in its development. Her willingness to support this kind of nontraditional book is greatly appreciated.

Prologue

Marv Alkin: I would like to welcome you all here. I can't tell you how much I have been looking forward to this. The thought of having a group like this assemble with a loose agenda and opportunities to do some brainstorming has been quite exciting to me personally. When Sue Klein, our NIE project monitor, and NIE first talked with me about putting on some kind of conference or meeting to sum up what we knew about utilization, I think that what they had in mind was a larger conference with speakers and participants. The more I thought about it, the less I liked that idea, and the more the notion of getting a small group of people who had been active in the field, who complemented each other particularly well, and were highly intelligent might prove to be more productive in coming to understand the various forms of evaluation and the problems they are meant to address. I must say, I didn't have this particular conference center in mind at the time that I originally planned this meeting. We might have been other places, like Palm Springs, where they happen to have an incredibly unusual inch of snow.

At any rate, you are here, and welcome! You have all had an opportunity to meet each other, and, of course, many of you knew each other prior to this meeting. But since someone will be taking notes, I would like to go around the room and make introductions, perhaps with a word or two as to how I put the meeting together. This is called "making it

13

appear rational after the fact." Although there was a good deal of rationality, says he.

I'll just go around the table here. Sue Klein is the NIE project monitor, has done some work at NIE related to evaluation and utilization-related kinds of issues. Although Sue is an educational psychologist, and has published in a variety of related fields, she has particular interests personally in sex equity and computer applications in education.

When I put the meeting together, I especially wanted to have people who were working in evaluation utilization. Mike Patton, of course, and Carol Weiss are notable in that regard. Mike has his book on utilization-focused evaluation, which is an attempt to take what he thought he knew about evaluation utilization and convert it into a manual for how evaluators ought to practice. Prior to that, he had done one of the earliest empirical studies on evaluation utilization.

Carol Weiss, of course, is probably the first person to have talked about evaluation utilization in one of her early articles, and has continued to comment on and be one of the leading scholars in that particular field.

Ross Conner . . . I wanted to have an evaluator who had looked at evaluation utilization but who had spent most of his career outside of education. Ross has been an evaluation person at U.C. Irvine, and has looked at evaluation utilization generally, both in the paper that he did in contrasting the various evaluation utilization research studies (not contrasting them, but comparing them, developing a matrix analysis). Ross, most of your work has been where? Criminal justice?

Ross Conner: Lots of places.

Marv Alkin: Lots of places, but primarily not in education, mostly evaluation of other social programs. Thus he provided a nice balance to many of the others here assembled.

Milbrey McLaughlin hasn't written about evaluation utilization per se, but what she has written about has been related to the topic. Her concern has been organizational change—the information processes related to change and so forth.

Jean King has done some very interesting studies on utilization along with several colleagues in New Orleans. She had been doing that work for about a 3- to $3\frac{1}{2}$-year period—has now concluded it—and I believe has some interesting perspectives to offer.

Ernie House . . . I wanted to have someone who was broadly participating in the evaluation community, who had broad understandings of evaluation, its philosophy, and theoretical underpinnings, but who had really not done very much work related to utilization. I thought Ernie could keep us honest.

Ernie House: Fat chance.

Marv Alkin: I wanted also to have several practitioners, people who knew about the way that evaluation is really practiced. Two very reasonable choices presented themselves in the persons of Mike Kean and Alex Law. Mike Kean was director of research and evaluation in the Philadelphia Public Schools and, after that, was at Educational Testing Service, Evanston, and is currently with CTB/McGraw-Hill in Monterey. Beyond that, he wrote an excellent survey article for the *Review of Research in Education* (Vol. X), in which he summarized research on evaluation utilization. So he's a practitioner who has a good deal of familiarity with utilization.

Alex Law is director of research and evaluation at the California State Department of Education. He has been looking at, understanding, and offering his perceptions of evaluation since time immemorial.

Alex Law: 104 years.

Marv Alkin: And beyond that, Alex has thought some about evaluation utilization and written an article related to the topic.

Joan Ruskus and Jim Burry are staff people working with me at CSE. Jim was primarily responsible for doing most of the research on the synthesis sheets that you all received in the mail.

That's my rationale for pulling us all together. It seemed like we could have a very reasonable meeting without a tight agenda, with just the opportunity to, as Milbrey says, "noodle."

Ross Conner: Is that a technical term, Marv?

Marv Alkin: I don't know. Milbrey acquainted me with it about two weeks ago.

Jim Burry: It comes from playing piano, usually. It's a jazz term. One term of noodling.

PART I

Evaluation Utilization

Participant Introductory Comments

Participants

Marvin Alkin: Evaluation utilization refers to the purposeful, planned consequences that result from applying evaluation information to a problem, question, or concern at hand. *Evaluation utilization* refers to the intentional use of evaluation information by those to whom the evaluator directs an evaluation. Use of the evaluation information by those *not* viewed as intended users and/or for purposes not planned and intended is *not* utilization; I would define it as "impact." Meeting the information needs of intended users is the raison d'être of evaluation. Utilization of a well-done evaluation is the goal.

Ross Conner: Utilization begins the first day of an evaluation project. Important kinds of utilization—frequently the most important—occur during the process of planning and implementing an evaluation, not simply with the delivery of a final report.

Ernest House: Two major problems currently confront evaluation practice. First, evaluation is being used more and more as an instrument of control and accountability by increasingly centralized and hierarchical governmental authorities; and, second, the extensive movement of evaluation activities inside the bureaucracies means that evaluation activities are removed from public and peer scrutiny and increasingly subject to the pressures that exist within those organizations. Given these two trends, the possibility exists that evaluation can be used as an instrument for concern rather than as a means of democratic enlightenment.

Michael Kean: As far as I'm concerned, there is no question concerning the utilization of evaluative data. Evaluations must be utilized. One should bear in mind, however, that the decision to *not* utilize data (the

19

measurement equivalent to a presidential pocket veto) is still an issue concerning utilization. In this instance, the alternatives have been reviewed and the decision made is not to make use of any of them. The failure to review and to consider the evaluative results, however, is an instance of nonuse and is inappropriate. Many people are familiar with the conundrum that asks, If a tree falls in the forest and nobody hears it, did it make a sound? If one were to apply this to measurement, they might ask, "If a product/program/process is evaluated, but the information is not considered, did an evaluation actually occur?" I would suggest that it did not.

Jean King: I speak from the perspective of the program. In the best of all possible worlds, people involved in programs would have sufficient resources and friendly assistance enabling them to structure practical evaluation studies on an ongoing basis. The results of one study would suggest possible actions; those involved would discuss these and make changes, dependent on available funds and approval by supervisors; then the next study would look at these changes as well as whatever other issues became important. Over time, program personnel would become knowledgeable users of both the evaluation process and its products. To use the latest buzzword, this is "empowerment" of the highest order as it enables individuals to reflect on and improve their own practice.

My experience suggests that this highly rational chain of events rarely represents the realities of evaluation use at the local level. Systems conduct many evaluations merely because they have to; these studies provide signals of compliance to outside agencies (most typically the federal government or a state department of education), and the outcomes have little to do with future funding or changes in the program. The notion of use implicit in such evaluations is coldly bureaucratic in contrast to the living and breathing notion of someone taking evaluation results in hand, reflecting thoughtfully on them, then doing what can be done in the constraints of a given setting.

Susan Klein: I think that governmental and professional organizations should do much more to help decision makers obtain and use evaluation information. In addition to using a wide variety of techniques to produce evaluative information, they should do much more to help organize the information so that users can make evaluation-informed choices about educational materials, programs, policies, practices, etc. This would mean that in addition to putting evaluation reports into major data banks such as ERIC, procedures should be developed to encourage users to contribute their evaluation information to computer evaluation banks. For example, these evaluation banks could be maintained on state-approved textbooks, promising and exemplary programs, school restructuring practices, etc. Organizations concerned with specific issues should also prepare "evaluation analysis products." These products would be designed to help users understand criteria that they should consider in making their choices, conceptual differences among the types of choices, and some understanding of how their own needs and requirements relate to the choices. These evaluation analysis products would also contain information on promising or exemplary products, programs, and/or practices so that a reader could learn how they address the criteria and their own needs.

Alex Law: The information generated by evaluations should have utility at multiple levels: for the program implementer, the program administrator, and the policymaker(s). Well-done evaluations will, if creditable and timely, convey to these audiences a sense of the program. With this knowledge, continuing or alternative actions can be taken. Many evaluations fail to be utilized because clients feel they are not responsive, lack credibility, or are not timely. Utilization of an evaluation is maximized when the evaluator clearly understands what questions need to be pursued or answered.

Milbrey McLaughlin: "Utility" joins validity and reliability as a standard against which the quality of an evaluation effort is judged. Technical elegance or virtue amounts to little if an evaluation is inaccessible because of language or format, if it fails to address clients' questions or information needs, if it is inattentive to the organizational field in which the evaluation takes place, or if it is too late. Utilization of evaluation poses requirements that are political and bureaucratic as well as substantive. Further, these bureaucratic and political demands sometimes operate at cross-purposes with the scientific requirements of design. At the top of the list as an evaluation gets under way, then, is discussion between evaluator and client about the inevitable trade-offs and compromises necessary to make evaluation as useful, reliable, and valid as possible given the context and constraints within which it is carried out.

Michael Patton: I define *desired use* as intended use by intended users. This means that evaluators must identify *who* the intended users are and then work with them to negotiate the priorities for intended use.

Intended use then becomes the goal of the evaluation and the source of the evaluator's accountability. The evaluation is designed, implemented, and reported based on intended use by intended users. Users and use will vary from evaluation to evaluation. What is constant is that attention to use is the driving force in the evaluation.

Carol Weiss: When I look at that title, it is (in Yogi Berra's immortal words) déjà vu all over again. One of the first academic papers I gave, in 1966, was titled "Utilization of Evaluation," and it proposed the test of alternative strategies to improve utilization. By now we know considerably more about what does and does not improve the use of evaluation, but we still have a way to go.

When we involve potential users in defining the problem and carrying out the study, when we report study results to them early and often and involve them in interpreting the results, when we communicate in intelligible terms using all the graphics of modern communications, we can increase the extent to which people know about and understand the results. We may even increase the use of results—marginally. But program decisions hinge on many things besides information, and even exemplary cooperation and involvement are not likely to make evaluation results the *primary* basis of program and policy decisions.

What we have learned in recent years, however, is that the direct and immediate application of evaluation findings to program decisions is not the only kind of use. Decision makers report that they value research and evaluation findings because these findings provide news; they alert people to new ideas; they show alternative ways of thinking about problems; they alter what is taken for granted as inevitable and what is seen as subject to change. Evaluation influences people's understanding of what the program has been doing. It widens the range of options they consider. It shifts priorities and helps decision makers focus on key problems. In effect, it can help to change what people think about and how they think about it. This kind of *conceptual* use is an important contribution which, in the long run, can lead—and has led—to significant program reform.

Discussants

Frederick Ellett, Jr.:   Given my conception of evaluation and my view of the political and ethical aspects of evaluation, I *reject* as being too simplistic the question "How should or can evaluations be utilized?" First, the question leads one to expect a general answer for all social-political contexts. But I maintain that differences in the particular social-political contexts lead to differences in what the evaluation should (and can) do. (I maintain, by the way, that the relevant sense of *should*—in "what an evaluation *should* do"—implies that the evaluator *can* do it.) Second, the question leads one to expect that evaluation itself is a rather specific (or homogeneous) kind of activity. But as my conceptualization of evaluation activities implies, there are *many* related but quite distinct kinds of activities that an evaluator, as an evaluator, could do. The important question should not ask about evaluation in general but about the specific *kinds* of evaluation activities (and their advantages and disadvantages in various contexts). Finally, the question suggests that there is a simple and general characterization of "evaluation *utilization*." But as my conceptualization of evaluator activities suggests, the evaluator acting in a particular context may be doing so for many purposes and with several views about the *utility* (or usefulness) of performing the activities. What is needed here is a careful explication of the kinds (or types) of utility and the contextual advantages (and disadvantages) of each kind. Thus the simple question must be replaced by a comprehensive, complex inquiry which is sensitive to the many social-political contexts, to the various kinds of evaluation activities, and to the various kinds of utility in order to provide a meaningful answer to requests about what the evaluator should do.

Michael Hendricks: Regarding evaluation utilization, I have used the same definition for the past ten years: Our evaluations are utilized when "the findings and recommendations from our evaluation are *considered seriously* by persons in a position to act on our information if they choose to do so." On the surface, this criterion seems too simple, but, in reality, it is quite difficult. Who are the proper audiences? What matters to them? What will they find credible? How can we best communicate our information? In my experience, these are the critical issues surrounding utilization.

1

Utilization Factors

Impact, Conditions of Use

Marv Alkin: There is no formal agenda or paper presentations or any of that kind of thing. I have three agenda items that I hope that we will accomplish within the several days. One is to look at what we think we know about evaluation utilization (including what we know about factors associated with utilization). Second is to consider what are the further research development, training, etc. needs to better understand evaluation utilization. Third, at some point in the proceedings, I would like us to discuss what we think are the implications for practice of these past 5, 7, 10 years that people have been looking at evaluation utilization. What differences could and should this research make? I hope we don't come to the conclusion that it hasn't made a damn bit of difference, but if we do, we hopefully would have had a good time at least. . . .[1] So, I would propose that maybe a way to start would be to take the first of the goals and have that as a topic for this evening. What is it that we think we know about factors associated with evaluation utilization?

Carol Weiss: I can't imagine resolving the question of what we know about evaluation utilization before 10:00 p.m. tonight.

Marv Alkin: Do you think we know that much?

Carol Weiss: I think we each know something and probably won't agree with each other.

Marv Alkin: What do you know, Carol?

1. *Ellett:* Not so. We should ask why it hasn't made any difference. Perhaps the answer to this question would enable us to make a difference in the future.

Carol Weiss: I think I know that there is relatively little direct and immediate application of evaluation results to programmatic decisions. I think probably you would agree. I think I also know that there is a considerable amount of use of evaluation results and research results in general in policy formulation and program development, in conceptual longer-term impact. I also think that the political and organizational context has a very strong effect on what is used, how it's used, and how much of it is used.[2]

Milbrey McLaughlin: Do you have some notions about the nature of the political and social contexts that are most related to conditions of use?

Carol Weiss: Yes. Very briefly, I would say that probably the most salient factors have to do with the distribution of interests of various groups and factions, the ideological commitments of the participating groups, and the nature of their previous information. By *previous information*, I refer to what they know prior to the evaluation from their own experience and from other sources of information; from reading, from conversations, from conferences, from books—all the various sources of information that people have. With experience probably being the most important way that they understand how the world works and the program works. I would say that those three things—interest, ideology, and information—set each person's limits of receptivity. Beyond that, it's the organizational processes—the way organizations work, the programmatic organization (the decision rules of the organization, the information channels, the standard operating procedures of the organization)—which influence which information is taken into account and how it's used. And that's what I think.

Evaluator-Influenced Utilization

Marv Alkin: Carol, I have had the impression that perhaps you and Mike might disagree on the extent to which the evaluator, as an active participant in the process, can influence the extent of utilization. I wonder if you would comment on that.

2. *Hendricks:* I wonder how Carol—and the other participants—are defining *evaluation*. I personally use a broad definition which includes everything from multiyear randomized experiments to scanning the Letters to the Editor. Obviously, "utilization" issues vary enormously along this continuum.

Carol Weiss: I have thought about that a lot, actually, because I use Mike's books in my courses. And I think we probably sound as if we disagree more than we do, because he's talking about decisions made at the program level and I tend to be talking about decisions made at the policy level. I'm talking about decisions made at some level removed from the actual evaluator and evaluation.

Marv Alkin: So you're saying that part of the perceived differences in your viewpoints is related to the extent to which the evaluator is distant from the decision makers/policymakers; it being greater at a policy level and less at a program level.[3] You would maintain that evaluators are able to develop greater interpersonal relations at a program level.

Carol Weiss: I think that's part of it. I think many of the critical decisions are made somewhere else. They're made not by the program that's being evaluated, but at other levels. For example, other school districts may or may not undertake similar programs if a program proves to be successful or unsuccessful, or decisions are made by people in state legislatures who decide on allocations of money and appropriations; they're made in Washington, and so on.

I'm agreeing with your statement, that part of the difference is that I am talking about these other decisions made beyond the purview of the immediate program being evaluated. In those cases, the evaluator does have less opportunity to talk with people, to interact with people, to engage people in dialogue. Other times the people that the evaluator engages in dialogue are not necessarily those that are going to make the more important decisions. I don't think that evaluators frequently can gauge who is going to be making the decisions that have the most effect on the program. We're not going to be very successful at identifying potential decision makers in advance, because so many people have a spoon to stir in the policy pot.[4]

Marv Alkin: Mike, I gather that, with respect to the possibility of identifying potential decision makers in advance, you might disagree with that statement . . .

---

3. *Hendricks:*   My experience at the Department of Health and Human Services tells me that the line between "policy" and "program" can often be a lot fuzzier than we're led to believe.
4. *Ellett:*   For example, who effectively controls the legislative decision process is often unknown. Those who are effective at one time may not be at another, etc.

Mike Patton: Trying to sort it out on the spur of the moment, it seems to me that what Carol is describing is probably a slightly different strategy than how I would be likely to work. Let me explain part of the difference. By the way, I agree with Carol and Marv's statements. Most of my work has been directed to the local level and clearly, as the number of potential decision makers and information users expands, the possibility of giving one person a piece of information and having impact is diffused.

I think that the way I work would affect that. My guess is that Carol is more likely to be problem oriented and I'm more likely to be person oriented. Therefore, even at a national level or a state level, I would tend to have a client on whom I would have impact, rather than a problem on which I would have impact. My gauge of impact would be on that client rather than on that problem. What you're saying [Carol] applies more to solution of problems or to writing specific legislation or to a particular action. My gauge of impact is more likely to be on my client, who is within that larger stew, more identifiable and therefore more manageable.

What Constitutes Utilization

Mike Patton: I would take credit, in other words, whether or not the legislation happened, if the person for whom I was doing it and worked with ended up doing something. That is still utilization, even if, in the short term, the larger picture didn't get changed as a result of the evaluation.

Carol Weiss: Even if the change were simply attitudinal, or modifications in that individual—but resulting in no legislation—you would still view that as a positive instance of utilization?

Mike Patton: It would depend upon what the findings were and to what extent the potential actions, or lack of them, were suggested by what was going on. The likelihood of some kind of change or action by the clients, I think, can be determined to a great extent up front by how you define the problem. But I would tend to define the problem *after* having identified the people, rather than identify the problem and then find the people who care about the problem. That's probably as much a style of work as it is a general prescription.[5] I don't think of it so much as suggesting that's the way it always will be; it's most often the way that I manage what I do and how I think about what I do.

Orientation to Users

Ross Conner: Would you generalize it, Mike, to say that if we agree that use has not been all we want, that part of the reason is because many evaluators have tapped in at the wrong level? They haven't tied into the people,[6] but have tied into the problem instead.

Mike Patton: It seems to me that tying into the problem may diffuse the responsibility for what happens a little bit more than tying into specific people, and may, by its nature, give the appearance of more of an intellectual process than it is. There's something different about grappling with an issue and trying to understand it than understanding the cast of characters and how to move those people along. My approach comes closer to an organizational change orientation than it does to the solving of conceptual problems about what ought to happen. For me, what ought to happen is never separate from the people for whom it's going to happen and who are going to do it. So I start with people, and that leads to the issues—and usually changes how the issues get defined.[7]

Press/Accountability for Utilization

Michael Kean: Perhaps the reason that evaluation use hasn't been all that perhaps we'd like it to be is because there hasn't really been a press

---

5. *Ellett:*   A "style of work" is quite different from a general "prescription." Perhaps society can allow some to do Michael Patton evaluations, but somebody has to do Carol Weiss large-scale evaluations if we want rational policy decisions. So, Patton could prescribe generally.
6. *Alkin:*   I presume that "tied into the people" means identified clients and started working with them.
7. *Ellett:*   Patton seems to think that one can first determine what ought to be done, and then worry about the organizational changes. Surely what ought to be done depends on what can be done organizationally.

to make it so; there hasn't been an accountability for use.[8] Look at school districts and consider why evaluations take place. At least until recently, historically, there were certain mandated reasons for evaluation, and there was little said that data use would be part of that mandate. It was a federal requirement that Title I or Chapter I programs be evaluated. It may have been implicit, it may have been actually in the regs—that the findings should be actually used. But ultimately, it was: "Is there an evaluation report for the Chapter I programs in district X or Y? Can you hold up a physical piece of paper, and has it been done properly?" That's the major initial reason—or has been historically—why utilization has not occurred. Beyond that there are certain people that have been interested in utilization, many of them in this room. And as one discusses and considers it, it only makes sense that utilization occur. On the other hand, initially, there's no organization precedent [for utilization].

Alex Law: I would disagree with that. One of the early motivating factors in Title I was the constant press that this information was essential for federal refunding decisions. Whether that was true or not, it existed. The explicit promise was that it was going to be used for funding decisions. It was used as a carrot with local districts.

Jean King: But typically, the final report was written in August-September, when refunding decisions had already been made in the spring.

Credibility of Evaluator

Alex Law: Let me pose another issue. One of the critical factors of use is the credibility of the person or the institution that is doing the programmatic evaluation. What's the extent to which the credibility variable—which both Mike and Marv have looked at—continues to be an important factor related to potential impact at the policy level?

Carol Weiss: I think it remains very important. I think that testing of information goes on at the policy level . . . because people are swamped with information, and they try to sift through it by taking what has been

---

8. *Ellett:* Good point; those evaluators who should be interested in *rational* policymaking are likely to be frustrated until the various levels become firmly committed to seriously evaluating their programs.

produced to those with whom they associate (both expert and nonexpert). They judge the credibility, in terms of the quality of research, through this network of contacts. It's critical. Nobody wants to be caught out on a limb with a study that is flawed. That just undermines people's faith in them.[9]

Marv Alkin: So when you say "a study" that is allegedly flawed, you're referring to the credibility of the evalua*tion* and not the initial credibility of the evalua*tor* or of the evaluating *agency.*

Carol Weiss: I think, as time and space increase, these distinctions between evaluator and evaluating organization become less important. In a sense they get dissociated from the idea. The fact, say, a notion that individual educational plans for handicapped kids consume much more time and effort than they're worth is a generalization that comes out of several studies; people have forgotten what studies those were. And it's the idea that they test: Is that true or isn't that true? And they will go around and check that out with groups and advocates and experts. So initially, I think, the evaluator and the evaluating organization give the basic ground for taking the single study seriously, but after time passes and after the ideas spread, creep, and diffuse into the policy arena, then it's the study and source of the data and the quality of the research from which the data are drawn that are most important.

Jean King: I think we need to separate the policy discussion from local school discussion. My experience in a large urban system is that the quality of the study doesn't matter. I have seen terrible studies in cases where people were so excited to have some information that they used this [study], even though methodologically we'd all retch. In other cases, well-designed, "good" studies were not used.[10] The question of quality and perhaps the credibility of the evaluation is meaningful to policymakers who have somebody who can evaluate: Is this a good study? Should you take this seriously? The people at the school level

---

9. *Ellett:* Carol Weiss describes the problem for a legislator studying a large-scale program, where the legislator probably doesn't understand research methods (and so on). So, the legislator must go with the "experts." (What else can he or she do?)
10. *Ellett:* When King refers to "good studies" not being used, what does she imply a well-designed evaluation to be? To consider the questions of interest? To consider the various outcomes? Or just to be statistically/experimentally "valued"?

don't have individuals like that around typically. So I think that those who are interested in using information will take whatever they can, and those who aren't interested won't.[11]

Marv Alkin: You're saying that people at the program level have fewer sources of reliable information that impact upon their decision. Do you really believe that?

Jean King: It's not that they have fewer sources of information, but that they have no way to evaluate, often, the quality of the information they're getting. They aren't trained in methodology. They don't like funding evaluations; typically, these take away money and time from kids.

Marv Alkin: But they still have alternate sources of information that play heavily upon potential decisions.

Michael Kean: Yes, but it depends on the nature of the question. If it's a policy question, then I think, Carol, you're on target. On the other hand, if it's a question about program X or Y—do we continue to fund it next year or do we add three additional schools to this particular program?[12]—then they're going to listen to the local evaluator, if he or she or if that particular office has credibility, even if the existing pervasive literature across the country may be somewhat different. And unfortunately they've been trained to do that, because they view that their situation is always a special situation. And sure, experts X or Y across the country have found these results, but they don't know New Orleans or they don't know Philadelphia, so what do they know? I'm not saying that's as it should be, but I'm saying I think that's the way it is.

Ernie House: And I think that's what the situation should be, myself. Carol's right that the interest, ideology, and the background of the people who are supposed to implement the decision make a difference. I'd like to ask a question. What about the interest, ideology, and background of the evaluator? Do those make any difference? What

---

11. *Hendricks:*   There's the famous (and, by now, tired) saying that policymakers use evaluations (or data) like a drunk uses a lamppost—more for support than for illumination.
12. *Ellett:*   What does Kean take a policy question to be? (Kean seeks to differ from Weiss.) Kean takes the policy question to be about whether (or not) to have, say, a science education sequence. Then the school board must decide whether to use X or Y science education programs. Kean is saying that the local level does not have good information about whether to choose X or Y (it is a *comparative* choice).

about the fit between the evaluator's interest and the ideology, background of those who implement it? Isn't that what we mean by credibility? If you have the same kind of ideology and interests and background that the evaluator has, then you may believe in the evaluator, maybe? The portrait we have here, from what's been said, is that we've got people who have ideologies; that is, people who are making decisions, they have interests, they have ideologies, and they have backgrounds. Those evaluation clients have to fit what those people believe. That's a picture I got. I agree with that to a certain degree. What about the ideology and interest and the background of the evaluator and the fit between that and what the decision makers have? I don't like the portrayal of the evaluators (and I don't believe the portrayal of the evaluators) being neutral in these matters. You wouldn't think they would be, would you? They would have their own ideology, and their own interests, and their own kinds of backgrounds, in a sense. And the more those fit with policy people or local people, the more those fit together, then I would think, the more there would be personal rapport[13] between the evaluator and those people.

Mike has a kind of a grass-roots, populist orientation. So he can go work with these local policy people, because that's the type of person he is. And lots of our evaluation colleagues have much more of an elitist approach to the world, and it seems to me, in some ways, that they would work better with higher-level policymakers. I'm just wondering if that's a possibility. It seems to me that there's some matching here, between the orientations of the evaluators and the decision makers. Some of the differences are really differences in ideologies and interests of the evaluators and the people implementing the evaluations.

. . .

Characteristics of the Evaluator

Michael Kean: I'd like to go into a discussion of the characteristics of an evaluator that enables him or her to be effective. I'm convinced that the real key variable in utilization is the individual, whether it's the evaluator himself or herself or the evaluation manager, depending on what level of information is being provided and at what level a decision

13. *Ellett:*   "Personal rapport" is not "credibility."

is to be made. And there are a lot of, I won't say unmeasurable, but difficult to measure kinds of factors related to that individual—personality measures or human interaction measures. Really, I'm convinced that what are important are the personal qualities of that individual and his or her interrelationship with the decision makers or the decision influencer or influencers who may not be the decision makers. The evaluator's ability to identify in advance, hopefully far in advance, who those key decision influencers are going to be and tailor, not the evaluation, but the information that's going to be provided to those influencers is critical.[14] The evaluator has to work at providing this information to the key decision influencers at the right time—almost like cheerleading the information through.

. . .

Marv Alkin: We have been using Mike [Patton] as the prime example of the kind of evaluator who would have tremendous impact, and you commented on the necessity for understanding better the characteristics, not in some strict demographic sense, of what makes someone like Mike effective. What are the things he does? What are the attributes of his personality? What are his various capacities? The ways in which he operates? Can we understand them? Are they necessary, and can they be replicated?

Michael Kean: Exactly. I think we can understand these characteristics. And yes, I do think they're necessary.[15] Now, as to whether we can replicate them: some perhaps—and some I think are very difficult. To give you an example: When I took over the office in Philly, almost a dozen years ago, the office was large, well funded, and not very well accepted out in the field, in the schools, for a lot of different reasons. And I spent a bit of time in the beginning going out, as the new executive director of that office, observing, and talking to principals and teachers. And I was fairly new and didn't have any reputation, good or bad, at that point, so I think I got a bit more useful information than I probably would have gotten six months later. I also observed some of my own

---

14. *Hendricks:* Is there a main effect here or an interaction effect? That is, are *traits* important or are *complementary traits*? If the latter, must an evaluator be an emotional chameleon, changing to fit the intended client?

15. *Ellett:* Are they *necessary*? Or just highly conducive to their ends? Need every good evaluator have every one of them? Most important, they are necessary to accomplish what? (What *kind* of utilization?)

people, my then-new staff, going out and practicing their trade or their craft or whatever it was. And there were some interesting things that I noticed. Those evaluators that were viewed as most helpful and were most easily accepted in schools were the less threatening, less formal. There were little things, like an evaluator coming into a school and saying, "I'm Dr. Kean from the Office of Research and Evaluation, and I'm here to look at program X," as opposed to coming in and saying, "I'm Mike and we've been working on program X, etc." And just simple things like that. They shouldn't really make that much of a difference, but it made a huge difference. Now sure, you can train a person not to say, "I'm Dr. So-and-so" when meeting the principal, but there are a lot of other things that are less obvious and less trainable.

Marv Alkin: Of course, the trick is to maintain a low level of formalism while still maintaining credibility.

Michael Kean: Well, again, it depends on who you're dealing with.

Marv Alkin: Right, so you're not only looking at each of these dimensions individually; you're looking at the interactions between these dimensions. And that's where the really interesting questions come in.

Milbrey McLaughlin: It seems that one step that can be taken is not to pattern Patton, but train evaluators to pay attention to the communication process, to the understanding of the possible problem, to the . . .[16]

Alex Law: Oh. But to add to the conundrum, what do our training institutions turn out? They turn out people who know how to do analysis of variance.

Milbrey McLaughlin: You're overgeneralizing.

Carol Weiss: You really are.

[overtalk]

Mike Patton: There's another perspective on what we're discussing, I think, and let me see if I can get at it a different way. It seems to me that what evaluators need to be clear about are the desired outcomes of the evaluation—what is meant by use in a particular evaluation—and then develop the evaluation process to achieve that use. How an evalu-

---

16. *Ellett:*   What purpose in what situations is the evaluator trying to achieve using what procedures? (Patton's talk about "processes" is a fancy way of talking about strategies or procedures.)

ator facilitates use, how one is going to get there, is going to be very much a matter of individuality. So you can't tell people in absolute terms all of the ways of behaving in the process: Don't use your first name or your doctorate. I present myself one way some times and another way other times, depending on who the group is and whether or not they're all wearing three-piece suits or in a wilderness setting or something else. So it is a match that one strives for, and the thing that you keep focused on is what you want to come of the process. If evaluators understand that they need to show respect for the people they're working with, the way you show that and what that's going to look like and the things you say are going to be different—all the time, every time. But it seems to me the outcome that one wants is to communicate that you have respect for those people somehow, that you're interested in them, that you care about them, that you understand them. And different people will get at that in different ways. It's not modeling any one style, but it is understanding where you're trying to get to. That's real situational responsiveness.

Alex Law: What you've described is almost a clinical model of evaluation. And I . . . I guess I'm old and cynical and pessimistic, but I . . .

Carol Weiss: Well, let me give you another example. It seems to me that some of the most influential evaluations have been influential in places that never saw the evaluator. Some of the ideas about whether federal models of school improvement have been picked up and maintained in local school districts came from the studies of Berman and McLaughlin and were used by hundreds of people all over the country who never set eyes on Berman and McLaughlin. [17] And yet that study had a great deal of impact. So it seems to me that this local interaction is important, and I've really gained some respect for it. But a lot of the most important uses of evaluation take place elsewhere. For example, the evaluators who looked at bilingual programs in Quebec. People who never set eyes on the evaluators heard that there were some good programs. They couldn't even have known who did the evaluation, but the word got through that somebody had found a successful program. So let's not lose sight of the fact that a good study or interesting data or at least hopeful findings have an appeal and an attraction that also encourage use.

17. Berman, P., & McLaughlin, M. (1978). *Federal programs supporting educational change* (Vol. 8). Santa Monica, CA: Rand Corporation.

Jean King: The question comes, though, How do we do studies that will become those? We can look backwards and say, Yes, that one really made it.

[overtalk]

Jean King: Yet, to look forward . . . that's very tough. At least we can say the evaluator will act a certain way. That we can control more.

Michael Kean: There's also the fact that, for every study like the one you just cited, there's probably a dozen equally good ones that have never seen the light of day, unfortunately. And if there in fact had been, I would guess, a champion—someone conversant with the study who had taken an active role in making the decision maker more receptive to the data—then perhaps things would have been different.

Alex Law: I'm not arguing at all. Let me give you another anecdote type of thing. An external evaluator did a study for school improvement programs in California. These evaluators had a lot of credibility and a lot of people read the report. Not much happened about this; pretty much status quo. We did an internal study with some graduate students, which started out to be a very modest study and grew beyond all proportions. The original thrust of it was to determine what changes were taking place in the high schools as a result of the implementation of proficiency standards. As the investigators got into the school, more questions presented themselves and they enlarged the studies. And we came up with certain kinds of findings which had a profound policy impact on what is going on now. For example, we found that more students failed to graduate from high school because they hadn't had the appropriate course work offerings than failed because of the test. We found out the school population is generally divided into thirds: the bright group, whose curriculum is prescribed by the University of California . . . no problem . . . ; the lowest group, whose curriculum really centers around remediation; but the large middle group wanders aimlessly. That then led to the conceptualization now being put in place of a general core kind of curriculum. So the modest study came to be used in a significant way. That's just one of the findings that had an impact.

. . .

Evaluator as Promoter

Alex Law: There's another aspect that's being talked about, and that's the evaluator as the promoter of his product, which again is sometimes referred to as the Fuller Brush man approach. A few years ago, we were doing an evaluation of migrant student programs, which was like all other special services evaluations. Now, if you're a Title I kid, you get a menu of services. If you're a migrant kid, also under Title I, you get a menu, but it's a shorter menu of services. It's not the full package, although ideally it should be. So we found out there are really great discrepancies in health services between what the migrant students received, and a variety of other social benefit kinds of programs. A key legislator felt bad things were happening to migrants. We sent the evaluation to his legislative consultant and said, Hey, look what we found. This is the one and only time in all of my experience that language of an evaluation report was literally lifted and became legislation. So here is an impact through promotion. I took it in my hot little hands right to a staff member, who had an interest in this particular target group. I peddled it.[18]

. . .

Issues in Utilization

Jean King: How do we, in thinking about evaluation use and trying to study evaluation use, get at the various issues?

Ernie House: What comes to mind for me is the study of Berman and McLaughlin, you know, the Rand studies—the timing of those was critical—plus their sponsorship. They were sponsored by the federal government. They were strongly plugged into the network at that point in time, and this network had produced a finding of failure and so everybody was perceiving failure. And Berman and McLaughlin offered an alternative explanation. Their timing was critical. They also

---

18. *Hendricks:*   This raises an interesting question of when or if an evaluator should become an advocate for change. Does discovering a problem morally obligate us to seek its resolution?

did a good job disseminating the findings. Those findings were plugged into the Harvard-Washington network, and to those people who determine policy. I don't think that stuff had much effect at the local level. The local people are not concerned with that. It affected them eventually, because the policy came in and . . .

Milbrey McLaughlin: You know, I have to disagree with you, because I have yet to go to a meeting—and this is what, eight years later?—even like the ERS[19] meeting in San Francisco . . . that someone doesn't come up and say, I'm so-and-so from such-and-such school, I've just got to tell you . . . . And I'm amazed. It's beyond all proportion that the findings of those studies have affected people at the school level.

Ernie House: Well, but most people who go to the ERS meeting are not school people . . .

Milbrey McLaughlin: No, no. This was a school principal.

[overtalk]

Ernie House: There's a real selection thing. Maybe I'm absolutely wrong about this. But I still think, even if that did happen, this study was picked up not merely because of the intrinsic way the study was done, but the timing and the sponsorship were critical in that particular setting. And Paul and Milbrey being plugged into the policy network.

Marv Alkin: But the success of that study was not merely because of the methodology, but because of the attempts by the individuals who performed it, to do so in a mode comparable to the collaborative kind of style that Mike describes at a local level—in terms of focusing on key people, understanding where they're coming from, and so on. From some things that I have read about the study as well as based on a conversation I had with Paul, it seemed to me that's what happened.

Milbrey McLaughlin: But it's also a function of methodology. I can't tell you how we had to battle to do case studies. And I remember people—not you or any of your friends, of course—who said, "Don't tell us about this process stuff, you know, these case studies, this qualitative data, yuk." And the only way we were able in 1973 to justify doing the casework was to tell them that we would use the case studies to validate the survey, and that was fine.

19. Evaluation Research Society (now the American Evaluation Association).

Ernie House: You say . . . it was case data, but I think that the significant thing was that you shifted to a political perspective. At that time you were saying, why doesn't this work? Because the districts are going to negotiate with the federal government; they're not going to take these guidelines literally. You shift to a different explanatory framework there. And that's why it was a seminal study, because it represents a shift. You had to fight the government, as we usually do, to make that shift.

Milbrey McLaughlin: The kind of data that people were able to connect with wasn't that . . . it was a methodological choice. They were kind of moving away from the beta weights and the *F* tests.

Mike Patton: Carol, do you have a sense that there's any hope of figuring out whether there's some depository of variables somewhere that are knowable?

Carol Weiss: I'm not terribly hopeful. I think that each policy arena has its own cast of characters and its own set of interests and its own organizational structure and its own communication problems. I think one by one we can probably get a better fix on which study makes a splash, but I don't think in general there's a crossover across fields or across time. I think it changes.

Ernie House: If you take Charlie Murray's report, [20] you know, in which he says all Great Society programs are no good. All the conservative columnists are now citing this book. Now, if you read the book from a social scientist point of view and from a methodological point of view, it's awful. It's an awful book. But you have a whole establishment there, waiting to say, These federal programs are no good. The entire Great Society was a loss. The Blacks lost their incentive during that period of time, because we were supporting them, which is what Charlie's book says. And he says we have to eliminate those programs so they'll get back to work again. Now, you know there are a lot of people out in Washington waiting to hear that message. So there's a receptivity there. If you read the book carefully and see what's behind

20. Murray, C. A. (1984). *Losing ground: American social policy, 1950-1980.* New York: Basic Books.

it, you'd probably be appalled. But when Pat Buchanan writes a column, he says, Brilliant, brilliant, superb . . . [21]

Mike Patton: One of the kinds of scenarios that seems to accompany utilization is the confirmatory scenario, where somebody sort of validates at the right time the paradigm shift and gives that credence in a research mode.

Carol Weiss: I can give you another example of a different type of scenario . . . where people are desperate for anything that works. People in schools, for years and years, who just did not know how to help kids learn better, and along came the effective schools research. . . . And it created hope, and there was something you could do that would really improve achievement.

Jean King: The problem oftentimes is the political setting. People simply can't act. I don't know how we deal with that. But then it goes back to trying to understand the evaluator and the user. But what do you do in those situations?

Ernie House: I don't know. In some ways it's so different from some of the other things we were talking about at a different level. You have a set of policymakers here—let's say, the president and his henchmen— who have a certain mentality and way they view the world. You get a study 'that fits into that mentality. It's consistent with the framework that they employ, and there's a sense in which there's a receptivity there already. And we also have people in social science who are willing to provide that, to meet that market. They take social science data, and even if it doesn't fit, they fix it up in such a way that it will meet the needs of those powerful decision makers.[22] Which may be one of the saddest things you can say about the social sciences. Now here we get information which is usable, right?

. . .

---

21. *Ellett:*   But it has a good and a bad side. One way it can "confirm" prejudices and biases, in another way it can "confirm" new facts and insights; "receptivity" depends on what one already believes!

22. *Hendricks:*   Politicians, whether Republican or Democrat, will *always* use data for their own purposes. To pretend otherwise is to miss an opportunity to understand their world.

Questions of User Concern

Carol Weiss: Well, I think if you have a little study that focuses on what is really going on it can make a big difference. For example, I know of a local study of deinstitutionalization of mental health patients in one community, and how badly they were faring in the community. Deinstitutionalization was the new policy that supposedly provided a higher quality of life to patients. But this study found that deinstitutionalized patients were not getting very much service, they were kind of wasting away in these group homes, sitting in front of the television set, taking their medication and zonked out much of the day, living on welfare, and not very much better off than they were back in the big mental hospitals. That study had a lot of effect, because it seemed to represent what was true, not only in this one community, but in the nation. And the people in Washington began to think and reevaluate the need for upgrading and expanding community services for people who have left the hospitals.[23] And I think that study sort of crystallized, again, a lot of unease and discontent and concern that people were feeling, but didn't have an occasion to think about together.

Jean King: Well, it seems like you're saying that this unease, this unrest, this uncertainty exists and then a study is done that either tells them what to do—for example, the existing policy isn't right, if you're going to deinstitutionalize people, make sure you provide them with adequate services. Or there's unease because I'm doing something and I know that it's wrong because social science tells me it's wrong. And suddenly a study comes and legitimates it. So what they have in common is this sense of unrest. And can we say then that as evaluators, we go out and look for unrest and say, Ah-ha, now is the time to do a little study on . .

Marv Alkin: Well, that's not a bad statement, because when you say, "Go out and look for unrest," you're really saying, "Go out and look for places where there are people who have real questions." The key is to find people—clients—who have real questions, instead of questions

---

23. *Hendricks: Which* people in Washington were concerned by this study? Budget analysts? Program staff? If only the latter, how might the former be persuaded?

that are just being stated and about which they don't really care about finding an answer.

Mike Patton: That uncertainty, if there's some dissonance about it, becomes unrest. It seems to me almost necessary for people to really get involved in what's happening.[24]

24. *Hendricks:*   But don't we also have an obligation to *create* some uncertainty when none exists but should? In other words, to shake some common misconceptions that are held too widely?

2

Other Utilization Issues

"Information" for "Decision Making"

Carol Weiss: This [information for decision making] is such a complex area. We're talking about decision making as if information leads to decisions. Decisions are the product of enormous numbers of interacting variables: how much money is available, who owes whom a favor, what groups are going to have the final say, what other decisions are being made at the same time. You know how complicated any fairly simple policy decision gets to be. Who happens to turn up at the critical meetings, how much time there is before something has to be done; so many things besides information. Even the best and the greatest evaluations only minimally affect how decisions get made.[1]

Jean King: I'm inclined to agree, but would like to go back and pick up on something that Marv said. That is, we're talking about different kinds of information here. The information resulting from the evaluation study is only one kind of information. The kind of information the practitioner has is another kind. It's an information about particulars, and that information will often (or perhaps usually) be more "correct" for what the practitioner has to do than the information the evaluation person supplies him.

Marv Alkin: Or more "relevant," because the evaluation provides some probable information, whereas the practitioner has a much better, richer sense of the immediate and local situation.

Jean King: I want to say "correct." It will be more relevant, but it will also be more correct for what the practitioner has to do.

1. *Hendricks:* I agree with Carol completely, and I often claim we're lucky to affect 10% of the discussion surrounding a specific decision.

Milbrey McLaughlin: When you talk about the information that the evaluator is likely to provide, you're generalizing about the nature of the evaluator, and the kind of evaluator he is and the way he or she operates. That generalization may mask some of the differences in information presentation, and credibility, that could make a world of difference in terms of the acceptability of potential information. So the portrait you painted is not of an evaluator like Mike, but an evaluator who is more research oriented. That's the kind of picture that came to my mind as you spoke.

Jean King: You're absolutely right.

Milbrey McLaughlin: But I think Jean is saying that there are such great differences between the kind of decision: whether to extend a program for the gifted in one school district, as compared to what to do about the funding levels for Chapter I in Washington. They're different animals. Let's not talk about them at the same time, under the same roof.

Susan Klein: I think one of the basic problems, at least in my mind, is that we're talking about all kinds of different information from evaluations. In some cases, people are talking about specific information that's relevant to a particular program, and in others they may be talking about bringing in a research-knowledge base.

Marv Alkin: I think that somehow or other in our discussions we'd better define where we're coming from. In addition to making policy decisions and program decisions, we're referring to different information bases, in different ways, for different purposes. What's the sense of the group about the extent to which we ought to make a group decision to try to focus on program-level decisions versus policy decisions, in order to make the subsequent discussion more focused?

Jean King: I would guess that both, in most instances, need to be taken into consideration. For the purpose of this discussion, you may want to say, let's discuss both, maybe segmenting them. I don't know if we can.

Michael Kean: I think something that has characterized evaluation at the local level has been a much greater focus on the program question. Is there any suggestion that maybe that's the way it ought to be? I don't particularly disagree with that. However, if the broader-scale questions are completely shunted aside and never paid any attention to, then perhaps that's not the way it should be. We evaluated early childhood programs for years, and at one point, had about 25 full-time evaluators in Philadelphia examining six different models of Follow Through. But nobody ever asked a broader question about the overall rightness of early childhood programs. We looked at each individual program and whether it was working and whether it was meeting its individual objectives. We looked at policy implicitly, I think, but that broader question was never raised . . .

Milbrey McLaughlin: But Marv, how do you then integrate the point that Carol made earlier this afternoon, that not all use is the result of a one-to-one relationship between evaluator and evaluatee?

. . .

Marv Alkin: I think one of the important points that's emerged out of our discussions this afternoon—and indeed your own studies support this—is that there is a need for those who are doing the evaluation to communicate at an early stage and not be in a situation where they have to say, We've got this report—what are we going to do to link? So I guess I'm not terribly persuaded by the applicability of that model . . . particularly for program evaluations. Milbrey, I think your own policy work demonstrates that there may be more applicability of the linkage model for policy studies, but there must be attention to developing questions and to communication at an earlier stage.

Mike Patton: I can share with you how I think about this issue because I raised it in a paper I wrote, a question about a hierarchy of utilization. In my own mind, there is one. And I think that my first responsibility, in the kind of work I do, is intended use for intended users. And that's what I call primary utilization. There is, beyond that, an ethic under which we operate for dissemination, for which I take no responsibility except to do it. That is, to make the information that comes out of an evaluation that is intended use for intended users available to a wider audience.[2] But typically, what unknown people do with that and how they use it is not something I take responsibility for. I think it's interesting to trace how dissemination affects people and what kind of things they pick up and what they respond to and what they don't respond to, but I don't take primary responsibility for what they do. In fact, I assume and expect that, in the dissemination process, the product will be abused and misunderstood and misused and will end up in places I never imagined, in different kinds of ways. I don't try to track that,

---

2. *Hendricks:*   Sometimes I deliberately *avoid* dissemination to anyone other than the intended user. Does Michael see this as unethical?

and I've stopped losing sleep about it. What I do take responsibility for is intended use for intended users—very heavy responsibility. And I focus my efforts on making that process successful. And the rest I leave more to serendipity.

. . .

Thoughts on Restructuring Evaluation

Marv Alkin: Based on what we now know about utilization, what needs to be done to improve evaluations? Ross, I think, had some thoughts on that. Maybe a good starting point would be for you to comment briefly on that topic, Ross, if you would.

Ross Conner: All right. I'll just quickly summarize some things I have in mind. Essentially, what I've tried to do was to lay out some pretty concrete ideas to make you mad, get you discussing things. The paper begins with an overview of my own evaluation efforts in the Evaluation Unit of the Peace Corps. The last two-thirds of the paper talks about some suggestions for structuring, well, knowledge production activities may be too grandiose based on what we were talking about earlier, but at least structuring some evaluation activities, to increase utilization. Based on some work I did in Washington a few years ago, I felt that, generally, people were producing some good stuff. Carol and I talked a little bit about this last night. These evaluations weren't getting used as much as they might, not because of some of the things we've been talking about this morning, although there were some of those problems, but more because of the way the time frame and whatnot of the researchers did not jibe with the time frame of the policymakers. The two were on really different paths that didn't very often intercept. So I have some suggestions in here for making those things intercept more— a lot of things that sound pretty similar to some of the things Mike talked about, in a different way. It's really a cooperative approach, working closely with programs.

Now let me be specific here: I have two areas, one where improvement is centered inside agencies and one outside. I should say, too, that these ideas pertain primarily to the federal agency level. I think it would also work on the state level. That's what Alex thinks. It also is perhaps more policy oriented than program oriented, as we've been talking about that distinction. From the case of improvements inside agencies,

I think that the evaluators have to establish and maintain direct links to decision makers. Nothing new there, I think we all agreed with that this morning. And I talk about some different ways that can be done. Also how evaluators have to become part of the regular order of business, not just come in at special times, but really be part of the programs and practices being studied on a day-in, day-out basis, to see these changes as they come, the different pressures that are brought to bear on the decision makers, and be there to be able to make adjustments in the studies, as well as to provide information that is already there.[3] I saw this exemplified in the Peace Corps, when I worked with them. There were decisions that came up where there was valuable information, but the decision makers didn't know about it, and if somebody had been there to say, "Hey, we've got something that will help on this," there could have been more use in that way.

Methodological flexibility that involves creative formative and summary approaches is another way to make improvements inside agencies. This reinforces some of the things Mike has said.

I guess maybe the most controversial suggestions I make are things for improvements outside agencies. And it was my idea, one that I talked about with some people when I was in Washington, that what we needed was an anchor for evaluation policy activities in Washington that doesn't really exist now. So I boldly proposed something that I grandly called the Institute of Evaluation and Policy Analysis, which would be established maybe in the Office of Management and Budget—outside of any individual agency, but yet hooked into the federal executive branch. A place where there would be some political appointees, no question about that, but there would also be more evaluator types involved. It would act almost as an anchor for evaluation activities that doesn't exist in Washington now. When I was there, there was an informal group of agency evaluators, who would get together every once in a while, mostly to cry on each other's shoulders, which was a useful function, and give each other ideas. But I think you could take that informal organization another step, and that would be to have an anchor for various kinds of evaluations that can be done, various methodologies, to provide a constituency for evaluation that doesn't exist now.

3. *Hendricks:* Does this suggest that in-house evaluators or consultants are more useful than occasional evaluation contracts?

Marv Alkin: Wouldn't this institute replicate the service now performed by GAO?[4]

Ross Conner: No. GAO's over on the congressional, the legislative end of things. The institute would be based in the executive branch, the operational branch. Most of the studies GAO does are more the checklist kind, where they come in and do the study. What I'm proposing here is that the study still stay in the agencies, that this institute not do the studies. Rather, the institute would help coordinate studies, to be an independent check, to provide some overarching consistency, to even fight for the evaluators, who get pushed onto the shelf.[5]

. . .

Practitioner-Evaluators

Ernie House: Another idea. What would you think about teachers and practitioners conducting their own evaluations? Does anybody have any faith in that whatsoever?

Marv Alkin: For what purpose?

Ernie House: Well, for the purpose of informing the programs and for reasons we usually do evaluations.[6]

Marv Alkin: Yes, of course teachers and practitioners can conduct their own evaluations. I have seen many situations where it takes place—but they'll need help.[7]

Milbrey McLaughlin: Are you thinking of that on an exclusive basis, Ernie?

Ernie House: Well, no. I stated it in a pure form to get a reaction and there would most likely be somebody helping with it. But a lot of the

4. General Accounting Office.
5. *Hendricks:*   I agree with Ross's instincts, and I've even made a similar proposal myself in the past. But he and I may both be underestimating the fear OMB instills in agencies. His proposed IEPA in OMB would have a formidable task convincing the agencies that they're really there to help.
6. *Hendricks:*   I find that we usually do evaluations for lots of different reasons, not just one or two.
7. *Alkin:*   A recent publication of mine is designed to train project administrators and others who commission evaluators to become more fully involved in the process (Alkin, M. C. [1985]. *A guide for evaluation decision makers.* Beverly Hills, CA: Sage).

responsibilities for the evaluation would be turned over to the teachers or whatever kind of practitioners or staffing we're talking about. The professional evaluator would work with those people, help them in some way, maybe guide them, but a lot of the responsibility would be turned over to them. To those people themselves.

Milbrey McLaughlin: Yeah. I think that's a fantastic way to go and, in fact, have seen it work. But what seems to have to go along with it is, in addition to responsibility for evaluation, is the authority to act on the results. That it not be seen as an empty, "formal" kind of exercise. And I'm thinking particularly of schools I've seen in Australia, in which I was blown away with the really hard-nosed look they were taking at their own school. I thought, God, how did this happen? They were asking tough questions.[8] When I asked them about that, it turned out that they also had the power to make changes—they could make their school better, based on their results. They worked with outside evaluators. They did a school-based review every two years. And it was really . . . it was tough-nosed.

Ernie House: When I was over in Australia this summer I saw it, too. Action research got a pretty bad name here in this country. And we've tended to give up on that, for the most part. There are a few people still dabbling around with it here, but in Australia, there seems to be a group working diligently on it.

Well, that's the Australian Teachers' Union that supported it. And I wonder what conditions are necessary to make something like that work.[9]

Milbrey McLaughlin: I mean, I think it's having the authority to do something about it. In the teacher evaluation process, we've seen the same thing: that in the districts where teacher evaluation has become meaningful, the district officials have given the evaluators, or the building principals or whoever, the authority to act on the evaluation information. And the evaluator's role, then . . . makes sense. And so principals, for example in the districts, think it's one of the most important things they do, as opposed to a desultory administrative ritual. But it's the attaching of authority to the responsibility.

8. *Hendricks:*   Anyone who has watched a figure skater practice quickly realizes the toughness of some self-evaluations.
9. *Ellett:*   Good point. What socioinstitutional *conditions* are needed for (or are highly conducive to) this kind of an evaluation? (This is an empirical question.)

Ernie House: It seems that you're saying in this country, it is going in the opposite direction—lots of responsibility and no authority.

Mike Patton: Many of the agricultural extension evaluations are being done by a county agent at the county level. And one of the things I've found is key in making evaluation work at that local level is that the people be involved in testing out real options for themselves, considering whether to deliver the program this way or that way, and really taking a look at those options. That is, not just be in a position of validating a single thing that they are doing. I virtually always find that they're playing around with some different ideas, and they're really prepared to put them to a rigorous test. Then they're not in the failure thing. If they're only looking at a single model and the data is negative, they look bad. The power of the piece has to be that they can make a real choice. They can do longer farm tours or shorter farm tours. They can do them at different times of the year. They can do them with or without videotape. Something that gets them turned on to exploring options. And those options are real for them. I think it brings a piece of integrity to it. There's no real reason to falsify. There's no question there and it's a win-win situation.[10]

Milbrey McLaughlin: There's not a failure option. That's important. This gets back, I think, to Carol's original question of last night, which is the question of how we make better decisions and how evaluation feeds into that.

Jean King: One thing we've got to ensure is that teachers do not do this in addition to all their other responsibilities—in their spare time. I would hope that evaluation activities might be something teachers could get involved in when they reach the top of the career ladder. They could assist the school principal, who probably doesn't have time for program evaluation projects.

Milbrey McLaughlin: That's what Tennessee's doing.

Marv Alkin: Tennessee is doing that?

Milbrey McLaughlin: They're especially training teacher-evaluators who are at the top. It's a meritorious kind of thing. And the teachers will now travel from city to city doing evaluations. This is a state to jump on right now, in terms of doing formative evaluation. They are teachers who are at the top of the career ladder, and they will be trained up the

10. *Hendricks:* Is it a coincidence that this is a formative sort of evaluation work?

kazoo. Talk about a policy that has been based on research. . . . They're amazing. Every objection you might raise, they have thought about it.

Marv Alkin: It's the supervisor model. It's the European supervisor model.

Milbrey McLaughlin: But these are all teachers who have been relieved of classroom responsibilities for a period of time and given special training. They're hoping that these teachers, when they return to their own classrooms, will bring with them a set of evaluative skills which will then reinforce their own situation.

Jean King: It's different from what I would want. I would want to see people stay in the same building because then they know the culture. They already know the kids and they've got a sense of the school. You also have all the norms. . . . I'm just devil's advocating.

Michael Kean: Where the remnants of the old alternative schools movement still exist, you'll find in some of those schools some really viable teacher-evaluator kinds of examples. Not a lot of them left, but some. I know in Philadelphia, when that movement was going full force in the early 70s, a number of schools, including the Parkway Program, the Pennsylvania Advancement School, and a number of others, had a full-time evaluator that was part of the school, doing both peer evaluation and program evaluation. And that individual became part of the school, I think very, very successfully. Unfortunately, it was also very expensive, because it was an additional FTE. It kept going in a number of schools for three of four years, but eventually, the money got tight, and it went, unfortunately. But I think it was . . . at least in the two cases I was most familiar with, extremely, extremely valuable. Schools just perked along beautifully, and I think largely as a result of what was happening.

Marv Alkin: Well, we seem to be at a natural breaking point—we're all breaking. Why don't we take some time for recreation this afternoon. Six p.m. for cocktails; dinner at 7:00 p.m.

Milbrey McLaughlin: Do we have to dress for dinner?

Marv Alkin: You have to wear clothes.

Milbrey McLaughlin: He knows I'm a Californian.

3

Research, Dissemination, and Training

Study of Evaluation Use

Marv Alkin: Why don't we start by considering the second question that I outlined yesterday, and that is: What are the implications based on where we are and what we think we now know for what needs to be done in research, demonstration, or training, related to evaluation and knowledge utilization (each in the broadest context of those terms)? Namely, based on what we know about research on knowledge and evaluation use, and what's been done: What are the directions? What do we need to do? What else should we study related to knowledge and evaluation use? Mike has already proposed that we need to have more demonstrations of evaluation use situations—that is, situations where what we know about utilization is systematically put into practice. All of us have insights on this matter because we've been looking at that field and are familiar with it, and have talked about it to some extent at this meeting. If Sue Klein were to offer the good offices of the National Institute of Education [NIE] to fund some research on knowledge, evaluation use in the next five years . . .

Susan Klein: Would that she could.

Milbrey McLaughlin: I'm sure if she could, she would.

Marv Alkin: And if it makes it any easier for you, you can even make your plea directly to her, instead of to the group. Use this as a forum.

Jean King: Well, I've thought a lot about this. I think it would be fun to go out and somehow identify people who are using evaluation information. It's kind of the effective schools approach. You go out and you find the effective users, and then you study their process. In other words, what distinguishes them from other people. I think we can probably talk a little about this already. But then we find out how information gets to them, in what forms, and what they do with it, and what pieces . . . what types of information somehow lend themselves to use more than others. We could study that. And then that way we'd have a better sense of what people who don't do this already might have to do and to go through, in order to become a good user. So that's one kind of a study that I think would be worthwhile.

Ross Conner: I think we know enough about some of the variables already that we could go the next step, which would be to try to do some planned variations, if you will.

Marv Alkin: To create good users.

Ross Conner: Yeah. To see if some of these things that we have hunches about really work. So I think we're ready for the next stage. Even though we don't have the first one completely set.

Marv Alkin: So, you're disagreeing with Jean. Ross, you don't think there's really a need for any more studies of effective practice—studies of evaluations which lead to use?

Ross Conner: No. I think we've researched that. Mike, in a sense, has done some. Marv has done a number of studies and so have Carol and other people. So we have some ideas about things. We could go the next step.

Carol Weiss: I think it would be interesting to take, as the target of analysis, a set of decisions, and see to what extent and under what conditions information, and particularly evaluation information, played a part in the decision role.[1]

Marv Alkin: What kind of decisions?

Carol Weiss: Well, you could take a set of decisions of different kinds.

Marv Alkin: Do you mean at different levels?

Carol Weiss: Decisions at different levels, of different scope and consequence. And see to what extent those decisions were driven by

1 *Hendricks:*   I wouldn't support this idea, for reasons mentioned earlier. Decisions are too complex to untangle the effects of evaluation information, plus I believe evaluation has many good effects over and above influencing decisions.

noninformational dynamics. And to what extent information played a part, and of that information, how much of it was evaluative.

Mike Patton: The test, it seems to me, would be more to know about a decision coming up, and try to take the best shot using everything we know about how to make information play a role, and see what effect it could have. I think we've stepped beyond the naturally occurring decisions, to some order of attempting to take our best shot at having a reasonable influence on a planned decision.[2] It seems to me we know what the results of what you're describing are going to be—an inconsequential, but moderate effect. Isn't that what you're predicting?

Carol Weiss: I would think there would be a lot of variability . . . depending on the arena, depending on the organizational structure, and possibly on the relevance of the evaluation information.

Ross Conner: That was what I did that year in the Peace Corps. That study. Looking at how decisions were made and how much of our information got used. Even though that was only one agency. Generally, I think the decision makers really wanted good information, across the board. It wasn't legitimating, really, their decisions. They really wanted . . . wanted to know. As Carol said earlier, they don't want to be caught with their pants down, so they'd like to have that information. But it wasn't there, and the decision had to be made quickly. My suggestions come out of that experience of realizing that the information, in a lot of cases, is there someplace, if decision makers only knew about it or had someone working along with them who could get the relevant information as they see the lens changing. But I agree with Mike. I think that, based on my experience, I'd push it even a little further. Try to load a structure, an organizational arrangement to increase many of the factors affecting information use. To even put in some—lobbying is too strong—but some advocates, I guess, some stakeholders for evaluation in the decision-making process, which are not necessarily there now.

Marv Alkin: And then what would we do?

Ross Conner: Well, I'd focus it centrally on looking at how decisions are made, as Carol was saying. When things get used. When they don't.

---

2 *Ellett:*   Should the evaluator always have an influence on the decision? Is it ever proper for him to provide the reliable information, and let the Congress, say, make the decision using it the way they see fit?

Marv Alkin: I don't understand that focus. Because I thought we just agreed we have a sense of that. So you're saying, given new structural relationships, you want to look at differential response.

Ross Conner: Yeah. With the structural arrangement, I think we can begin to affect a number of the different variables, such as . . . well, an earlier interest in evaluation in the planning process, for example. It doesn't come at the eleventh hour; that sensitivity is added at the first stage, for example.

Understanding Practitioner-Users

Ernie House: I don't disagree with anything that's been said so far, but I don't think we really understand how practitioners think about their world. If we take teachers, I don't think we really understand how teachers make decisions. And there's a sense in which that isn't absolutely necessary, in order to come up with information that they might find useful. On the other hand, it would be very valuable for a whole lot of reasons, not only for evaluation utilization. I would encourage that kind of work. It would be good to know how teachers think about the world, if you're going to try to affect their thinking somehow. We could try several things out. Maybe we should try to set up some situations in which teachers would do a lot of the evaluation, and then see how much they use that—the evaluation they themselves engaged in. We already know enough to set up that kind of variation, as Ross suggests. So, you could actually do that; try some kind of, I don't know if you want to call it experiment, but an experiment of sorts . . .

Jean King: Not in this group.

[laughter and overtalk]

Michael Kean: Ernie, do you view teachers as a primary client of evaluation?

Ernie House: Well, that's a good question. I said practitioners, so I wanted to make it broader than that, to include, for example, administrators. But I think teachers should be evaluation clients. Until we come to the place where teachers are actually changing something, I don't believe education is going to change very much. I believe that underneath the whole thing, there is the teacher in the classroom. And we can horse around with all this other stuff—these projects and these pro-grams—but until the teachers themselves begin to conceive of their task differently, I don't believe that education is going to change very much.

I think other practitioners view the world differently. I would pre-sume that administrators are practitioners of a different sort, right? So understanding how they think would also be important. They're proba-bly a more likely audience for test scores and various kinds of informa-tion that we have to offer at this time than the teachers are. But that's partly because how teachers think is pretty much a mystery to us.

Mike Patton: I get worried about the extent to which that implies the ability to generalize about such a thing, at virtually any level. I've recently gotten to know the situation a little more in St. Paul, my own community. There are about 40 school principals, and I've spent some time interviewing some subsection of them. I mean you're talking about the full range of humanity in that group. And to begin to generalize at all about anything other than their title would probably take one farther afield from understanding than closer to it. The schools are quite different from each other, as are their situations, the size of the schools, and staff that they have. When you start talking about teachers, there's even more variation. At most, we may learn some generic questions to ask to understand specific situations. If that's what you're suggesting, that makes some sense to me. But to hold out any promise of there being generalizations about kids, teachers, or principals and how they think seems to me not to hold much promise.

Ernie House: Well, I think there are some modest kinds of generaliza-tions one could arrive at.

Mike Patton: On the order of what? Can you give a . . .

Ernie House: Well, on the order of . . . How do teachers conceptualize the world, for example. Is it in terms of . . .

Mike Patton: That's a modest question?!!

Ernie House: What does this import to a teacher? For example, take the Shavelson review.[3] He found that teachers think in terms of activi-ties, and they think in terms of certain categories. I presume that teachers do have a cognitive structure that they think about the world

3 Shavelson, R. J. (1983). Review of research on teachers' pedagogical judgments, plans, and decisions. *Elementary School Journal, 83*(4), 392-413.

in terms of. That will probably generalize at a modest level from teacher to teacher. I don't think they think totally differently. Same thing with architects. I think there is a professional kind of knowledge that they develop in working in the job themselves. But that doesn't resolve the problem for us. If we knew what their cognitive structures were like, that still would not enable us to know exactly what to do in order to influence them. We need to pay them the respect that they actually have some kind of in-depth understanding of their situation, which I think we are not now doing.

Mike Patton: I think one can do that with an individual, but I wouldn't think it would be respectful to be thrown into a stereotype generalization of how I was like all the other teachers in how I approached the world. I don't think teachers would respond well, from the ones I know, to that kind of research.

Ernie House: I disagree. I disagree with you. I may be wrong about this, but I think some modest generalizations can be made about how they structure the world and go about things. For example, when teachers try out something in the classroom, they tend to look to see how their students are involved and how the students talk about what they're doing and how they react. Rather than look at the test scores . . . Even that's a generalization. You can find teachers who do the other thing. But generalizations at this kind of level could conceivably be important. I don't think that teachers walk in off the street and have only the knowledge that any street person would have. I don't believe that's the case. They develop a certain kind of technical, professional knowledge by being in the classroom.

Marv Alkin: Ernie, I think that you—that we as evaluators—sometimes fail to understand what people in schools view as the significant occurrences. I did this study several years ago, with Brian Stecher, a student of mine, where we looked at 20 elementary schools. And at each school we did interviews with principals and two other administrators. We didn't talk about evaluation initially. We talked about significant occurrences in the life of the school and tried to get them to identify those significant occurrences. And they were not the kinds of things that we think of as significant—for example, whether to have the Cinco de Mayo festival in the afternoon or in the evening, what color to paint the school cafeteria. The cases that were identified were decisions relating to day-to-day functioning of their organization. And from that, we tried to identify the kinds of information that influenced the way they thought about that issue. And formal evaluation goes way down the line. But they did identify other kinds of informal information sources that had impact on those kinds of situations.

Mike Patton: Part of my skepticism comes from the data Alex was telling me about—the results of the teacher examinations. To generalize to any kind of cognitive structure, when we can't assume a common core of basic arithmetic in teachers, seems to me to call that possibility significantly into question.

Ernie House: It's an empirical question. And I bet that you can generalize . . .

Mike Patton: Well, I don't doubt that researchers can impose some generalizations and then get at it . . .

Ernie House: One always imposes definitions on the world. And the question is whether those concepts also make sense to the teachers.

Mike Patton: Alex, you've looked more at trying to understand some of this than I have, to be sure. What's your sense of the level at which one might get at commonalities?

Alex Law: This is an indirect answer to your question. But as you two were talking, I was going back to what we used to call our high-low study. We matched about 20 pairs of schools as closely as we could on every indicator we could find. One member of the pair had scores that were going up, one had scores that were going down. The interviewers went in blind, and spent three days in that school. They talked to the teachers, the staff, the parents. Came back and made a description of the school. One of the main things that stood out was the difference in the value systems of the teachers at the two sets of schools. For example, at one school the faculty was quite young, was dressed shabbily. Their thing was to communicate with the kids. Classrooms were in pretty much of a shambles; kids were coming and going; there was a lot of freedom of expression. That was the sense of the school that the interviewers came away with. This school was matched to another school where the ethnic characteristics of the staff were the same— heavily minority. The evaluation team got back to the hotel and during our initial debriefing the first remark that came out about the comparison school was: It looks as if they had just been shopping at I. Magnin's. The staff was older, extremely well dressed, very quiet in their demeanor. The classrooms were controlled, generally quiet although there was some interaction going on, but you could sense which was the highest scoring school. And we got down to it in questioning their teachers. They said: We have an expectation that these kids are going to learn. And we communicate that to them as soon as we can. And it's not as explicit as: You are going to learn this. But it's the expectation that is set. Two different value systems. Two schools less than a mile apart.

_____ :   Which was the highest-scoring school?

Alex Law: The one with the well-dressed teachers. I mean, their value was learning. Their value was discipline. Their value was an expectation, and a particular ethical system that was not present in the other school. So this is a laborious point—that teachers are truly different in more than cognitive style, but also in their value systems and their approach to the situation.

Carol Weiss: You were right when you said it's not the individual teacher. It is the social system of the school. But the question we never got answered was, How did those teachers become so homogeneous in those two schools? Was it the instructional leadership of the principal?

[laughter and overtalk]

Alex Law: We had another school. It was a high-scoring school. The principal, by everybody's definition, was an absolute loss. He was the kind that would come in and lock himself in the office. And yet, that finding violated the other principles we had seen. So what happened? There were three teachers that took over for him, and they performed the principal's functions; they were the acknowledged leaders of the school. So yes, the system within the schools is, I think, really different among teachers, between schools.

. . .

Carol Weiss: Yeah, but it's not the idiosyncratic individual, but the system in which that individual is a member. My experience is that teachers are not likely users of evaluation, and I don't think they'll ever be. Except maybe if they are their own investigators, with their own data. It seems to me that this is because of what you were saying earlier, Ernie. That they have so much direct, rich daily experience with these children. They know so much about them that the little bit of probabilistic information that evaluation can add isn't going to be that much of an increment. I don't know how much we can add to what observers who are immersed in a situation already know, except to help them think more analytically and reflectively about their own experiences. But as far as information input, I'm not sure that evaluators can produce something and transfer it to them, that will have much of an incremental value.[4]

Susan Klein: Has anyone systematically looked at the research from dissemination, for example, about linkers, and applied that to evaluation use? Because we know that there are some high-use people that perform that kind of linkage function in a normal situation with regular research-based knowledge. Do they do the same thing with evaluation-based knowledge?

Marv Alkin: I personally don't find that work productive, because that assumes a utilization model that starts the linking process *after* the data have been collected rather than at the beginning of the evaluation as part of a collaborative relationship with users in the development of the information. And so, I don't think the linkage model holds much promise for utilization purposes.[5]

Milbrey McLaughlin: But Marv, how do you then integrate the point that Carol made earlier this afternoon, that not all use is the result of a one-to-one relationship between evaluator and evaluatee?

. . .

Training Users

Michael Kean: One issue you may not want to deal with, Marv, and that is the role of the evaluator in training potential users in the appropriate use, when the user is not the primary client.

We used to run media seminars in Philadelphia, and they weren't wildly successful, but I think it made some difference. We would bring

---

4 *Hendricks:*   This strikes me as a radical statement with far-reaching implications. Can we really *not* add any more information to the discussions? I certainly think we can, if we recognize our limits.

5 *Ellett:*   Alkin doesn't find that work productive. But couldn't it work in a limited way and be of some benefit?

the folks from the media in ahead of time, train them before the tests were ever administered, and try to get them minimally conversant with what testing is about. And then do another training session at the time that the scores were released; actually, right before. The notion being that, if they had some knowledge of testing, that the chances were a little bit better that they wouldn't make wild statements. And it worked. It really worked to some degree. It wasn't perfect and pristine. And they always changed education editors.[6]

. . .

Utilization and Reporting

Marv Alkin: Why don't we start now, since several people need to leave early. It seems that there is maybe one other utilization topic that we had said we might talk about—changes in the program policy framework that would facilitate knowledge and evaluation utilization. We really have sort of skirted around it on a number of occasions. We

---

6 *Alkin:*   My colleagues and I noted in a report on Title I evaluation utilization that evaluator assistance in developing use procedures was a critical factor. Drawing on case studies by Richard Williams and Jean King, we noted:

> Mr. Leonard, Suburb West's evaluator, believed that "school administrators, teachers and parents who serve on Title I advisory committees often do not have group process skills and decisionmaking skills. They must be given assistance in how to read, analyze, and make decisions upon evaluation data." To this end, Leonard has outlined a planning and decision-making process which lists the specific steps in sequence, the data that are available to inform the decisions, and the specific decisions that must be made.
>
> Small Town's evaluators have a slightly different approach. According to King, Mrs. Lopenia regularly encourages others to use evaluation data by giving them information and a related task or problem such as "suggesting changes in the program, planning next year's workshop, developing a dissemination plan, and creating a meaningful attendance policy." She is in essence training Small Town's personnel to use data in making school decisions by giving them practice with the process.

See Alkin, M. C., Stecher, B., & Geiger, F. (1982). *Title I evaluation: Utility and factors influencing use.* Northridge, CA: Educational Evaluation Associates.

might want to talk about evaluation strategies (the ways in which evaluation might be conducted by practitioners) and other kinds of changes that would facilitate knowledge and evaluation utilization. That's pretty broad, but I think you can just jump in any place that you happen to feel comfortable and go from there with your thoughts. As a matter of fact, Carol mentioned the General Accounting Office practice of the agency responding to the evaluation, which is a kind of intent to utilize statement, isn't it?[7]

Carol Weiss: Yes. Facilitated by the fact that the Congress holds the purse strings.

Marv Alkin: Well, that's right. That's a particular instance where the evaluator is in a very unusual position, because of the administrative and budgetary authority the evaluator happens to hold.

Ross Conner: In fact, all the GAO studies were commissioned by Congress . . .[8]

Mike Patton: A lot of the agency response is why what GAO did is nonsense. It's not always, "How are we going to use it?"

Marv Alkin: Oh, yeah, I understand that.

Carol Weiss: Well, a lot of it is how they've already used it.

Mike Patton: And why it never needed to have been done, because they'd planned to do it even before GAO did the study.

[laughter]

Carol Weiss: And we also talked yesterday about this collaborative style that Mike has written so eloquently about. And you, as well, Marvin. I guess one thing we haven't talked too much about is dissemination. Susan mentioned it as part of the NIE Joint Dissemination Review Panel [JDRP] effort. But if we think again, not only of the up-close users, but of the distant users as well, efforts to get the word around are important. And it's important that findings be disseminated in the scholarly literature, in the popular literature, and in the profes-

---

7 The U.S. General Accounting Office requires the agency recipient of evaluation studies to present a formal response to the report.

8 *Hendricks:*   Actually, this isn't completely true. A good percentage (in fact, I think a majority) of GAO studies are initiated by GAO itself, but sometimes with a pro forma request by Congress to justify the funds being spent.

sional literature—the journals and newsletters that practitioners see. Getting information into things that teachers and principals and school board members read. I don't know how may evaluators ever make half an effort to get their results written up in those kinds of practice-oriented publications, but it seems to me that it's a possible way to go. What do you think, Alex? Is that worth doing?

Alex Law: Well, I don't know, I've just been sort of musing while you were talking. The scholarly literature, I think, skims a very, very small population. There are a lot of evaluations that my shop does that I think you'll find are going to be uninteresting to anybody; they probably shouldn't go any farther than immediate dissemination. There is a clump of local evaluations which probably should stay local. I mean, they're narrow programs. But there's this vast middle ground, and if there could be some kind of extracting service, like dissertation abstracts . . . I don't think anybody in their right mind wants to go through the full ones.

Marv Alkin: Well, but they find their way into ERIC,[9] don't they?

Alex Law: Very few of them. Very few.

Mike Patton: My concern with that process—and this might be something that a center or lab or combination of them might take on—gets to the synthesis that you were talking about. I don't trust the paper or the reports as the synthesis base. It seems to me that the best kind of synthesis and real wisdom would be generated by bringing together key practitioners and evaluators who had done a number of these things, and having them try to sort out—the way we have around utilization—try to sort out the collective wisdom. You might well commission somebody to do the paperwork synthesis ahead of time, or as part of that process, and then take a bunch of these generic reports and make some sense out of them. But I would always want that tempered with some face-to-face interaction between the people who have done the evaluations and relevant practitioners. There's a model for something like that in what US-AID[10] is doing. US-AID began what are sometimes known in the field as rapid reconnaissance surveys; they're evaluative in nature. Twig Johnson, who ran that unit, was the mastermind behind it, and he assembled teams—partly internal, partly external—who would

9 Educational Resources Information Center.
10 U.S. Agency for International Development.

go into AID projects and spend a month to six weeks in the field and put together an evaluative report about that project. They've accumulated, over the years, about 160 of these, many of them well done. One of the limits is that the body of the report can only be 20 pages long, and then they attach whatever appendices they want to it. When they get eight to ten of those in an area, they do a synthesis. They bring back key members of those separate teams and they take the documents and they say, "What have we as an AID institution learned about doing public health, well digging, or water projects in the last five years?" They write a synthesis piece on that; that is, a collection of the working knowledge of the key people who were involved in the evaluation reports. Those are really quite good documents. They have, I think, five of them now that I've seen, that, in conjunction with the individual reports, are a rich source of working knowledge, interspersed with empirical data about what we know. It's a very nice piece.[11]

Marv Alkin: Well, you know, it seems to me that this is what ERIC is supposed to do. Now ERIC does more than document collection. They also do synthesis summaries on particular topics. At least I know that the ERIC Clearinghouse on Community Colleges at UCLA does this. They put out periodic pieces which represent syntheses of the literature. They pull the syntheses out of the ERIC documents, and so, if some evaluation reports never made it into ERIC, they won't be included.

Michael Kean: In terms of all the new stuff, it's at best an annotated bibliography. And there's just so much that never gets into ERIC-TM [Tests and Measurement] because of parameters of what they'll accept.

Marv Alkin: What kind of synthesis papers do you think you would like to see done on evaluation reports? Focusing on the topic of the evaluation?

Mike Patton: It seems to me the utilization potential is greatest around some area of practice.

Ernie House: I'm not very optimistic about the idea of generalizing from these evaluations to other settings. It just doesn't seem to me that's how we think about these things. If we do it, I think you need to get

---

11 *Hendricks:*   I'd like to see someone survey the internal evaluators in federal and state agencies for the sources of their information. I'd predict that most evaluators get little or no information from the "outside world" of evaluation.

somebody who would think about it afresh. Computerizing objectives and computerizing outcomes—I don't think that would go anyplace. I'd like to see somebody give it a try, try to figure out how to put this information in useful terms. I think it requires a lot of creative thinking, if you're going to try to do that. It just doesn't generalize.

. . .

Michael Kean: Until recently, with the exception of large-scale evaluations, much of the existing evaluations were not published in normal, accessible kinds of channels.

Jean King: Yes. They're hard to get hold of.

Milbrey McLaughlin: Yeah. But with the Freedom of Information Act, if you have any leads at all, you can usually spring loose a whole batch of reports that the agencies had conducted earlier. And they sometimes are really helpful.[12]

Jean King: I hate to say it, but the evaluators I have known—and I admit that I come from an unusual city, a less-than-ideal situation—they aren't going to do this [go seek out reports from other cities or agencies]. No way. I mean, they just aren't going to do it. And we can say . . .

Milbrey McLaughlin: I would respond, "Their evaluations would be less useful than they might otherwise be".

Jean King: I'm not sure. . . . Less useful to whom? To you?

Milbrey McLaughlin: No. To the client.

Jean King: Let's go back to the lousy Chapter I studies. Those are very useful studies. People use them. They believe in them and they take them and they use them . . .

Milbrey McLaughlin: What do they use them for?

Jean King: Typically, for going up to the next level of administration and saying, "We need this, this, and this, and here we have proof that this program works." I mean, that's instrumental use, that's valid. The fact that it's a lousy study doesn't seem to matter . . .

---

12 *Hendricks:*   One good way to start, and a nice political way to boot, is to ask program officials what information *they* have relied on so far. By starting at their starting point, an evaluator can understand their viewpoints and then begin to broaden.

Marv Alkin: Is it a *lousy* study, or is it an *incorrect* study?

Jean King: Incorrect. I mean, the program doesn't work. So here's an example on Mike Patton's misuse scale. It's high on the misutilization end. But speaking against literature reviews is like being against motherhood. I would be in favor of relevant literature reviews too, but how do we change Joe Q. Evaluator out there, who's producing poor evaluations?

Carol Weiss: Well, we do what we do. We teach and we write.

. . .

Ernie House: It's not immediately apparent how to take evaluation reports and make them useful to somebody else. Because the variables that we're dealing with are particular to a given situation. That's what makes the success of a program; the particular situational variables in that situation, as Mike said from a couple of sides. And so the things to generalize about in our evaluation studies don't leap out at us right away.

Michael Kean: There's a problem that precedes that, Ernie, too. And here you really, I think, need to differentiate between research and evaluation, at least in terms of the means by which the information's available. As you pointed out before, most research at least tries to find its way into some type of published journal or something of the sort. The great majority of evaluative information, evaluation reports, is never published. It may be provided in terms of a report. And published, with a little p, by that school district, or made available, but it doesn't find its way into a journal at all. And the big problem is getting hold of it. That's not to say that, if I asked the director of research in City X for a copy of his or her report, that they wouldn't provide it. Yes, they would. But it's not available. We've tried through the directors of research of the large cities, for about close to a decade, to come up with a vehicle that would provide it. We even, when I was at ETS,[13] got some money to bring some people into Princeton for about four days to try to hammer it out. And we came up with what we thought would be an idea. And it was very much utilization focused. We figured if research director X were to receive a hundred evaluation reports from a hundred

13 Educational Testing Service.

cities across the country, that they'd never have an opportunity to read thoroughly through the stats. And, unfortunately, many of those reports never had prologues or whatever you want to call them. So we worked out a deal whereby people could become part of the network, and the only cost to receive reports was that every evaluation report that . . . that their school district produced would have an abstract written and that they would send one copy of that abstract to a central clearinghouse at ETS. And we contacted all the directors, hundreds of them, and fewer than 20 of them expressed an interest in doing it. Well, it was certainly an easy enough thing to do, no cost, the whole thing. The stuff is out there, but it's tough to get. Someone would really have to make an effort to obtain the reports and then to . . . to really sit down and either read them and abstract them. Even those with abstracts, I think, it'd be necessary to read through them and find out what's not included in the abstract, etc. So it would be a gargantuan job to do.

Marv Alkin: Do you think that the reason that the directors didn't send the reports was because they didn't want to put forth the effort of writing the abstract? Or do you think they had other reasons?

Michael Kean: I think it was more the former, Marv. I don't think it was a reason of, "Gee, I'm trying to cover up something."

Marv Alkin: No, no. I didn't necessarily mean cover up. I wasn't implying that they were doing it because they had things they were trying to cover up. I think many of those directors may have had the feeling that what was done in their district did not have applicability elsewhere. That's what I'm searching for . . .

Michael Kean: That's possible, but I don't really think so Marv.

Jean King: I think they haven't got time. That's another thing that you've now got to require and getting the copy made and sent out to . . . My sense would be that it's just not enough payoff. It goes back to the discussion we had yesterday about theory. This is kind of a grounded theory, I guess, from other places. My experience, in a couple of like programs in Louisiana, is that they haven't got time or aren't interested in that.[14]

---

14 *Alkin:*   Because they don't see the relevance for their situation.

Evaluation Training

Marv Alkin: Okay, why don't we return to other possible changes in program policy—the framework that might facilitate knowledge and evaluation utilization. I think that we have already covered to some extent the topic of dissemination and the means of facilitating the dissemination of information about evaluation reports . . . which could be used both by decision makers in making judgments about programs they were about to initiate and by evaluators as a theoretical framework for thinking about the way in which they conduct their evaluations. I'd like to get on to some other potential changes in program policy framework or mechanisms for potentially increasing evaluation utilization and practice. Are there some you want to mention just so we can get them on the table? Focusing a little more on improving evaluation practice, if possible? The "if possible" did not refer to the improvement of practice, but to suggestions.

Jean King: Don't chuckle, but I do think that we should work on putting together a program evaluation course for principals and superintendents.

Carol Weiss: Terrific idea.

Milbrey McLaughlin: I think it's great.

Jean King: Evaluation. Just so they have some sense of how it happens and if you could really make it user focused.

Marv Alkin: Any hints for administrators on the way in which they can organize evaluations that they commission, or ask the evaluator the right questions in order to make the evaluators more use oriented?[15]

Mike Patton: The whole area of how to train evaluators outside of getting the Ph.D. pieces is critical. CSE,[16] at one point, did some work in developing the evaluation kit, and offering a couple of published workshops, some of which had potential for being self-supporting. But there's not an opus of high-quality evaluation workshop kinds of training. There's a huge demand.

---

15 See Alkin, M. C. (1985). *A guide for evaluation decision makers*. Beverly Hills, CA: Sage.
16 Center for the Study of Evaluation, UCLA.

Alex Law: We trained over 3,000 mid-level administrators in three- or four-day workshops. It focused upon what questions they asked. Marv was the consultant to our staff in developing these materials.

Milbrey McLaughlin: I think it's really exciting. If I see a change in what evaluation is coming to mean, I would see it pretty much moving in the direction of usefulness.

Michael Kean: To go back to something that you mentioned before, Mike, that I suspect may be very important and well taken in terms of school district evaluators: There's a good solid nucleus out in the large cities of yeoman evaluators, that have been doing a decent job for a while, but my guess is that the great majority of them are not particularly utilization focused. They've been doing it the same way for a while; they're not anti-utilization. They just don't think about it very much.

Mike Patton: They haven't thought about it. That's the issue.

Michael Kean: Yes. And if a means could be developed whereby they could get more active . . . It may be consciousness-raising. Maybe it's a one-day kind of thing or a renewal kind of process, whereby what they know can be . . . just slightly fine-tuned to make them sense the real importance of the utilization factor in what they do. I think . . . working with those people, who already know what they're doing pretty much, could increase the quality—if one likens utilization to quality—of our product immeasurably. And how we do that? Maybe through AERA,[17] a lot of them go to that. There are a number of different ways.

Marv Alkin: I did something at CSE a few years back, that some of you may be aware of. We created a little newsletter, called *Using School Evaluations.* And the focus of this newsletter was that there would always be one centerpiece article about what we know about evaluation utilization. There was always one headline article, from a practitioner, describing an experience that he had, and there was always a letters column in which we invited people to comment on their experiences. And we got the initial mailing list through AASA and ASCD,[18] just to get a practitioner audience. And that got quite a bit of attention.

---

17 American Educational Research Association.
18 American Association of School Administrators and Association for Supervision and Curriculum Development.

Review and Commentary

Part I

The three chapters in Part I are drawn from the discussion at the Malibu seminar. For the most part, the discussion has been presented sequentially, but some editing has changed the time sequence of various discussions in order to place related topics closer together. Chapter 1 examines known factors related to utilization. Chapter 2, loosely titled "Other Utilization Issues," examines a variety of other utilization-related topics discussed within the course of the seminar. Finally, the discussion of Chapter 3 relates to the research, dissemination, and training activities that might enhance knowledge about utilization and improve the extent of utilization of current evaluations.

Utilization Factors

Chapter 1 considers the issue of evaluation utilization generally and begins with a discussion of some of the factors identified in the research literature as associated with utilization. A substantial amount of research has taken place within the past 15 years on the topic of evaluation utilization, and some excellent summary articles have been published (in particular, the reader is referred to Cousins & Leithwood, 1986; Leviton & Hughes, 1981).

The research literature on evaluation utilization is also synthesized and reviewed in Alkin (1985). That review identifies some 50 factors associated with evaluation utilization. These factors are generally categorized into four groups: (1) evaluator characteristics, (2) user characteristics, (3) contextual characteristics, and (4) characteristics of the evaluation (the way in which it was done). *Evaluator* characteristics that are highlighted include the evaluators' commitment to use, their willingness to involve users, the kind of rapport they are able to develop with users, their political sensitivity, and their credibility. While a number of *user* characteristics are identified in the literature, the most important noted is the interest of users in the evaluation—that is, the extent to which they believe evaluation is likely to make a difference. Perhaps this could be referred to as a general receptivity on the part of potential users. Various *contextual* characteristics come into play as well. Typically these involve characteristics of the organization, including its complexity, legal requirements, and organizational structure. These contextual characteristics place bounds upon the evaluation that serve either to enhance or to limit the possibility of use. Finally, the fourth set of factors is related to the *evaluation* itself, including the procedures used, the substance of the evaluation information (e.g., its relevance), the extent to which information dialogue takes place, and the nature and timing of evaluation reporting.

The discussions at the Malibu seminar essentially used this knowledge base as a starting point. That is, most of the participants were very familiar with the research on evaluation utilization and sought either to explore or expand on aspects of this literature or, in more personal terms, to define the situational meaning of some of these evaluation utilization factors. The free-flowing discussion presented in Chapters 1-3 has the advantage of spontaneity and of demonstrating the thinking process of evaluation theorists as well as the nature of the interaction between theorists when they're simply "talking." As in any conversation, people tend to stray from the topic—perhaps to return at another time. The purpose of this and subsequent review and commentary sections is to provide a recap and a "guided tour" of some of the main themes that emerged within this discussion.

A recurring theme of the discussion in Part I is the extent to which the evaluator, as an individual, influences utilization. Initially, Carol Weiss differentiates between program and policy situations, seeming to acknowledge that it is possible for the evaluator to have greater influence on program-level evaluation than on policy studies (or policy evaluations). While *program* and *policy* are not specifically defined, the group comes to think of program situations as primarily local (possibly state) and referencing specific ongoing programs. On the other hand, policy situations are viewed as more broadly focused, typically federal, and having less identifiable clients. Policy evaluation is viewed as a situation in which it is more difficult for an evaluator to have specific impact because, as Weiss notes, "we're not going to be very successful in identifying potential decision makers in advance, because so many people have a spoon to stir in the policy pot."

General agreement exists that a local program evaluator *can* have enormous impact; that is, there is a stronger possibility that local program evaluations will be utilized. However, the way that the evaluator conducts a program evaluation is important. Utilization will occur if the evaluator plays an active role in fostering evaluation utilization. In essence, this active role includes factors noted in the literature: the evaluator's commitment to use, willingness to involve users, political sensitivity, and the like.

While recognizing the lesser likelihood of obtaining utilization in large policy evaluations, the participants cite examples of large-scale policy studies that did have impact. However, not all examples of utilization are viewed positively. For example, in one instance it was believed that the primary reason for a particular study was to obtain confirmatory data or evidence for beliefs already widely held. The evaluation subsequently provided that evidence and, in turn, was used. But this pro forma utilization is not considered exemplary. As Ernest House notes, "You have a set of policymakers here—let's say, the president and his henchmen—who have a certain mentality and way they view the world. You get a study that fits into that mentality. It's consistent with the framework that they employ, and there's a sense in which there's a receptivity there already." House and other Malibu seminar participants recognize such contextual characteristics as being extremely important in utilization, although not always a positive influence.

The impact of other policy study examples is viewed more positively—particularly the Berman and McLaughlin change study. Among the reasons for the acknowledged importance for this work is the methodology that was used. As Milbrey McLaughlin notes, the investigators "had to battle to do case studies" to accompany more traditional quantitative data. Berman and McLaughlin strongly felt that case-study data would provide evidence that would persuade policymakers to use the study results. Other important factors associated with high levels of utilization were the study sponsorship and its timing. The Malibu participants cite the importance of federal government sponsorship in this study, although recognizing that many federally sponsored studies do not see the light of day. Timing, another acknowledged factor, is related to the extent to which the study serendipitously fit into a timely schedule when people were doing or thinking about these issues.

My own view about the factors leading to high levels of utilization in the Berman and McLaughlin change study relates to the presence of what Michael Kean refers to as a "champion." By this he means an evaluator willing to work at providing information to potential key users at the right time—"almost like cheerleading the information through." In this instance we apparently have more than the "evaluator commitment to use" noted in the literature. Berman and McLaughlin had a good feel for the potential users and the relevant issues because they had worked systematically at understanding them. McLaughlin, for example, notes that the evaluators put forth a good deal of effort to "pay attention to the communication process." Another participant notes that Berman and McLaughlin were well connected to appropriate dissemination channels and that this connection also enhanced the possibility of use.

This discussion about "dissemination" is particularly intriguing because it marks a primary distinction between program and policy evaluation. In program evaluation, particularly when one employs a utilization-focused approach, there is strong effort to identify primary users. Consequently, the evaluation information provided is highly focused and tailored to the needs of those particular users. On the other hand, in broad-based policy studies, where it is less clear who will be stirring the policy decision pot, "dissemination" takes on increasing relevance. The reporting duties of the evaluator are less focused and demand greater consideration of the myriad users who might participate in the policy process. These potential users become the targets of information dissemination. Thus the evaluator needs to consider the avenues available for getting the evaluation findings into general circulation. Likewise, the credibility of the evaluation—viewed in terms of the quality of the research—takes on greater importance than in a program evaluation. Simply put, the evaluation is more public, and those taking stands don't want to be "caught out on a limb with a study that is flawed" (as Weiss notes). The individual evaluator as a person with high or low credibility, or with high or low rapport with users, and so on, becomes a much less meaningful concept in policy studies.

What else do we know about utilization at the local and/or program level? We know a great deal, as much of the available literature emanated from program evaluation studies and therefore is quite relevant. Seminar participants aptly summarize the primary local utilization factor as "situational responsiveness." Comments about local program evaluators take into account that those seeking high levels of use are forced to recognize situational differences, to be "champions," and to "communicate" actively. The word *communicate* implies respect for potential users, interest in their situations and concerns, and care and understanding.

The notion of evaluator credibility, which is prominent in the literature, is also a topic of concern. We know that evaluation credibility is not inherent in a static sense but is, in part, acquired in the conduct of the evaluation (Alkin, Daillak, & White, 1979). But does credibility consist of certain personal characteristics, traits, and abilities or is it, as House has suggested, a fit between the characteristics of the evaluator and those of the decision makers/users? Yes, we know there are important characteristics associated with credible evaluators. To some extent also, credibility is determined by the fit between evaluator and user. Given this fit, Hendricks asks whether the evaluator must be an "emotional chameleon." I would venture to say that this is not necessary: Skilled professional evaluators can understand clients, work with them in identifying issues, communicate with them, and come to understand to some extent how they think and act, and in doing these things develop high levels of credibility without having perfectly matched values.

In summary, Chapter 1 provides additional insights (and raises questions) about some recognized factors associated with evaluation utilization. It provides a better understanding of the distinction between program and policy evaluation and the differences in evaluator actions associated with high levels of utilization in each instance.

Other Utilization Issues

A major issue discussed within Chapter 2 is that of "information" for "decision making." In the literature, this topic has been widely misunderstood. Advocates of evaluation oriented toward decision making have been criticized on the belief that they view the relationship between evaluation and the decision process as direct, immediate, and having sole impact. These criticisms are ill directed. Those who view evaluation as having potential impact on users have never conceived of evaluation as the sole source of information that might come to play within decisions—or even as the most important source of information in some contexts. They recognize that contextual setting, including the user's knowledge of the current program situation, provides an information base that is only elaborated upon by evaluation information.

Moreover, what constitutes evaluation information is not clear. Evaluators' perceptions of evaluation information varies and thus the degree of formality of presentation varies. Information presentation may range from written reports presented in the best research style to informal conversations of shared perceptions. Content may vary from quantitative data derived from highly sophisticated statistical analyses to brief anecdotal data. As McLaughlin notes, information presentation is dependent upon "the nature of the evaluator, and the kind of evaluator he is and the way he or she operates." It is almost as if there is no such thing as "pure" information: The evaluator and the way in which he or she functions act as a filter for information presented to potential users.

Finally, Mike Patton raises the issue of "decision making by whom" and outlines a hierarchy of utilization. In this hierarchy, he defines his intended users and notes that he takes primary responsibility for providing information relevant for *their* decision making. This distinction between Patton's view of which decision makers he takes responsibility for (a highly focused approach) is further elaborated in Part II of this book. But Patton, after delimiting those decision makers he views as potential users, strongly commits to satisfying their information needs. These information needs are related to preidentified user issues, although both the issues and their associated information needs are subject to modification throughout the course of the evaluation. This view contrasts with the views of others in the seminar who perceive that evaluators have responsibility for serving the information and decision-making needs of a wider audience.

Aside from evaluation information and decision making, Chapter 2 raises a second important issue regarding teachers and practitioners as evaluators. Ernest House, apparently contemplating the relationship between information and decision making, asks whether information is more likely to be used if practitioners act as their own evaluators. He discusses this issue with teacher practitioners in mind. The underlying issue is, What happens when practitioners conduct their own evaluations? This question seems to have two parts: first, whether it is reasonable to expect that teacher-practitioners can do evaluations; and second, whether they are more likely to use the results of evaluations that they conduct.

Mike Patton and other participants agree that practitioner evaluations are indeed viable, with an important proviso: that "there's not a failure option." In essence, teachers and other practitioners as evaluators of their own programs must be placed in situations where the evaluations involve selecting among options for program change rather than in situations that force evaluators to make absolute judgments about the program. That is, the evaluation question in such instances must not be, Did the program (meaning the teacher) pass or fail? Self- (or own-program) evaluation can be successful if evaluation issues are couched in nonthreatening terms that offer the possibility of program modification and improvement.

The general idea of practitioner-evaluators is thought by some to encompass using teachers as evaluators in a variety of educational settings. However, several participants at the seminar noted (and I strongly agree) that the greatest benefit is derived when practitioner-evaluators conduct evaluations in their own schools, "because then they know the culture."

Research, Dissemination, and Training

Chapter 3 poses the question, Where do we go from here? What are the most promising directions for further research, dissemination, and training on evaluation utilization?

With respect to further avenues for research, substantial disagreement exists, although participants put forth a variety of innovative ideas. Jean King, using the effective schools approach as her model, suggests that researchers identify effective evaluation users and study them in order to gain insights for improving evaluation. Ross Conner suggests planned variation studies that vary aspects of evaluations from setting to setting in order to gain insights into the relative importance of each aspect. Personally, I am not optimistic about such an approach because of the difficulties of generalizing from idiosyncratic settings. Carol Weiss proposes a modification of the effective users study; researchers might start with specific decisions that have been made, and then—through interviews, document analysis, and so on—determine what information influenced each decision. Such a study would provide insights about the influence of evaluation on specific decisions. I note that Brian Stecher and I conducted such a study in elementary schools and found it to be highly illuminating. Nonetheless, a series of similar studies in a variety of decision contexts could be quite informative. Finally, Mike Patton proposes an action orientation to the study of evaluation use—a suggestion that seems altogether fitting and consistent with his general orientation to evaluation. Patton feels that researchers might learn more about evaluation by attempting to do an evaluation that incorporates all we know about how to obtain high levels of utilization. His focus is on learning from the implementation of a "best case" example.

While several participants focus on users (either to identify effective users or to start with the decisions they make), Ernest House extends his thinking about teachers and practitioners as users. House feels that evaluators do not understand how practitioners think about their world, and specifically notes, "How teachers think is pretty much a mystery to us." The implication is that we need to conduct research on how teachers think—and, more specifically, how and what they think of various kinds of evaluation information. A number of the participants disagree with that assessment and maintain that is not a valuable line of research, in part because teachers are such marginal users of evaluation.

Carol Weiss dismisses the importance of studying the practitioner-user's world. She does not view teachers as probable users, because "they have so much direct, rich, daily experience with these children. They know so much about them that the little bit of probabilistic information that evaluation can add isn't going to be that much of an increment." Evaluation information is seen as a part of the total information flow that relates to decisions. And Weiss concludes that the richness of information already available to teachers, for the kinds of decisions they are likely to make, far overwhelms in importance the additional information that might be derived from evaluation. Weiss's view characterizes information as macro in nature. House's assertion suggests a more micro view. Surely teachers can (and do) benefit from evaluation information on their classroom processes and classroom achievement.

Others, like Patton, simply think it is a mistake to conduct research seeking to generalize about such a thing as how teachers think. Concern is expressed about asking such a generic question and whether the "modest generalizations" that could come from such study would impede the evaluator's ability to be situationally responsive. Stated simply: How helpful would such a study be, really?

Another theme discussed within Chapter 3 is that of utilization, reporting, and the recurring "D word," dissemination. The broader issue has been discussed earlier in this section. Here discussion focuses on improvement of dissemination procedures in order to increase potential utilization. Weiss describes potential modes of disseminating evaluation findings—with primary emphasis on situations involving policy studies. An unresolved dissemination issue addresses the value of seeking and incorporating evaluation data from other contexts into a particular evaluation. Questions about access to such information and the issues of generalizability and data applicability also are raised (but not resolved).

Finally, having discussed research and then dissemination, seminar participants briefly discuss evaluation training. They conclude that the primary means for increasing evaluation utilization is by providing program evaluation training for principals and superintendents. Research on evaluation utilization factors highlights the importance of informed users who understand and appreciate the importance of evaluation. Other research provides case-study examples of situations where identified potential users were, in essence, more utilization oriented. A major means of enhancing the possibility of evaluation use, then, is training decision makers in the way in which evaluation information could be beneficial in the decision-making process. Seminar participants also note that many experienced evaluators could benefit from training. There are many evaluators who have come to view their job in a strictly technical way. Evaluation training that emphasizes known utilization factors might humanize the process and, in so doing, lead to enhanced utilization.

References

Alkin, M. C. (1985). *A guide for evaluation decision makers.* Beverly Hills, CA: Sage.

Alkin, M. C., Daillak, R. H., & White, P. (1979). *Using evaluations: Does evaluation make a difference?* Beverly Hills, CA: Sage.

Cousins, J. B., & Leithwood, K. A. (1986). Current empirical research on evaluation utilization. *Review of Educational Research, 56,* 331-364.

Leviton, L. C., & Hughes, E. F. X. (1981). Research on the utilization of evaluation: A review and synthesis. *Evaluation Review, 5*(4), 525-548.

PART II

Evaluation Theory

Participant Introductory Comments

Participants

Marvin Alkin: The term *evaluation* refers to the activity of systematically collecting, analyzing, and reporting information that can then be used to change attitudes or to improve the operation of a project or program. The word *systematic* stipulates that the evaluation must be planned. This plan should be aimed at obtaining information that will answer the specific questions of specified potential users. The steps include an agreement about questions to be addressed, identification of the appropriate information, collection and analysis of the data, and drawing justifiable conclusions from the data.

Ross Conner: To paraphrase Lewin, there is nothing as practical as good theory. As the theoretical basis of the evaluation discipline has developed on such topics as planning an evaluation or ways to foster utilization, we have seen better outcomes from our work.

Ernest House: Evaluation is the assignment of worth or value according to a set of criteria and standards, which can be either explicit or implicit. It has its own logic and can serve either private or public interests. As practiced in late twentieth-century America, public evaluation should be an institution for democratizing public decision making, for making decisions, programs, and policies open to public scrutiny and deliberation. Hence, as a socially institutionalized practice, it should conform to the values and ethics of a democratic society. Considerations such as social justice, impartiality, and equality, while subject to disagreement and debate, are neither arbitrary nor relative.

Michael Kean: I tend to view evaluation according to a definition developed almost two decades ago. The definition is somewhat simplistic and is purely decision oriented. I believe that it was Dan Stufflebeam who initially articulated the definition; although I seem to recall a *Phi Delta Kappa* monograph (that perhaps Stufflebeam edited) that further refined the definition. Evaluation, according to this definition, is the process of delineating, obtaining, and providing useful information for judging decision alternatives. The definition "works" because of the built-in assumption that decision alternatives *will* be judged, and therefore will be easier to use by the decision maker.

Jean King: My notion of evaluation stems from my involvement in Louisiana schools and social programs for the past decade and reflects a local (as opposed to systemic) orientation. In my mind, program evaluation is directly tied to the outcome of changed practice, although such change may occur as much in the individual's mind and future actions as in observable alterations in a program. Evaluation is a three-part process: It raises questions about a program, ideally on issues that matter to someone directly involved in its administration or operation; it collects information to answer these questions, ideally with the involvement and cooperation of program personnel; and it reports results, ideally so someone will act appropriately on them. My experience suggests that most evaluations fall short of the ideal because resources for such activities are simply unavailable at the local level—if a choice must be made between serving students or clients and conducting an evaluation, there *is* no real choice—and because most practitioners feel uncomfortable with a process about which they know little.

Susan Klein: Evaluation is the use of disciplined inquiry to help people acquire and use information to make reasoned decisions about the relative value of a product, program, practice, policy, person, etc.

Alex Law: My conception of evaluation has been evolving over the past decade from the rather traditional view that evaluation is a process which judges the worth of an endeavor to the view that evaluation is a process that provides information, both at the program and at the policy level to a client system. The traditional constructs of formative and summative are subordinated to an evaluation which delivers timely and useful information for decision making.

Evaluators should keep in mind that policymakers who commission evaluations typically want the answers to three questions: (1) Did the project do what it was designed to do? (2) How well did it do it? (3)

What happened as a result of it being done? A process that provides relevant information to any or all of these questions is an evaluation.

Milbrey McLaughlin: Evaluation is the process of providing reliable, valid, relevant, and useful information to decision makers about the operation and effects of social programs or other institutional activities.

Michael Patton: I prefer a broad to a narrow definition. A great deal of diversity now characterizes the professional practice of evaluation. I include as evaluation the following elements: (1) systematic collection of information (2) for use by specific, identifiable people or groups for the purposes of (3) making decisions about and/or improving program effectiveness. This broad definition focuses on gathering data that are meant to be used for program improvement and decision making.

Carol Weiss: Evaluation is a type of policy research, designed to help people make wise choices about future programming. Evaluation does not aim to replace decision makers' experience and judgment, but rather offers systematic evidence that *informs* experience and judgment. It illuminates the current program situation, shows how things are working, what is going well and what is going poorly, and how the varied sets of participants conceptualize the meaning of the program in their lives. Such information helps stakeholders of all kinds plan more appropriate and effective interventions.

Evaluation uses the whole array of social science research techniques in its quest for systematic evidence. It draws on qualitative and quantitative paradigms; it uses observations, surveys, unstructured interviewing, tests, questionnaires and inventories, review of documents, and reanalysis of existing data files; it draws on historiography, ethnography, and statistical modeling. Perhaps its highest creative effort goes into framing the most appropriate questions about the given program in the given situation at the time. This is a tall order, but then evaluation is not for sissies.

Evaluation is systematic and data based. While we recognize that there is no single objective reality "out there" that evaluation can "find," evaluation strives for impartiality and fairness. At its best, it strives to represent the range of perspectives of those who have a stake in the program. The data that evaluation collects can be used by different stakeholders to answer the questions to which they seek answers. The aim of evaluation, as Cronbach and associates have written, should not be so much to point out the "correct" decision as to support negotiation and accommodation among the range of groups who have a say in the program.[1]

Discussants

Frederick Ellett, Jr.:   Evaluation activities characteristically are concerned with the intrinsic, extrinsic, or instrumental value of something (and such valuings are typically comparative). In order to accomplish this goal, the evaluation must employ certain conceptions of value and must employ certain empirical methods to show that something *has* the appropriate value-laden properties. These activities that are typically or usually performed to carry out the goal of evaluation eventually come to be called evaluation activities themselves. Thus the term *evaluation* has come to refer to a cluster of distinct but interrelated activities. And as evaluation activities take place in a special context, the evaluation will also be framed with its potential uses in mind.

Michael Hendricks: Must a program evaluator understand program theory in order to conduct good evaluations? In my opinion, the answer is, "It depends." For the type of goal-free evaluation which Michael Scriven has encouraged, no—theory is not that important. In fact, a knowledge of the theory behind the program can even be counterproductive. But for more goal-based evaluations or other evaluation-related activities such as evaluability assessment, yes—a knowledge of program theory is absolutely essential.

1. Cronbach, L. J., Ambron, S. R., Dornbusch, S. M., Hess, R. D., Hornik, R. C., Phillips, D. C., Walker, D. F., & Weiner, S. S. (1980). *Toward reform of program evaluation.* San Francisco: Jossey-Bass, p. 4.

4

Purposes and Function

Purposes of Evaluation

Ernie House: The current thought I've been having this evening listening to the discussion is the discrepancy between the world of the practitioner and the world of the evaluator-researcher. (I've been working on this recently, so it's not unusual that I hear that in the discussion. Like most of us, people who work on information systems are hearing that, people who work on strategies for evaluators are hearing that. That is a problem in any discussion.) My own thought is that we've got our epistemology turned upside down probably. This is not a meeting about the philosophy of evaluation, but I just think we've got things turned around backwards in terms of what's important and this has some implications for utilization eventually.

Marv Alkin: Do you want to set us straight as to how we are going to turn it around?

Ernie House: No. Read my next paper.

. . .

Marv Alkin: It seems to me that there are several interesting linked questions that I hope we can explore fruitfully tomorrow. And, of course, I want to hear from Ernie how we have our epistemology turned around.

Ernie House: Couldn't we save that for the cocktail hour?

Marv Alkin: I think I could take it better in the morning . .

. . .

Marv Alkin: Ernie has had an evening to think about it so we want to ask him to clarify how we can improve on our epistemology.

Ernie House: Without getting into a detailed discussion, part of the problem, as I see it, is that the practitioners, for the most part, know more about what they're doing than we know about what they're doing.[1] Teachers know more about teaching than what researchers and evaluators do. And, in a sense, the knowledge base that we really should be developing is what the teachers or the practitioners themselves have, rather than trying to find a knowledge base away from them and tell them how to do it. That's a thumbnail sketch of what I mean. There is a knowledge that exists there (with teachers). Now, the evaluator-researcher comes along and might be able to help assist that person in what she's doing, but at the same time, really doesn't understand actually how to do the teaching. The best that the researcher-evaluator can do really is to assist the practitioner somehow. But that's not how we act. We act as if we go out to discover knowledge, principles, techniques, which we then are going to tell to the practitioners, and that will make their practice better. Sometimes it works, but most of the time, it doesn't work very well.

Milbrey McLaughlin: How does that fit with the sort of scheme that I think Mike raised in his paper about the multiple purposes of evaluation, leading to multiple notions of utilization. Could you imagine a purpose for evaluation in which an evaluator, coming from the outside as you suggested, might be not only inevitable, but appropriate?

Ernie House: Well, I'm not saying the evaluator isn't appropriate, but I think you can't expect the practitioner to pick up on the stuff that we (as evaluators) generate. Practitioners know some things that we don't know and they are more correct in their knowing. That doesn't mean that we don't have a function.

Milbrey McLaughlin: Is that assuming that the purpose and the substance of evaluation is to elaborate practice? Are there other purposes as well?[2]

---

1. *Ellett:*   This is an important claim. Is it true? How would House defend this? Note: This form of knowledge at the local level *won't* be *scientific knowledge*, although it would be *commonsense knowledge*. There are different kinds of knowledge.
2. *Ellett:*   Good point: Evaluation is hardly limited to *elaboration*. Here evaluation elaboration is a kind of descriptive-explanatory account of what's going on. But can't we ask if it is successful and if the stuff is worthwhile?

Ernie House: Yeah, right, yeah. There are other purposes. For example, informing the public as to what practitioners are doing. Or making the practitioners or the professionals more accountable to external audiences. That's where the test scores and other kinds of indicators come in. But, it seems to me, one of the difficulties is when we collect test scores in districts, and then when we turn around and tell the teachers, you've got to raise these test scores—then you start intruding. That somehow doubles back on the practitioners themselves.

Marv Alkin: It strikes me today, as with a comment that you made yesterday, that you base your comments and discussions on some idealized notions of how evaluators act and what they normally do. So when you talk about the way the evaluators go into the field, and their relationship to practice, you may have in mind evaluators that you have seen and that you think represent the traditional mode. And you may be right—but maybe you aren't. At any rate, the picture that you have in mind about how evaluators operate, if typical, is not exclusive. And it is different from what I have in mind when I think of "evaluators." There are other kinds of evaluation strategies. There are evaluators who act in other ways, and that aren't exemplified by the criticism you bring forth.

Ernie House: Yeah. I agree, yeah. I'm taking one particular mode and one particular notion.

Marv Alkin: And it seems to me that we do a lot of this in the professional literature and our discussion. We create caricatures when we talk about evaluation. We talk about evaluators who are insensitive, evaluators who distance themselves from programs, we talk about evaluators who are this, that, or the other thing, who view their task as a research study not to be contaminated. And I think our descriptions are often wrong and tend to perpetuate a particular view of evaluation.

Ernie House: I don't think it's a caricature. There are an awful lot of researcher-evaluators, and that's exactly how they proceed, the way I'm describing. If you look at this book of Donald Schon's,[3] what I'm talking about is what he calls a model of technical rationality. The kind of stuff that Mike does isn't quite that kind of evaluation. If he goes in and talks to the people and tries to get more personal with them, what he's actually doing is trying to ferret out the kinds of ideas that are operating. And, therefore, that makes the evaluation material that he

3. Schon, D. A. (1987). *Educating the reflective practitioner: Toward a new design for teaching and learning in the professions.* San Francisco: Jossey-Bass.

collects more relevant, presumably, to the people that he is doing it for. I don't think the kind of stuff that he's doing is the prevalent form of evaluation.

The Knowledge Production Point of View

Carol Weiss: I think what Ernie's saying is not limited to a relatively small number of cases. Just to take the work that Ross used here and that is very common in the field, the transfer of knowledge from researchers to the managers and policymakers and practitioners. Consider the whole notion that evaluation generates knowledge, which is then transferred, to be utilized by practitioners or policymakers or program directors. Underlying that is a notion that we produce knowledge, and that somebody out there in the field has a responsibility to use it, if he/she wants to be a good effective person.[4]

Marv Alkin: That's one point of view. A view, incidentally, that the language in the field (and our assumptions that that is evaluation) tends to perpetuate. Personally, I find that language offensive and not constructive. A knowledge production point of view implies a static model with practitioners as passive receivers of information.

Ernie House: But I think that is a dominant view. I think that's the view of most people—knowledge production then utilization is the dominant view.

Carol Weiss: Knowledge production, dissemination, and utilization. The field tends to see it as starting with the knowledge production, and then getting to dissemination (or knowledge transfer) and to utilization.

Michael Kean: When you say these notions are widely held in the field, how do you define "field"? . . . Do you mean university professors or do you mean folks out there in schools that are evaluating?

Carol Weiss: I think evaluators, widely.

4. *Ellett:*   What is knowledge? Is this just another word for information? Science is the knowledge game that is after causal laws and causal explanations of the phenomena. I don't believe that Patton does that at all. What *kinds* of *information* does Weiss have in mind? Some evaluations generate knowledge, some don't, depending on what you take knowledge to be. If knowledge is some kind (or other) of *information*, then all evaluations produce it. But this is a trivial platitude. If you mean scientific knowledge, then most evaluations don't produce it. (Compare this to L. J. Cronbach's early views, where he was seeking a scientific explanation!)

Michael Kean: Then, I would disagree with you there. I don't think folks in the schools feel that way.

Carol Weiss: Well, perhaps the evaluators who work for a school district don't follow that model, but anybody who does research and evaluation, who isn't an employee or a staff member of a program unit, I think tends to see it that way. Almost all the outside contractors in evaluations, I think feel that way.

Ernie House: I agree with Carol. I think that is the dominant view. I don't know what percentage of people hold that view, but that's much the overwhelmingly dominant view. But a significant number of people don't hold that view. Let's say it's much more prevalent in some place like the Evaluation Research Society than it would be, maybe, in a school district. The closer you get to formal social science the more that view is held, I think. And the closer you get to practice, the less that view is held, perhaps.

Carol Weiss: Yes. I think that's true, because I remember talking to a session at an Eastern Evaluation Research Society meeting a number of years ago, and we got into a discussion on the uses of evaluation. There were about 80 people in the room. And I asked the group, "How many of you feel that your first responsibility in the evaluation is to the purity of the research and the knowledge that you're generating and to the field of knowledge, and how many of you feel that your first responsibility is to the agency and the staffs that you work with. And if there were a conflict, which way would you go?" And about 80% of them would go with the program and the staff, the agency. Because these were mostly people who were on the staff of mental health institutions. But that's very different from the people who write in the journals, and who write about utilization, and who write the books.

Marv Alkin: I don't believe that is totally correct. Some of the same discussions are found in the literature and among those who write about utilization. There are those who write about utilization but view the process as "knowledge utilization"—that is, use of knowledge that has been produced by the evaluation researcher and who is concerned about knowledge transmission and hopeful about the prospect of utilization. Others, like Michael, Jean, and I, have written about utilization but view that it requires continuing attention throughout the evaluation process—that utilization is not solely dependent upon transmission of a report and instead requires continuous evaluation attention.[5]

Research Use Versus Evaluation Use

Marv Alkin: Carol, I presume you make a distinction between research utilization and evaluation utilization. And you feel that the researcher and evaluator have different responsibilities . . .[6]

Carol Weiss: No, I don't. I think evaluation is a kind of research, evaluation is a kind of policy study, and the boundaries are very blurred.[7] And people who are going to use it don't categorize it in those categories. So I think we have a responsibility to do very sound, thorough, systematic inquiries.

Marv Alkin: Aimed at generalizations?

Carol Weiss: Not aimed at generalizations, necessarily. Aimed at specific situations. Aimed at specific target populations. I think of what Alex talked earlier about—specific Hispanic groups, not all . . .

Marv Alkin: Aimed at specific situations, or aimed at generalizing about specific situations?

Carol Weiss: Aimed at whatever . . . You can't generalize about things you haven't studied, all right? Because you study Cubans, you can't generalize about all Hispanics. You've got to go in no further than your data will carry you, in generalizing. If you study two programs, you can't generalize to all math-science innovations.

---

5. *Hendricks:*   In fact, transmitting the report is usually the *least* important part of being utilized.
6. *Alkin:*   I agree with Weiss's description related to research and research utilization. Lots of research will have very little utilization, and this I can accept. But I view evaluation differently.
7. *Hendricks:*   I agree that evaluation is a form of inquiry, but I'm less certain that it's also a form of research. Lines get fuzzy here.

5

Audience

Knowledge and "Working Knowledge"

Susan Klein: Carol, when you're talking about knowledge, are you talking about generalizable, research-based knowledge, or are you just talking about information that . . .

Carol Weiss: No, I'm talking about research-based, usually evaluation-based knowledge.

Susan Klein: That is somewhat generalizable?

Carol Weiss: Hopefully, yes.

Ernie House: Well, you see, that's where we start getting into difficulties. I think we're talking here about what we call knowledge. What the practitioner, what the teacher does, or the social worker, what they do in their work every day, we tend to think that that's not knowledge. Now I'm saying that is a fairly elaborate, fairly exquisite, highly developed form of knowledge that they have, which they arrived at in some other way. We've got this set of techniques over here, which we all know and which when used produces "knowledge." That's what we tend to call knowledge, and we expect practitioners to take what we've generated and use it in their setting. Actually, they have a whole other knowledge base that they're operating on.

Marv Alkin: We don't expect them to use it, Ernie. You're generalizing again to the one point of view that you say is "predominant" in the field. My point of view and, I suspect, perhaps a few others, is that it's not that we're in the business of producing knowledge and then trying to effect strategies that will help to assure that knowledge is utilized by them—someone. To too many people the utilization "problem" is getting those folks in the field to recognize the worth of the good stuff (research) that we have produced so that they will use it. Utilization by that definition is "end-loaded." Concern for utilization requires a much greater "up-front" effort to work with potential users to determine what it is that they "know," and want to know—with less of a concern for generalization.

Jean King: I want to label this idea [what practitioners do in their work every day and what they have come to "understand"]. Mary Kennedy has already labeled this. She calls this "working knowledge,"[1] and I think that notion is very helpful.[2] Every person in the field, and we all have our own version, has something that we can call working knowledge. That's how you get through the day. And it's bits and pieces of information that you've gotten from evaluation studies, from research you read when you were in college, from your next-door neighbor. All of that is put together into this set of assumptions, beliefs, and values, and that's what helps you to make decisions when they come up. And I think that if we frame our discussion using that idea, then we have a much better chance of coming to some useful conclusions here. Because if we can't get into that "working knowledge," if we can't change people's working knowledge, then we're not going to change practice.[3] If I as an administrator believe that evaluators have this mistaken approach, and I believe that they're not going to do me any good, then until that attitude is changed in my mind, I'm not going to take what you have to say. Evaluator, I'm not going to work with you. So, what I am interested in is the "working knowledge" of those people who are heavy users of evaluation information.[4] There are people out there who are doing that, with or without Marv's help, Mike Patton's help, or my help. There's an approach to knowledge, whatever we want to call this stuff that they use, that works.

Mike Patton: I take a somewhat different slant on that. I think I begin with the assumption that there is a "working knowledge" and practition-

---

1. Kennedy, M. M. (1982). *Working knowledge and other essays.* Cambridge, MA: Huron Institute.
2. *Ellett:* Why call it knowledge? Why not be neutral and call it mere *belief*?! Knowledge implies that one is *justified* in believing it; but one can believe unreasonable things.
3. *Ellett:* Even if we do get into it and change it, it need not be a change for the *better.* Are you folks just interested in any change whatsoever?
4. *Hendricks:* Sometimes, however, you can show people that the current situation should be considered an exception to their "working knowledge."

ers "know what they're doing," on the whole. In fact, the things that they believe that they know about are not easy to change. So what I look for with them are the pieces of "that perceived reality" that they're not sure about, that they are willing to investigate themselves. That only works if one assumes that, on the whole, while they have put together some things, there are some other questions that they still have that they're willing to take a look at. That's different from providing knowledge to people; it's also different, it seems to me, from a research stance that is trying to elaborate people's "working knowledge" for them. While going in and documenting the "knowledge" that these people have is a valuable task, it strikes me not as an evaluation task so much as research. Instead, working with them is a matter of figuring out which pieces they're still investigating and helping them do that more rigorously, to help them find out what they do and don't know and put it to a test—to do their own "reality testing." The powerful combination is respecting the things that they do know, and helping them find the things that they're mistaken about, to put those to a test, to increase that "working knowledge."

Carol Weiss: I'd like to get back to the policy sphere. I think that the exact same process is applicable at the higher reaches of policy. People have a great deal of knowledge about the substantive area that they're dealing with as well as the modes of negotiation and implementation. And what I have said is that the problem is not to increase the uses of evaluation or research, the problem is how to make better decisions, how to help people make better decisions. And are there ways that evaluation can help? And what are those ways? I think that, if I were to name the epistemological backwardness, it would be that we start by thinking that we have this golden chalice of evaluation to offer the world, and they are not making good use of it. I would just turn the thing around. People are making decisions and setting policies and doing practice, and how can we help them improve what they're doing?

Ernie House: Well, that's exactly what I meant by epistemological backwardness—we've got it turned around backwards. I think that policymakers in our system have an added encumbrance of having to justify publicly their decisions. Up to now, people like teachers don't really know evaluation and research to justify to their various constituencies why they're doing what they're doing. And that seems to me an additional burden that policymakers have, in addition to trying to decide the right thing to do. Often, a lot of policy evaluation is in the service of legitimation. And so, the policymaker thinks: I'm going to take this action; I know it's the right action to take; but how in the H___ am I going to convince people that this is the right thing to do? So the policymaker may have studies done to prove that that's the right thing to do—he already knows it. Up until now, for the most part, the teacher is in her classroom—and she's shut off and hasn't had to make those justifications. She doesn't have somebody on her back all the time asking her to justify every move she makes and, in a sense, she lives in a much more private world. (I think that's changing to a considerable degree.) But, I do think that policymakers have that additional burden.

. . .

Mike Patton: Particular studies and approaches do make a personal connection with people on the firing line. They speak to people about a place that they're coming from and a place that they're going to. Clearly the timing is part of it, some kind of shift of thinking is going on from one place to another place, and what happens to appear and is understandable at that point in time will make the difference.

. . .

Carol Weiss: But I did this study in the use of mental health research and evaluation, and looked at the factors of studies that people in federal, state, and local mental health agencies said were useful.[5] And it turned out that one of the characteristics of the studies that people found useful was that they challenged existing agency policy. And this was just by having them rate studies on descriptive characteristics and then having them rate studies on the usefulness of the data, and we did the analysis of the relationships between the two sets of ratings. In many cases, the people were in sympathy with the challenge, and they felt that the program wasn't working or the policy wasn't working, from their own experience, but didn't have any data that supported their concern. And having a study come out and show that there was something wrong with this program, or that there was something better about another policy, made the study very useful.[6]

5. Weiss, C. H., with Bucuvalas, M. J. (1980). *Social science research and decision-making.* New York: Columbia University Press.
6. *Hendricks:* I believe that one of the useful functions of an evaluation is simply to *create a discussion* around the topic, whether the evaluation confirms *or* challenges the working knowledge.

Marv Alkin: I'm thinking of Jean's comment about the Title I study: that in essence, the study fit into and was compatible with the working knowledge of some individuals within the organization. And that working knowledge . . .

Carol Weiss: Yeah, but in many cases, they hadn't crystallized it; they hadn't articulated it; they just had a vague sense of unease, and the study clarified what the issues were, what the alternatives were, what was wrong, what was right.

Marv Alkin: But, Carol, the unease was part of the working knowledge. And so the clarification was the expansion from that base.[7]

Carol Weiss: Absolutely, but evaluation never supersedes people's working knowledge, ordinary knowledge. Never. There's no way we can change . . . we live and die by our ordinary knowledge, even as social scientists.

Mike Patton: Can I write that down? Let me see that in print.

. . .

Understanding the "Audience"

Marv Alkin: I saw an interesting analogy . . . something that you said that helps to demonstrate the complexity of the issue. For some time, I've been aware of the image of evaluators acting in certain ways. The common image that most evaluators have some agenda, that they are going to try to do this evaluation, and then get people to use the information, as opposed to what I view as a more constructive way of performing as evaluator. But at the policy level, it seemed to me that the knowledge production-utilization mentality was the operational evaluation mode. But, you have pointed out that that's only part of the situation. Juxtaposed against evaluators who may have certain conceptions of their purpose in an evaluation are policymakers who commissioned the evaluation with a very different purpose in mind. And this adds enormous complexity to the consideration of the utilization issue.

---

7. *Ellett:*   Remember, *working knowledge* is just a fancy term for the practitioner's beliefs and attitudes—some of which can be quite unreasonable! (The group has already conceded this point.)

Milbrey McLaughlin: I'm puzzled about the distinction being made because what Mike described is really the policy analytic mode. Part of what a policy analyst would do, just in the course of evaluating, is to probe issues of feasibility and implementation, which are very much pragmatic and user centered: What's feasible in this setting? We're not going to go with a set of recommendations that suggests that all things would be better if you spent four or five zillion more dollars. That's not what a decent policy analysis does.

Marv Alkin: I understand that. It's perfectly reasonable to me. It seems to me, however, that you are describing the probing of issues related to the feasibility of doing what the evaluator-analyst believes to be appropriate versus what the user believes he needs. There is a difference in starting point. But beyond that I have a hard time juxtaposing the previous discussion about the activities of knowledge production utilization against that framework. That is, you talk about evaluation researchers with knowledge production concerns and then talk about policy analysts who you say act differently.

Carol Weiss: I have trouble with the word *knowledge* in this context, because so much of what we produce in research is very partial and time specific and not generalizable into the future very far. For now, it's pretty good. It's the best we can do and it's better than most people know, but somehow there's an aura about the word *knowledge* that makes it beautiful and noble for all time. We produce good information—I think I'm a little more comfortable with "good information."

Ross Conner: I don't see it that way. I guess for me, knowledge production is much more modest. That's why I see Marv setting up kind of a false dichotomy between what Mike was talking about—where you find out what questions are of interest to the local folks. Then there is a point where the evaluator has to produce some knowledge, essentially: Were those hunches right? They're not sure about certain questions. So then, it's our job to produce that knowledge. Now maybe it's too grandiose a term, as Carol was saying. Maybe we need a little more modest term. But I guess I don't see it in a grandiose way. It's at that point that it's on our shoulders to produce something. So then Mike goes back and says, "Hey the divorce thing is much bigger than you thought" . . . that's knowledge to me; that little chunk.

Marv Alkin: Yes Ross. But there is a difference in the extent to which the evaluator works with decision makers and policymakers to find out what they know, think they know, want to know, etc. For this group, we're all saying that it's those *other* folks who behave simply as researchers and produce knowledge but don't function as "evaluators." Not us . . .

Milbrey McLaughlin: They don't deserve to be here in Malibu.

Carol Weiss: And we all do.

Alex Law: It serves them right.

Carol Weiss: And we all do. After you invest three years of your life in study, you're sure you have the answers. But in our finer moments, we recognize the limitations of what we produce, and the limited understanding of what practitioners are. I like the way Mike tries to surface their uncertainty. And I think that's exactly what happens at the policy level. Staff people on congressional committees will talk to researchers and, if the conversation goes on long enough, they'll surface their uncertainties. They've got a program and they've got a political position and they know generally where they're going. But they've got some problems and they've got some uncertainties and they really don't want to make a major blunder, so they're willing to go along with people who have come up with some good information, and they'll pay attention and learn. You can change their minds if you're very credible and convincing, and you show them things that they haven't worked out before.[8]

Milbrey McLaughlin: But what you're both talking about is the importance of shared language. That, at the policy level, the analyst or the researcher is able to speak policy. And, at the classroom level, the importance of the evaluator being able to hear and converse in that setting.

Ernie House: But I don't think most of us are, for the most part, very conversant at the classroom level. We're much better able to talk to policymakers, who share our background, share our interests, as Carol said, and who, for the most part, share our ideology and we share theirs. And it's easier for us to do credible things with policymakers because those are the people we went to school with. You know, we interchange

---

8. *Hendricks:*   And if you spend enough time with them, which too many evaluators seem unwilling to do.

positions with them often. We're very similar to those people in many ways. We're not very similar, I think, or at least a lot less similar, to practitioners, like teachers. While there are some of us who have been teachers and may remember what it was like, there's a reality they engage in every day that we're not very conversant with. We don't understand their categories; we don't understand what they're doing. Lots of times it doesn't make sense to us, when it would make perfect sense if we could get into their shoes. Now, I think that's one of the differences between evaluation at the level at which practice actually occurs, as opposed to policy level.

Carol Weiss: But I teach. You teach.

Ernie House: But do you read the studies of educational research? When you go in and face your classroom, do you pull out the *American Educational Research Journal* and read what the correlates are with successful student outcomes, and base your teaching on that?

Carol Weiss: No. But what you're saying is that we don't understand teachers teaching. And, clearly, they don't read education research journals either.

Ernie House: That's right. We do understand teachers at a different level. But, we compartmentalize our lives. When we go into the classroom as teachers, we do things that are intuitive, but are not unsystematic. I know how to teach a certain kind of course, and make it come out pretty well for the kinds of students I get. That's phrased in very particular terms: I know the kind of students I'm going to get; I know the kind of material I'm going to deal with, and so on. At the same time, I don't think I'm able to go into a high school and tell a teacher how to teach something. And also, when I do research in evaluation, I'm off into another field altogether. It's a different kind of knowledge.[9] I do think that each is knowledge. I think it's knowledge in knowing how to teach a class—real knowledge, that we don't respect very much.

. . .

9. *Ellett:* Why is it a different kind of knowledge? Where are House's empirical data? From what Weiss said above, it isn't really knowledge at all. Furthermore, what is printed in journals isn't knowledge!! It only *claims* to be knowledge (future research may show that it is not knowledge).

User Focus and/or Broader Focus

Mike Patton: I'm bothered, I guess, by what seems to be an assumption that being responsive to an intended user for intended use would make one somehow less rigorous in one's work. Was I misreading you on that?

Carol Weiss: Well, I think I understood from what you said earlier, that you would take the theory of your client and you would try to explore the assumptions that your client was making about the program, and not go beyond that, not introduce other theory or other understandings. But really test your client's understanding and assumptions.

Mike Patton: But I'm going to test that rigorously.

Carol Weiss: Test that rigorously, but only in terms of the cognitive frame of your client.

Mike Patton: That's right. I'm not directly trying to speak to a wider audience. But that doesn't mean it's less rigorous.

Carol Weiss: No. But I don't . . . I think it's less . . .

Mike Patton: It means the questions are different.

Carol Weiss: It's less comprehensive an investigation of that program than I would think would . . .

Mike Patton: Well, how comprehensive the question is depends on what they're trying to find out.

Carol Weiss: Yeah. But I don't think it . . . I wouldn't be content with what they're trying to find. I think I would want to find out as much about that program as they want to know, and I want to know, and explore issues that people who have studied programs like that in the literature have raised . . . I wouldn't want to generalize to all times and all places, because I don't think social science, at it's best, ought to do that. But as an evaluator, I think I would like to milk that situation for as much knowledge as I could.

Mike Patton: Well, there's one of our utilization experiments [discussed in Chapter 3]. I don't know how we could set it up. But if we were able to construct a set of cases and allow these two approaches to interact, we could see if we came up with anything different. I really don't know that we would. But we might well. It would be interesting to see. If there were some way of running identical scenarios, where I worked with one and you worked with one, to see what kind of differences came up.

Carol Weiss: It would be interesting. There's one of Ross's planned variations.

Mike Patton: I think these are two really different orientations, different ways of ordering priorities. And whether or not that makes a difference and to whom is an empirical question that is hard to predict. You would speak to a larger audience than the stuff that I do. I think that's likely.

Carol Weiss: And I would want to be sure that there were some critical assumptions tested, as well as the practitioner's kind of faith assumptions. I think most practitioners believe in what they're doing. As you said earlier today, the kinds of things that they're interested in are differences in one modification versus another—should you do it in groups of three or in groups of five? And I guess I would hope that an evaluation would take a more critical approach to test the very assumptions underlying the program.

Mike Patton: Well, you see, if my client is the person who is making the decision about those two program choices, then that's where I would begin. It's a specific level of decision making. My client could be a congressman/woman who wants to decide policy for the whole country, and that would lead me to a different set of questions, on a higher level, but the process would be the same, user oriented, client oriented.

Ross Conner: I wonder if we could have Carol do your approach and you do Carol's approach. That's the planned variation I'd like to see.

Marv Alkin: Yeah. Well, I don't think that would be too fruitful. Because I don't think either one would be committed to the other approach.

Ross Conner: Which is what I was going to say. I wonder how much it anchors in the *evaluator*, so that these other variations we're talking about would sound nice, but it really wouldn't work out because we're talking about a very different kind of evaluator mentality.[10] And that's the crucial thing. Yes?

---

10. *Ellett:* Background beliefs and attitudes are part of the *kind* of UFE evaluator one is.

Carol Weiss: For utilization?

Ross Conner: I think Mike would say that.

Carol Weiss: Or for design?

Mike Patton: Well, these aren't nonpersonal strategies. If I can personalize for a moment . . . If one looks at Carol Weiss, and me, we have different reference groups, at this point in time and historically, that we're responding to. And Carol's strikes me as more the scientific approach with the higher policy-level reference group. And my most responsive reference group and the one I've had the most success with is the individualistic local clientele. And in terms of classic reinforcement theory or however one wants to look at it, our strategies are not happenstance in terms of the experiences we've had and what works.

Carol Weiss: But in terms of utilization, Mike, I would bet that your notions about utilization-focused evaluation have been used by people and studies that you don't even know about.

Mike Patton: I hope so.

Carol Weiss: Your influence is really irrespective of your personal charm and charisma, the way you would work with a client. . . . It's based on the intellectual appeal of your approach. And I think that's true of evaluation studies generally. That they go beyond the individual or the individual interaction. And I think we limit ourselves too much if we think of that interpersonal interaction as the critical component in utilization.[11]

Mike Patton: I don't disregard what you're saying, but from my perspective, I place a higher responsibility on serving the clients than on the broader aims. And that frame of reference does have potential for getting into some different orientations and doing things differently and that would be interesting to put to the test.

Ernie House: Well, how far would you pursue this orientation? Surely, you can't consider your only purpose to be meeting your client's interests?

Mike Patton: Tell me why I can't.

---

11. *Hendricks:* I think there's a logical difference here between generalizing an *approach* and generalizing a particular *study*. The former seems much more defensible to me than the latter.

Ernie House: Why? It's an immoral position.[12]

Mike Patton: I could argue it's immoral to take anything else into account when that's the person who supposedly . . .

Ernie House: You can't. You can't. It would be a long argument which you'll lose.

Mike Patton: Go for it.

Ernie House: There are too many counterexamples. For example, who has the money to purchase evaluation? The most proper people in society. You serve only the most proper people in society? You wouldn't condone that.[13]

Mike Patton: That's not my experience.

Ernie House: That's usually the way it is . . .

Mike Patton: That's not part of the theory, to me, in terms of the way I work . . .

Ernie House: That may not be what you think your experience is, but that would be empirically demonstrable somehow. Well, take medical care. If the doctor is only concerned with a particular patient and not concerned with the distribution of his or her services across the society as a whole . . .

Mike Patton: Which does seem to be the dominant motif, does it not?

Ernie House: Absolutely. Would you approve of that? Medicine for the richest? Surely, you can't condone that kind of position.

Mike Patton: But you're attaching clientele to the monetary system. I do evaluations where there's no money involved, and I have clients whose interests I . . .

Ernie House: Well, you may. But it's not really separate from the monetary system, you see. It can't be. It's not separate from the power

---

12. *Ellett:*   I believe House overstates it. Surely Patton's position seems unjustifiable, unreasonable, and *perhaps* immoral.
13. *Ellett:*   I believe House has brought up some very important issues on these pages. He has raised the issue of social justice. Is this a legitimate standard for UFE? House is also facing up to some of our problems in a supposedly democratic society. This is extremely relevant. UFE can't go on in a vacuum!

system. Not in this society. You must ignore the entire structure of the society in order to believe that. And you don't.

Mike Patton: What I am talking about, in terms of my personal responsibility, is . . . [14]

Ernie House: That's what I'm talking about.

Mike Patton: . . . is this set of people that I can work with, who will be different from case to case. What I take immediate responsibility for is what they do, the things that I do with them. I recognize that there's a broader set of things that are going to happen, but I don't take responsibility for what happens with that broader set of things.

Ernie House: Well, you must. Then . . .

Mike Patton: Because I can't . . . It's not my . . .

Ernie House: Then you are immoral. Right? You'll back off that position. You cannot possibly justify that position. You don't hold that position. I mean, you say it, but you can't hold it.

Mike Patton: My sense of responsibility . . . What I mean by that is that I take action and try to control what goes on. When results get into the dissemination network, and I lose control over that, I also don't take responsibility for it. That's what I mean.

Ernie House: Well, yeah, I understand . . . Yeah, maybe we're arguing a little bit at cross-purposes, but at other times, you do worry about the distribution of your services.

Mike Patton: Yeah, I've stopped answering distortions of my work.

Ernie House: Yeah, well, I'm not talking about distortions.

Mike Patton: That's what I'm talking about.

Ernie House: But see, you have to have a concern beyond the immediate welfare of the immediate client. I believe you do that.

Mike Patton: I think I build that larger concern that you're talking about into my interactions with that client. But the person I'm directly and immediately taking responsibility for bringing that to bear on is that

---

14. *Ellett:* But the issue is not what Patton is "willing" to take on. We're talking about the legitimate responsibilities of a UFE!

client. There is a moral concern. There is a moral and value context that I bring to bear in that interaction. But I don't take the responsibility for what goes on outside that interaction.[15]

Ernie House: But we have to.

Mike Patton: I take responsibility for bringing that in.

Ernie House: You have to do it sometime. You may not do it right then, working with that client. But you have to show concern for the rest of society. You can't just sell your services to whoever can purchase those services. That would be an immoral position.

Mike Patton: I resist confusing the monetary issue with the approach that we're talking about. They seem to me to be separate issues.

Ernie House: You have to be concerned with the monetary and the power issues sometime or other, at some point . . .

Mike Patton: Yeah. That's right, but . . .

Ross Conner: You probably also pick and choose your clients, right?

Mike Patton: That's right.

Ross Conner: My concern would be with the student who picks up, say, *Utilization-Focused Evaluation*,[16] reads it, believes it, goes out ready to do it, and then they're willing to work with anybody. And maybe they don't have the luxury of picking and choosing who they work with. Would this fit in with what you're saying?

Ernie House: It's easy to construct preposterous examples. Some guy has a concentration camp and comes to you and says, "Look . . ."

Marv Alkin: Why don't you give us a real-world example, so we don't look preposterous? Give us a real-world example of how you work with a client, but still show an expression of concern for interest groups beyond the client.

15. *Patton:* There is an exception that may help clarify my position. One of the options I present to clients is to speak to a broader audience. If that's what the client wants, I'll help him or her to do it. But if the client wants an idiosyncratic, nongeneralizable study, I'll also do that, and then I wouldn't worry about the larger dissemination audience.

16. Patton, M. Q. (1986). *Utilization-focused evaluation.* (2nd ed.). Newbury Park, CA: Sage.

Ernie House: If you do a Follow Through evaluation, or whatever kind of evaluation you do, sometime or other, I say that you should be concerned about the interests of the less advantaged people in society.[17]

Marv Alkin: And Mike has said that he can't do that directly.

Ernie House: I think he does. That's not the same as the situation where the person who can afford the evaluation comes to you and says, "Here's what I want you to do." And you work only with that person, serve that person's needs. That's not saying what I just said.

Mike Patton: No. And I've resisted tying it to the monetary relationship. I said I would take responsibility for intended use for intended users. There can be a broad range of types of people within any particular evaluation problem, as one runs through the stakeholder laundry list and it shakes out. Whoever is in a task force or whoever I'm dealing with, at some point, they become the intended group. They are the ones who are going to use this thing and who I aim my efforts at. And what I'm saying is that I take primary responsibility for working with that set of people on the evaluation. We build in some things that they're going to do with it, but nevertheless, there are some limits to it. We also attempt to package it and disseminate it in ways that other people can pick it up and use it, because that's part of the ethical context within which it is done. But that is a secondary effect. It is a luxury.

One of the things that I regularly ask people now, quite seriously, in the evaluation consulting enterprise, is whether or not there's a need for a final report in this evaluation. Now, our scientific canon would say that, of course, there has to be a final report, because that's the disseminatable document. But my situational responsiveness is such that I don't find the need for a final report.[18] I don't have sufficient commitment, even to the dissemination process, that I would ask people to spend that five grand that it takes to produce that, when we might well spend that five grand better on the immediate information that's needed for the situation. There's a cost involved in meeting the larger dissemination function. A high cost in a lot of cases.

17. *Ellett:*   Here House reflects his John Rawlsian view of justice. Perhaps what he has in mind is that the UFE should foster such dissemination.
18. *Hendricks:*   In my own work, I find a rough draft report to be much more powerful than the final report. In fact, I often include sections in the draft that I have no intention of leaving in the final, just so I can make points I feel are needed.

Carol Weiss: How about a journal article?

Mike Patton: Well, the journal article usually presupposes sufficient monographic reporting of the data that people can get more methodological detail. But I would be very reluctant to ask people to pay for the cost of producing an article that I was going to publish. I often do that on my own time, but that's part of the negotiation. The issue is how much it's worth paying the cost of that larger dissemination function versus the other potential uses of that money and time and effort for elaborating the information needs of the situation. And by raising the question of whether or not we need a final report, or even a written report of any kind, the real merit of such a product can be evaluated and costs can be attached to it. This should really be looked at because we know that a great deal of utilization occurs informally and verbally and in the process of the thing. There are a number of situations in which I now work that do not involve a report.

Ernie House: Which almost ensures that there won't be the kind of indirect use by unanticipated users that Carol's talking about.

Mike Patton: Well, it'll be difficult. It doesn't ensure that this type of use won't happen. But it will be more by word of mouth and it will spread.

Ross Conner: Well, that's risky business, because what gets remembered may not be the exact words of what you meant . . .

Mike Patton: Well, what gets quoted and often misquoted out of the reports is just as bad.

Ross Conner: Yeah. That's true.

Ernie House: I think the issue of unintended use is a difficult one. It's easy to think of misuse. For example, to what degree is Coleman responsible for the misuse of those studies? He does them in such a way that he lays himself open to people picking up on and generalizing far beyond probably what they should.[19]

Mike Patton: But the evaluator's ability to respond to that stuff is very difficult when it gets widespread. Two issues of *Evaluation Review* came out within the last year that quoted me as representing the position

19. *Ellett:*   I think House is arguing that the real merit must be seen to involve social values and consequences beyond Patton's client!

that utilization is direct immediate use on major decisions. They did this because there's a quote in *Utilization-Focused Evaluation* that says, "The dominant view in evaluation has been that utilization is direct immediate impact on major decisions." And the whole thrust of the book is to argue that that's not what it's about, that much important use is incremental, conceptual, and formative. And two articles attribute that narrower position to me. I just stopped answering them.

Ernie House: I can see why you stopped writing things down.

[laughter]

Mike Patton: But the same thing happens with specific evaluations. Part of the empowerment process that I want to convey to the people I work with is that they take responsibility for the indirect use because I'm typically not working in a substantive area where I have a long-term commitment. That's part of the difference between the specialist and the generalist. And that may be a difference which determines how much one looks at the unintended use. But I really work to empower people who do have that disciplinary or professional commitment. And I look to make them the disseminators and the people who are going to look after the unintended use, and answer the distortions, and follow this thing through, and champion it. And I want to provide them with the set of skills to do that, rather than doing that myself. Then they take the responsibility. In fact, there's a whole shifting of responsibility in this collaborative mode, where it is less the evaluator's responsibility and more the stakeholders' and users' responsibility, not only for the immediate action, but for the secondary use, tertiary use, and on down the road. And I leave them to track it, and lose track of the thing altogether myself. And they've done that.[20]

Ernie House: Well, you've probably . . . I think that's where you bring your notion of justice and ethics in. You're still talking about empowerment.

Mike Patton: So I sneak some morality back in.

Ernie House: Well, no . . .

[laughter and overtalk]

20. *Hendricks:* I think Patton's point about specialists versus generalists is important. Generalists may feel more loyalty to the entire field. Obviously, some of each kind of loyalty would be ideal.

. . .

Responsibility to Client and Audience

Carol Weiss: One confusion I have is . . . Help me understand why you see the responsibility to the client as almost exclusive of other responsibilities. Why can't one be faithful and responsible to a client, but also in an evaluation, leave in place the mechanisms whereby there can be other kinds of knowledge building?[21]

Mike Patton: It's simply a matter of priorities, because it takes resources to do that other piece. It is different to speak to a wider audience. It costs a lot of money to do that.

Carol Weiss: Well, not necessarily, it depends on how the problem's framed. It can be framed in a way that is intelligible and responsive to people in Peoria, but also to anyone who's interested in the question of, say, agricultural research methods. They can then take your case and build on it and learn from it. I feel like I'm missing . . .

Mike Patton: I don't object to that. As I said, I don't object to bringing in the other stuff. It is, for me, a lower priority than the more immediate problem solving, at whatever level. It can be a policy level.

Carol Weiss: See, what I'm seeing as exclusive, you're seeing as a question of resource constraint.

Mike Patton: And of the client's choice of how much to bring that in. I don't bring that ethic with me automatically. That is, I am prepared to . . .

Marv Alkin: Well, it's more than their choice, Mike, and you've said that. And you're really underplaying your role. It's their choice, but since you bring a working knowledge and a set of beliefs, you, in your consultation with them, try to—if you believe it to be appropriate—influence the way in which they look at the situation.

Mike Patton: That's right.

21. *Hendricks:* Sometimes a responsibility to the client can exclude larger knowledge building. For example, what if the client wants (and honestly needs) a private report? This obviously excludes secondary or tertiary use of the evaluation. I saw this once with HHS Secretary Richard Schweiker, at a completely off-the-record briefing that was attended by only six people.

Carol Weiss: For example, if I were called in to evaluate a displaced homemakers program, I would be enlightened by your observations of today, that staff tend to promote divorce and getting on with one's own life, and that clients don't necessarily level with staff. That whole story that you provided us I would find very useful as an evaluator of a new program, a new displaced homemaker program. And if you hadn't written that or told people about that, that would be an insight that would disappear. [See the section headed "Data for Whose Questions" in Chapter 7.]

Ross Conner: It would also be an expenditure of resources in a redundant manner.

Carol Weiss: Yeah. We'd have to reinvent that finding.

[overtalk]

Mike Patton: That example's a nice one, because bringing in the larger audience would have created confidentiality problems for some of those groups, that would have involved risks for them. Well, telling that story even, certainly putting it in print, doesn't make that program look real good from their point of view.

Carol Weiss: Well, who knows what program it is?

Mike Patton: You can find out. I don't know. It's not compelling to me to bring in a larger audience, unless it's negotiated up front as one of the options.

. . .

Jean King: The research I've done shows that there are cases where collaboration just doesn't hack it. I mean, even Michael Quinn Patton would have a tough time in some of the situations we have.

Marv Alkin: Well let's take situations where, perhaps, there's reason to hope for success. I don't know how we decide that in advance. This brings up the question of, can you take somebody who's not a likely user—and you can identify those people pretty well, I think—and turn him or her around? That's a very interesting question and worth studying.

Jean King: Or should we [turn them around]?

Marv Alkin: Well, I would say, yes. If we don't try, then why be an evaluator?

Mike Patton: I have too little time and energy to work against the impossible cases. There are times when I do an evaluation for the money and don't expect anything to happen—any use to occur.

6

Role of the Evaluator

Framing Questions

Milbrey McLaughlin: Microcomputers are threatening to a teacher [and others]. There's this new technical capacity to give you all you need to know about some of the effects of some of your curricula choices . . .

It means that, in a few years at least, one really can move away from a special program-type evaluation. That given six people, for example, you can have all six of them moving along in quite a different mode. The whole issue of program versus policy or special project will really no longer be applicable, because it's going to be information on a continuing basis. In this situation, the stakeholder issue becomes crucial. Here, you have this ability to get information as needed. As stakeholder 1, do I want stakeholder 2 to have anything to do with my information? And what does this mean as it aggregates its way up through the system?

Mike Patton: I'm not sure that I see that as a change. I'm not sure that the technology difference makes that much of a difference. I hear it talked about a great deal. But, generally, in current practice, there is the challenge of bringing together the different values [or different questions] of different people with whatever kind of information is going to inform them. And at both the program and policy levels, these things both occur. How complicated is it? How much information is accessible? Maybe those things have changed with new technology. But it doesn't seem to me that the values piece is more important or different with the new technology, just because there's more information to filter. The thing that hasn't changed is the human ability to make sense out of information. So, the more complex and the more pieces of information you get, the ideology and the value system are necessary to put the pieces together. The problem and the trick in this whole information business is precisely the problem of figuring out what's important. What is worth looking at? What's worth paying attention to? And that's a values question. That's not something that we can address empirically. Once we figure out what's important, we can bring our procedures in and deal with it. But it's all nonsense outside of the question of what's worth finding out, what's worth making sense out of? The danger, it seems to me, with the microcomputer is that it trivializes the whole thing. People don't make the important values decisions, because they're so busy putting in their bits, just gathering endless pieces of information.

Milbrey McLaughlin: Yes, that's true. I guess that the piece of it that I was looking at, Mike, was the multiple-use issue . . .

Marv Alkin: I would like to play the devil's advocate on this issue. If you look at what we know about evaluation and our experience, I don't find it persuasive that the display mode of evaluation information has been terribly influential in the decision process and in determining the extent to which evaluation information, in fact, is used. It seems to me that there are a host of other factors, elements, that are considerably more important. That being the case, why should we be persuaded that new information technology is likely to have any more impact?[1]

Milbrey McLaughlin: One thing to ask about it is what's driving it? Is it simply punching in frequencies or is it, in fact, question driven? The systems that I was talking about were systems in which an evaluator sat down with a classroom teacher, began to talk about interesting questions and what sorts of evidence would begin to inform those questions, and ways in which the classroom teacher could begin to be more active in the evaluation process. What sorts of things would begin to provide evidence on questions of student competencies, on a variety of discussions.

Marv Alkin: What you're really describing as the virtue is not the information system per se, but the way in which the evaluator operates within the system. What you're talking about is the way in which an

---

1. *Ellett:*   Information available on new technology might contain more *relevant, reliable,* and *timely* data! Surely Alkin can't generalize over all forms and kinds of information!

evaluator "creatively operates" in performing an evaluation, using this . . .

Milbrey McLaughlin: It's the notion of "an evaluation" that I'm beginning to resist. In framing these questions for a variety of implementers and deliverers using the new technology, you're moving away from "an evaluation" to an ongoing sort of information-informing activity. And it's not just information display at all. It's rather, moving toward a more continuous kind of evidence.[2]

Marv Alkin: When you frame questions and provide information and evidence related to those questions, *that's* an evaluation. At some point in the continuous flow of information a user feels that there is sufficient evidence to answer the question.

Mike Patton: I find that, to deal with the issue, one has to break it into some discrete pieces. And this notion that infiltrated the previous discussion—that the goal is "ongoing evaluation" . . . seems to me fairly mythical. "Ongoing evaluation" still needs some discrete stopping places to figure out what has happened over time. One of the things I get called on to do most often is related to this problem of people routinely getting ongoing masses of information. The sheer volumes of information make it harder for them to figure out what they know. They need focus to get a handle on the data. They need help learning how to deal with that.[3] Help may include bringing some decision rules to bear and deciding "when do we sit down and make sense out of this thing" and monitor those trends. Where there may not be a project with an end-point (and the classical endpoint) evaluation, one has to artificially introduce something like periodic focused reviews to make the process manageable. There have to be some kinds of timelines imposed on the data, to see how we got from here to there, and what's happened during that time. Over the course of such a process, the questions will evolve— as we figure out some things, we get on with some other things—it's ongoing in that sense, so that there's never an end; there are new questions. But each one of those new questions is a mini-project. It needs focus.

2. *Hendricks:*   Where's the line between "evaluation" and "monitoring"? Where's the line between "a series of evaluations" and "monitoring"?
3. *Hendricks:*   Car makers have recognized this problem and have completely replaced meters (for oil level and the like) with "idiot lights" that can be ignored until they light.

Milbrey McLaughlin: You bet. That's exactly right. Such issues as: What about the evenness of distribution of X.[4] This data can inform multiple levels of users. For me, that's why the program-policy distinction is becoming less and less useful.

Ross Conner: It looks like the evaluator is becoming less and less useful in that system, too.

Milbrey McLaughlin: The evaluator becomes a framer of questions, an interpreter of data, and someone who looks forward. The user can't do all that, nor can the policymaker, nor can the state-level person.

Marv Alkin: And who is to say that that wasn't, all along, the most constructive role that the evaluator played, even prior to the new technology?

Milbrey McLaughlin: Good point. And this technology really facilitates that kind of activity.

Marv Alkin: It *reinforces* that kind of activity.

. . .

Susan Klein: The responsibility of generating . . . and using information is two-sided. The evaluators have a major responsibility in both activities. Administrators, in helping to figure out what information to collect as well as what they'll use, also have major responsibilities. But administrators also have the responsibility for helping other groups of users tap into this information in responsible ways for educational improvement.[5]

Marv Alkin: That is, a data base may have multilevel uses if potential users at various levels have had the opportunity to really develop issues or questions of interest. But that isn't always so easily done.

Mike Patton: I don't think it's that hard to get people to generate "the" questions. The difficulty comes when researchers have their own questions that they really want other people (their "clients" or stakeholders) to buy into. And the resistance is that the clients aren't buying into it.

---

4. *Hendricks:*   Too often, however, state-level managers don't look beyond the data to ask *why* resources are distributed unevenly or *why* problem areas exist.

5. *Hendricks:*   Let's not let ourselves off the hook by assigning too much responsibility to administrators. *We're* still responsible for serving *them*, so let's remember that it's *our* job to find effective ways to have information generated and used.

And they spend all this time to get these other people to buy into their questions.

I think it is highly feasible to really help clients or stakeholders discover the questions that they have, and to move from there. But it is much harder, and much more typical, to see researchers trying to sell questions to the people—questions that they have predetermined. And frequently they can't hear the other questions, because the only thing they're waiting to hear is that their questions are the ones that are important. They will go at it and at it and at it, until their question finally emerges, and the clients are eventually browbeaten into understanding that there is a limited set of acceptable questions here and the only way out of this game is to come out with those questions. Which they eventually do; they're good folks; they'll eventually come around to the researchers' questions. They won't use the results, but . . ."Yes, you can get on with your questionnaire now," or "Yes, you can put those items into your data system now."

. . .

Types of Decisions

Mike Patton: It seems to me part of our role is that we're helping people make better decisions.[6] That strikes me as perhaps more accurate at the policy level than it is at the practitioner level, because what they do at that level would not be thought of as *Decision*. The evaluation role is partly making them more conscious and deliberate and aware of what it is that they're doing, because this knowledge you're talking about is too often passive, even to them. They often know that they're doing good stuff and they can see the results of it, but they can't lay out to you what they actually do. And one of the ways an outsider can help is to figure out what they're doing—and by so doing to enrich their practice, to help them be more deliberate and knowledgeable about what it is that they do and which pieces seem to be working. That's one of the most common kinds of observation work that I find myself asked

---

6. *Hendricks:*   But "helping people make better decisions" isn't our only way to contribute. Sometimes we can provide background information, or comparisons, or reconceptualizations—none of which affects today's decisions, but all of which may help eventually. To focus only on specific decisions underestimates our potential, I believe.

to do, because people really appreciate the feedback of having somebody else say: This is what it seemed to me you were doing and this is what I saw happening. I ask them: How conscious were you of that? Was that planned? Do you do that often? How does it work in other situations? And they begin to become conscious about previously passive knowledge. They're willing to use it more effectively, because the options become real to them. They can start to make some conscious choices about what to do in situations that go beyond intuition. That kind of learning is different from making decisions.

Carol Weiss: That's very similar to what goes on at the policy level.

Milbrey McLaughlin: Let me support Carol, because I have been doing both ends of the thing. What I heard you talk about is just what we're seeing. A major problem policymakers have is understanding what the question is, What is the problem? Even being able to diagnose what a situation is [is helpful]. And this is again where being able to talk about it, and to illuminate the choices, and identify really in a systematic way what the problem is.

Jean King: So, the evaluator's task then is to go in, meet with a decision maker (or multiple decision makers), and try to figure out their "working knowledge"—gaps in it, strengths in it—and then tap in where there are choices or questions or weak spots, and gather some "information," and then somehow come back and present that "information." Would we agree that that seems like a reasonable description?

Ernie House: That's one strategy. Yes. It's not the only possible strategy, but that's one strategy.

Jean King: Is that one strategy that will work? Is that a better strategy?

Milbrey McLaughlin: Better than what?

Jean King: Well, certainly better than our straw man.

Ernie House: Our straw man is 80% of what people are doing . .

Alex Law: The white-coated scientist who comes in to tell you the answers, create some information, or create knowledge.

Modes of Evaluation Practice

Marv Alkin: This is incredible. We all seem to be in agreement about what appropriate practice is, and yet we concur that most of the field isn't doing it.

Michael Kean: I think that it's one mode; and it's appropriate. But it's only one. It's like saying that it is appropriate to have prime ribs instead of lobster. I mean if you're in the mood for prime ribs tonight, then it's appropriate, but there's nothing wrong with lobster either. I think there are three or four other appropriate modes.

Marv Alkin: All right. What are those three or four? We've spoken of two so far.

Michael Kean: And it's not a matter of wrong or right. What's the two?

Jean King: Just for simplicity, let's call the first one the "appropriate" approach.

[laughter]

Michael Kean: And, the scientist approach, you know, the typically quantitative outsider who comes in to find knowledge.[7] Most typically this evaluator/analyst comes in and defines the appropriate questions as the outsider's interpretation of what happens.

. . .

Mike Patton: There are different kinds of questions. The more scientific mode is aimed at more generalizable kinds of knowledge. The other one is more situational, more situationally specific to people and to places. The scientific mode is looking for generalizable knowledge. Any specific situation is simply a place to generate information that's really relevant through generalization to the larger world. And part of the tension, then, between the researcher and the practitioner, at whatever level, whether we're talking policy or classroom, is that practitioners tend to be less interested in serving the purpose of generalization than in getting their own answers. So the researcher who's driven by the desire for generalization tends to be (it seems to me) likely to be somewhat less responsive to practitioners' situational needs, because

---

7. *Hendricks:*   It will be interesting to see if the discussion labels the "scientist approach" as quantitative and the "appropriate approach" as something else.

they recognize that these needs are very situational, and won't yield as much generalizable information.[8]

Ernie House: Let's remember one thing: Some of these formal kinds of methods of experimentation have been highly successful in some areas. There are certain diseases that we have cured. Some formal experiments find out what causes different kinds of things. Although the formal approach hasn't been terribly successful in improving education or some of the other social areas, it has been elsewhere.

Mike Patton: I don't find that to be the case in medicine or agriculture. I've been working a great deal in the agricultural field recently. Now, it turns out that the problem in agricultural research, when you get inside it, is the same as what we're having here. One of the main arguments now in agricultural research is whether it ought to be done on an experiment station or on a farmer's farm. And the difference is precisely the difference we're talking about between practitioner needs/interests and researcher needs/interests. Because the experiment station results are not working well on real farms. And so now there's a push for on-farm research. But the experiment station researchers don't like on-farm research because the controls are bad, there's so much variability . . . [9]

Marv Alkin: You might say there's so much dirt in the data.

Mike Patton: And the field is split. Agriculture seminars in farming systems research are caught between the experiment station folks and the on-farm research folks. And the experiment station folks have clearly been the dominant figures up to this point. They say they're looking for tight scientific findings. And then they say it's the problem of the agricultural extension service to take research and figure out how to make it work on the farmers' farms. It's not the agricultural scientist's problem to do that. They get the research results and then somebody else translates that to the farmers. And the other side is saying, "Yeah, but the experiment station's stuff isn't relevant, so we ought to start on the farms, where the real farming is going on, and do the research there and combine it with extension and make it one piece."

8. *Ellett:*   M. Scriven made this point in 1967 ("Methodology of Evaluation"). He argued that the evaluator can just determine whether *this* program really works (to degree D) in *this* situation. This is called a singular causal statement. It is *not* a *universal* (general) *law* or causal statement.

9. *Hendricks:*   Many states are having the same problem transferring pilot studies of welfare training programs to full-scale state programs.

Carol Weiss: That's wonderful. I didn't know that was happening.

Mike Patton: I find the same thing going on in the medical field. The big thrust in medicine now is compliance studies: finding out why people don't follow medical advice and studying what people actually do with their medications. Compliance studies reveal a major discrepancy between what the prescriptions say and what people are actually doing.

I was at a conference the other day concerned with medication regimens. They were honestly talking about building into the medications continued symptoms until you've taken the whole ten-day prescription. This would be a way to get people to take their full regimens of things like penicillin—because people stop taking it as soon as the symptoms go away. The only way to get people to continue to do these things is to keep them sick until they've taken the whole dose, and then they can be well. The point is that it's a different approach whether you start with how the clients view the sickness and work on that perspective versus treating them as simply biological phenomena. And folks are arguing both sides of that across the board.[10]

Carol Weiss: I'd like to comment on the scientist approach, which seems suddenly to be in very ill repute around here. I'd say that that [approach] can be very responsive to people's real questions as well. If you're sitting in the Congress of the United States, you may want to know whether, say, Head Start is still worth supporting. You have a question that needs some generalizable knowledge about nationwide programs that is not responsive to practitioners and their needs.[11]

Marv Alkin: Is that generalizable knowledge or is it simply knowledge required by a different practitioner—Congress? Therefore, because of the nature of this practitioner (Congress) and the differences in not being able to have close interaction, the evaluator requires more scientific-appearing data to attain credibility.

Jean King: We can go back to the point that Ernie made earlier, that the closer you are to kids or programs, the less likely it is that a scientific study will yield you usable information.

10. *Ellett:* It seems to me that several issues are being run together. *Medical science* has clearly established the procedures for taking various drugs. But, of course, the *public* is not following the procedures. So *public health* officials (and *social scientists*) must figure out how to get them to comply.
11. *Alkin:* I do not feel that it is necessarily not responsive to practitioners. These practitioners may need/want/require the "certainty" of a scientific study.

Marv Alkin: And if you're making a decision about whether to re-fund a national program ... .

Jean King: Certainly. Then you're up here [holding hand high], and you want to know information for 50 states.

Marv Alkin: Even in that circumstance, the extent to which the scientist has met with legislative aides or members of the key committees to try to understand the way that they perceive the problem, to try to determine what they think are the critical questions, is likely to increase the possibility that the scientific research findings will be, in fact, significant and relevant in framing future legislation.

Carol Weiss: Exactly. And that's what I'm saying. The scientific mode can be responsive.[12] I don't see the dichotomy being between the responses to your questions and being a scientist. I think we can do both. . . . It seems to me that what you're talking about now is making it a methodological issue rather than an operating issue.

The scientific paradigm seems to be one of a disembodied, white-coated person, who comes to collect data, goes back to the lab to analyze it, and then delivers an "objective" report.

I don't think one can use the paradigm to answer certain questions. For example, I would want to disabuse the congressional folks of the idea that they can answer a question like, Is Head Start working? Because there isn't such a thing.

Ross Conner: But it seems to me that the research that needs to go on and ought to go on—the scientific piece as opposed to the evaluator piece—is basic knowledge about how children learn and when and in what kind of environments. That is important, but it seems to me that the evaluator piece that becomes different has to do with what people are doing with that in programs, what kind of variation is being applied. What kind of generalization of knowledge would that be.

Mike Patton: That still seems to me to be the collaborative mode, because what you're doing is making that time and place decision. You're saying, in October of 1985, given the information we have right now, what seems to make sense? That is different from the scientific statement that says: Do these things to kids, forever, and you will get these kind of results. And a lot of that logical positivism is what has

---

12. *Ellett:* Surely—but the scientific research will be an important and essential *part*. Alkin's point is that it should be seen as *only* a *part*. Other things still should be done to make sure it is the *relevant* research.

driven the scientific perspective. That, it seems to me, has gotten us in trouble, because policymakers have thought we were going to deliver those kinds of *Truth* statements, and scientists pretended like that's what they were going to do.

Ernie House: Also, you just made something very clear, because I don't think that science and relevance are necessarily diametrically opposed. But are you equating scientism with positivism as some of the images here suggest? Because that's something else entirely.

Mike Patton: I am equating them, in terms of strategies.

Ernie House: That's very different. And I want to cue in on it. [overtalk] Because the scientist can also be a phenomenologist.[13]

Mike Patton: The Follow-Through Experiment, for example, was built on a positivistic model in that it purports to discover that there is a "model" out there of education that people ought to be adopting, and the researchers were going to find out what it was.

Ernie House: You're quite right. But that's an epistemological choice, not necessarily a scientific choice, because it can be equally scientific.

Mike Patton: That's why I said we weren't talking about methods . . . quantitative versus qualitative or something. We are really talking about the kind of message one can deliver. The issue here is approach and strategy, not the methodology that one employs.

Ernie House: I guess I was beginning to disagree a little bit with Jean's comment—the closer to the client, the less scientific. Because for me, being scientific is the notion of disciplined inquiry, which can either be phenomenological or positivistic, and I don't want to move away from that, even if I'm being as relevant as I possibly can.

. . .

Generalizability

_____ : My social science colleagues . . . [have a] dominant commitment to the role of generalizability across time and space.

13. *Ellett:* I think the term *phenomenologist* might be confusing. House probably just means that it is scientifically okay to consider the people's beliefs, purposes, and values. In my view, it is wrong to contrast this with logical behaviorism.

Mike Patton: Take, for example, the students being trained to do dissertations. I've had students warned away from my supervising their dissertations because I do not teach them that the only purpose of a dissertation is to generate truth across time and space. And one cannot do a dissertation in most university social science departments unless that is the purpose of the dissertation. Students may do them in applied settings, and call what they do applied social science. But, applied social science typically means you get data from real settings to generalize across time and space.

Susan Klein: I've always wondered, though, why we can't go from what Carol was talking about, the scientific approach, and apply it to multiple field settings. Let me use an example—the Joint Dissemination Review Panel [JDRP]—which you're all probably familiar with. The purpose of the JDRP process is to find something that works, that has some limited claim for generality. Okay, you find that a model works pretty well in certain situations. Why can't we, as scientists, especially now with getting more access to information via computers and more collaboration across the country, systematically test some of these models out in a wider variety of situations. You could then feed this information back and say, Okay, well this model works with certain kinds of students, it doesn't work with these; it works in this kind of situation, but not in that. And sort of build your knowledge base at the same time that you're serving your practitioners. But you would be doing it from a scientific inquiry base, with a focus on replication, to get at the wide diversity there, and still really contribute to the field.

Mike Patton: Let me try and use that example to show you what I think would happen in the two approaches. If one is interested primarily in the generality question, what you would do with the joint dissemination approach to replications is go replicate findings somewhere else. The thing that you get worried about is any deviation from that model in the replication process. And what you have to implement and test is *that* model as true to form as possible in this other setting. What happens in practice is that replication doesn't happen. It rapidly deteriorates from what that model was supposed to have been. And the struggle becomes, on the scientific side, trying to keep the model pure so that you can really test its generality versus working with the practitioners to do whatever the hell they want to do with the model, adapt it any way they want to, and study that new piece that emerges. The tension at the implementation level is the discrepancy between what is really being implemented in the new situation and trueness to the original model.

The field really struggles with that when we get into issues of dissemination. How much of something has to be there in order to say the original idea was tested out in the replication site? And on the scientific side, if you're really looking at that, you want to keep it as pure as possible. The practitioners, you can guarantee, will screw it up every time, will change it and do their own thing. And then you're not sure if you have that model anymore, or something else that's specific to them. So in terms of JDRP, you may not know any more about the model you started out to test than you did before . . .

Carol Weiss: I think that's absolutely right, Mike. And yet, I'll give you a counterexample. There has been 40 years of programming for delinquents, trying a whole range of programs to reform and rehabilitate kids who have gotten into trouble with the law: through counseling, through job training, through psychotherapy, through group therapy . . . you name it, they've tried it. And there must be, at this point, several thousand studies that have been done, about 500 of which have been judged reasonably good evaluations according to the criteria of Cook and Campbell.[14] And people have reviewed the whole body of the literature. And basically, they say, across all kinds of local variations, that they don't work. Now there's a generalization that has enormous consequences, if people take it seriously. Really significant implications. Everything we think we know, everything practitioners know from their own experience, suggests this is true. We don't know how, given our accustomed modes of operation, to keep these delinquents out of future trouble with the law.

Mike Patton: I think that's not the conclusion to draw from that. It seems to me that what we're saying, in the positive sense, is that there is no truth, there is no model. It doesn't mean that there aren't any effective programs, situationally. It means that there is no generalizable model, across time and space—which I would have expected.[15]

Carol Weiss: I think that it's more generic than that. I mean, most of these programs have been counseling programs of one kind or another,

14. Cook, T. D., & Campbell, D. T. (1979). *Quasi-experimentation: Design and analysis issues for field settings.* Chicago: Rand McNally.
15. *Ellett:* Not so. I believe that Weiss's point is that research can sometimes firmly and soundly *eliminate* alternatives as not being effective. And this is an important thing to do.

and there are many variations and very different local implementations, and yet they don't seem to be able to do that much for delinquents.

Mike Patton: Across the board, that's true, but I mean individually, some of the local programs *do* work. They get lost, though, when thrown in with national aggregate data.

Carol Weiss: No. I mean, for a few kids, there may be some positive outcomes, but there are almost no program success stories. And that's sort of an unexpected generalization. . . . They found what the evaluators were looking for. They may have been looking for the model that worked, but to find out that, given the current modes of dealing with these kinds of kids, we don't know how to do it. I think this is a conclusion of enormous significance, both for policy and for intervention programs.

Mike Patton: I would interpret it differently than you did. I did some of that work in Minnesota and we found, within the Minnesota context and with Minnesota kids and the Minnesota staff that was available, that there were better and worse ways of going about it. And practitioners changed some of what they were doing, in terms of our findings. I wouldn't apply what we found in New York City or someplace else. But I think, within the Minnesota setting, we were able to come up with some things that were less effective and more effective with the Minnesota population, and that had an effect upon those programs. But I would not expect these finding to hold on an aggregate level. A lot of work in synthesis and meta-analysis convinces me that overaggregation disguises more than it reveals. I think that conclusions generated from this type of aggregate analysis are misleading. In a like manner, there isn't a model of evaluation or a method of evaluation or some technique that can be generalized. It is the situational relationship that emerges in the interaction between your policymaker and evaluator, and it's what happens there that is going to lay the foundation and be the basis for utilization.[16]

Carol Weiss: What you just said is a generalization that may help. I mean, I don't know whether the whole relationship issue is viable, but there's a generalization that might come out of a lot of situation-specific evaluations that would be very important to know. So I don't think you can give up at least some hope of generalizing.

16. *Hendricks:*   Which is why I'm a big fan of spending lots of time understanding the policymaker's world.

Mike Patton: Well, I think the change literature would confirm what you just said, that there's no specific inviolate model that works across settings. But what that literature can generalize is that it seems to be *how* something is put in place. This led to the kind of nihilism of content-free process. I don't think I'd go that far, but in general it seems to be how something is done and the process by which something is done that is more important than the what of it. That's another generalization, I suppose, but it changes the focus in an important way.

. . .

Role of Theory in Evaluation

Marv Alkin: We spent some time this morning exploring the general issue of how much of evaluation is an art, how much a science. Ross, you raised this topic. Did we satisfy your interests? Specifically, did we talk enough about what we bring to an evaluation, what do people think we bring, etc.? Do you think we still need some more exploration on these issues?

Ross Conner: Yeah. We definitely need some more information. I don't know if we can productively do it now. Maybe if we keep circling around we'll work it out. Part of my thinking was to determine if there was enough science or substance that we could anchor that somehow, so that we could have a point to agree on, and then we could incorporate the art around that. But I'm not sure what we're getting into right now, which is art and which is science. Or how much is theory . . . Milbrey and I were talking a little bit about that at the end of the lunch. We just started in on some ideas about the theoretical or nontheoretical.

Milbrey McLaughlin: About the importance of theory in doing this kind of work. That unlike basic research, where theory plays a prominent role, I would argue that in evaluation policy analysis, theory is absolutely crucial but it serves a different purpose. And I guess what I was saying was that one thing I would use to distinguish good evaluation research from not-so-good evaluation research is the role that theory has played in formulating the problem. Go on, hit me.

[overtalk]

Mike Patton: I am going to have to ask, unfortunately, for the inevitable definition of the question.

Milbrey McLaughlin: Oh God. What's theory?

Marv Alkin: And I rather suspect you would disagree with that.

Mike Patton: Well, that depends on how she answers that question.

Milbrey McLaughlin: This reminds me of a discussion I just had with Liz Cohen.[17] You're laughing. By theory, what I'm intending is kind of a systematic body of information that can be focused on something. Return to the change-agent study as an example. I would suggest that one of the reasons why it turned out to be as useful as it was, beyond the obvious kind of serendipity in time, etc., etc., is that it had a very strong theoretical base, which wasn't always apparent, but it really helped us focus on some things and understand some likely relationships that people hadn't looked at before. We began to use what we knew—both Paul and I are organization-type people—what we knew about how organizations behaved, to begin to frame change agents. That's what I mean by theory: kind of a systematic volume of information that you can use to focus on an issue. I don't necessarily mean theory as abstraction.[18]

Mike Patton: The piece of that I would agree with, I guess, is that theory most often comes from working with clientele. The theory I'm interested in is *their* theory, testing out *their* theory, as part of evaluation logic. I work with them in identifying what their theory of action is, how they think the world works. I tend not to link that to an academic body of knowledge, although such a body of knowledge might well exist. But to be heretical on the other side, there are very, very few evaluations that involve any search of the literature. *They* are the literature; it's that working knowledge Jean was talking about—whatever is operational in their minds. It's often tacit, not very explicit. That's what I work with in the program design piece. I ask staff: "What do you think happens? How do people change?" It's usually some variation of anticipated, or "theoretical," linkages from knowledge

17. Elizabeth Cohen, Stanford University.
18. *Ellett:* This is an important conception of "theory." Notice that this is *not* an adequate characterization of a *scientific* theory. McLaughlin is merely saying that it is a coherent set of beliefs and generalizations about something, that is, a commonsensical theory. I trust she would add that the beliefs and generalizations are *probably true* (else, a theory could be most false!).

change to attitude change to behavior change. It is implicit in their educational effort or structure that they're trying to set up. And it seems to me that one of our roles is to flesh that out. That's where the sources of uncertainty are: Well, what is this linkage here between knowledge and attitude? Why do you think that if your clients in the program understand something different, then they're going to behave differently? What in your mind is the connection? How long does it take? When are we going to see that? What's it going to look like? If you accept that as theory, then we're saying the same thing. But it's not an outside body of knowledge. It's an internal piece of knowledge from the clientele's perspective, for the most part.

Ross Conner: Mike, I start the same way and try to lay out their theory of what they're doing. Then, using theirs as an anchor, I will go to the more traditional theory to see if there has been some other thinking about some of these links that may be useful in how I will go about the evaluation.

Milbrey McLaughlin: I was thinking about what I would go through in asking the question of what's going on here. Part of that would be what you just described. But for a lot of the work that I've been involved with—and you can't always do this—I would go to something else. And again, you know, it would never surface explicitly in any kind of evaluation report. But just framing questions, trying to think of connections that might not be apparent in asking, What's going on here . . .

Marv Alkin: You know, some of this is somewhat abstract and would be much more understandable if it could be framed within the context of a real example that you could cite. Can you give an example of an instance where you use clients' theory as a base and then look at a larger or related body of theory for a broader context? I would be interested in a real example.

Ross Conner: I was able to do a little theoretical, quasi-experimental study in conjunction with a citizen dispute settlement project I was involved with in Orlando, Florida. The idea was that they would bring in people who were having neighborhood disputes—barking dogs, post-hole diggers being stolen, kids throwing rocks at the neighbor's house (these are all actual cases I sat in on), things that can sometimes escalate into misdemeanors or even into felonies. The complainant would file a form and the two parties would come together and bring witnesses and pictures, and they'd all seen *Perry Mason,* so they all approached it that way. There were volunteer attorneys who served as hearing officers. And after, oh, two or three hours sometimes, they would try to resolve these disputes and write out a resolution for different parties and so on. Well, my job was to assess this thing. So what I did was to listen to the director's ideas about how this would work and what the links would be. Then I looked into the citizen dispute literature and anthropology literature . .

Marv Alkin: Let's talk some more about looking into the director's theory. Could you expand on that? What kinds of things did he ask you? What kinds of things did he tell you?

Ross Conner: Well . . .

Marv Alkin: What I'm trying to do is understand what you mean by the client's theory in this situation.

Ross Conner: In this case, it was his idea of how bringing these people together would solve some of these disputes, what would happen, and the links that were involved—these people talking in a neutral setting with someone who had not been involved in it but who had some status, an attorney who mediated the process. It also was held in the civil court. They held it there intentionally because they wanted the aura of legality, even though these hearings had no legal status, no legal restrictions on them. So that was part of the idea. That kind of thing; without clear links, but all those components were going to be important in this. They would have one side present the situation with no interruptions from the other; then the other side would present rebuttal; they would be back for a response, and then back again; and then, at that point, the attorney, the hearing officer would begin to play . . .

Marv Alkin: Now you're talking about anticipated procedure (i.e., the way the program is "supposed" to work), right? And when you talk about the theory that was in the head of people who were responsible for this, you're talking about what they felt were the anticipated links within the system that led to an agreeable adjudication of the issue.

Ross Conner: That's right. No theoretical ideas of the sort we're usually talking about, but they had a theory . . . a theory of action. Then I began to look into the anthropological literature and some areas I had never even looked at before, and discovered that there was this whole argument in the literature about whether this kind of informal dispute settlement would even work when the hearing officer did not know the people. It was contrasted with a situation over in Africa, where this also goes on, but you have a wise person who's the hearing officer, who knows the parties and knows the families and can lay out solutions that don't really exist for somebody who doesn't know anything. So here is a case where we had a hearing officer who had no interaction with the parties, and according to the anthropology theory, this should not have worked at all. And lo and behold, it did work in some cases.

Marv Alkin: So why did you look at the other kind of theory, and in what way did looking at it influence what you did as an evaluator?

Ross Conner: I looked to get even more ideas, I guess.[19] I think what Milbrey was saying . . . to see what other people were thinking about it, to help my planning in terms of the kinds of data I would try to collect for them.

Carol Weiss: To identify some of the critical variables. For example, if it turned out that this kind of process worked in communities that were very interactive and not in places that were not, you could work with a hearing officer who knew both parties. So that's what the literature suggested, and that identifies certain kinds of data that one would collect. One would try to identify the relationships within the community, the degree of association between the hearing officer and the parties involved and so on. It just alerts you to what are the factors that may operative in this situation.

Milbrey McLaughlin: And also, what their significance might be. I'm thinking of a little piece of a research project I'm in the middle of now. Something puzzling came up about teachers' willingness to engage in new activities that sent me to the theoretical literature on adult learning and development. And what I brought from that was the understanding of the need for adults to have a high degree of safety and the notion of rehearsal, etc., etc. So this then helped me understand some of the things I was seeing and, I think, interpret them better. We were seeing the importance of collegial kinds of meetings with adult learners, teachers who were trying to change. But what this literature suggested was that it wasn't the meeting *qua* meeting as much as it was the provision of an opportunity to rehearse that was important. So if that's the case, are there other structures in which this can happen? And we started looking for that factor. So we saw it. Without looking at that, the policy

19. *Hendricks:* This is the second time a participant has suggested that evaluators can be useful by broadening the array of possible actions.

recommendation might have been: You've got to have a whole series of meetings and do this and that. When in fact what seems to be going on is the importance of the rehearsal opportunity in any number of guises. Just like instructional leadership doesn't have to be located in the principal; it needs to exist in a building somewhere. It is identifying variables and thinking about interpretations that are relevant.

Marv Alkin: Well, to what extent did the outside theoretical concepts lead you in directions that may not have been compatible with the theory framed by those in charge of the program? Or was the research/evaluation successful in this instance because there were no strong theoretical concepts internally?

Milbrey McLaughlin: Well, can I use the change-agent study again? Both Paul and I, as I said, are organization theorists and this is what we do. And we tried to understand the theory of action that was behind the federal programs. It was our kind of grounding, our theoretical position, that led us to begin to look inside the black box, which people really hadn't done before.

Jean King: Are you saying then that any conceptual literature that a person in the world uses then becomes part of evaluation theory? That makes me more anxious than I typically am.

Carol Weiss: What you're trying to do is understand, to explain why programs work or do not work. You not only want to find out what works, how it works, but you also want to know why. And the theoretical literature in the field will turn up some of the important variables to examine in order to know why something works and why it doesn't.

Ernie House: Isn't that, though, suggesting the logical positivist business again? That's "causality."

Carol Weiss: That's not what I mean . . . No, it's not necessarily causality at all. None of the examples that I've just heard have to do with causality.

Ernie House: Well, I don't think causality is necessarily the word that the logical positivists use. Logical positivists believe things like . . . that the only knowledge which is legitimate is scientific knowledge. Other people might believe in views of cause and effect without being positivists necessarily.

Carol Weiss: Let's take a very specific example. We all—the society—believe that it is a good thing for parents to come to school and talk to teachers; that some conference between teachers and parents is good. And somebody decides to evaluate this. Okay, when you talk to the participants you might ask: What's good about it? What makes it good? What will happen because the teacher and the parent talk to each other? And you can get this implicit theory from the participants. The teachers think that maybe it'll turn the parents on to understand what the teachers' expectations are and then parents will help the students with their homework and encourage them to learn. And somebody else will think something entirely different: that the teachers will learn something about what the parents' expectations are, and the culture in the family, and the problems the kid is having at home. There are a whole lot of different understandings about what this contact means. Well, then you can look at some of the theoretical literature in social psychology about what this kind of interaction means to different people in different settings. For instance, *where* the interaction takes place might be very important: If it takes place in the teacher's classroom, where the parent is the outsider, it may mean one thing; if it takes place in the child's home, it takes on a whole different kind of thing. You know, there's a set of understandings that have emerged from years of social psychological research. Knowing about this work broadens the evaluator's understanding of what the possible outcomes are and what the variables are that should be taken into account and studied.

Ross Conner: You know, that's what could be another one of these lists of rules we've been coming up with from time to time, and that is, if this is done in the early phases, as Carol highlighted, you could feed this back to the program planners and say: Let's not hold it in the classroom; why don't you also do a little bit of this, because in some cases it's turned out to be better to hold it in this neutral territory . . .

_____ :   A perfect example . . .

Marv Alkin: I don't know how we can carry on this discussion without having some notion as to what the original question was. Let's just take the parent conference example. Now that's just kind of an overall issue, but without some understanding as to why the evaluator was brought in, and what the pressing demand was that led to someone saying, Would you come in and do an evaluation of X, I can't see the justification for getting so involved in looking at all the literature and the theoretical bases and so forth. You might be barking up the wrong tree.

Milbrey McLaughlin: I feel very strongly that some kind of content knowledge is really important to choosing the tools that you're going to use for the evaluation. I could no more go in and do an evaluation of, I don't know, water fluoridation programs, outside of asking somebody obvious questions . . .

Jean King: And how does this relate to use? I mean, that's what we're talking about now. I think you would probably agree that we can make the evaluation process better by doing some background work in the area studied.

Marv Alkin: Better in terms of the quality of the data?

Jean King: Right.

Marv Alkin: But not necessarily better in terms of impact. That's really the question. We don't know. The evaluation might be technically more scientific and "theory" based, but will that make it relevant and likely to be used by the program client/users?

Carol Weiss: But if the practitioners or the program directors know their program, and we show that we really don't understand the underlying premises, I can't imagine that they could take the evaluation seriously . . .[20]

Jean King: I can give you a good example. I'm doing a computer science training evaluation for a large computer company and while I know a bit about computer science, these are highly technical courses, well beyond my understanding of the field. So, I come in and ask what to me is a trivial question—Do you have a pretest and a posttest?—and they're excited about this fascinating concept—Oh, you can see how much the people have learned. And by doing that in kind of a collaborative mode, I have yet to feel the need to go out and learn the content of the courses. Now, that may just be an odd example, because the people involved know little about the educational process but I . . .

Carol Weiss: But you might want to know something about continuing education, to begin to ask certain, more fine-grained questions about

20. *Alkin:*   How is studying the research literature demonstrating that we "know their program"?

the long-term impact of learning in that setting, the extent to which it seems useful, the extent to which it's made a difference . . .

Jean King: I don't feel a need for a literature search. That's part of working knowledge that an evaluator would have, I would think. About education and . . .

Carol Weiss: Well, let's go back to Mike's very simple example about parent participation. It seems to me that, if you talk to teachers or principals or school people generally about why that is important, you get very simplistic responses. First of all, they've never thought about it before; they just know it's good. And if they have to make their tacit assumptions visible and accessible to somebody else, they will give you really a quite simple set of a few linkages. It would maybe be different from one person to another, but there are relatively few linkages in the field. By just sitting down with them and making available a whole set of alternative theories, which I think any one of us could do without a lot of literature review, I think we could help them understand . . . begin to question. Maybe in Mike's case, we could begin to raise some of the uncertainties, to surface their questions: that they don't really know as much as they thought they knew about this whole operation; that there are whole elements of it that are very problematic; and that it may be counterproductive, in some cases; and that there are all kinds of interactions and backward loops that they'd never even thought about. If we did a little more search of the literature, we might go out with even richer possibilities, and I think that that kind of inspiration can't help but enrich a research environment. And it doesn't involve months of library work. To specify several models of how a program works or is *expected* to work allows us to do a more relevant inquiry. We can better understand *why* it works or doesn't work. And on the other side, if we don't really push for alternative explanations of the "program theory," of the expected linkages from inputs to outcomes, we risk misunderstanding and misclassifying the program. We're likely to miss major variables in the evaluation. I guess I'm pressing for us to ferret out and surface the alternative program theories—the different assumptions that people make about how programs are expected to reach their goals. I'm thinking of parent involvement, right? Everybody said they aren't involved because they're apathetic. You know, it wasn't until the late 70s that people began to look at alternative institutional explanations about psychological accessibility and other factors that depressed involvement. This gave rise to a wholly different set of evaluative conclusions.

Ross Conner: I agree, Carol. I think its a matter of how people look at us as evaluators. And I know in some of the evaluations that I've done, they have wanted me to kind of be the devil's advocate. What they've wanted, at the outset, was: What do you think about how we are thinking about this or what are the gaps in our program? What are other ideas? How do other people handle this issue?

Mike Patton: I really want for them to do that. I expect them to do that.

Ross Conner: But that flies in the face of what you said earlier about helping them with the program development process. And it seems to me . . .

Mike Patton: I think it's a logical process. It's not a substantive knowledge process.

. . .

Marv Alkin: I'd like to play the devil's advocate for a moment, Ross. It seems to me that they want you to tell them how to do the evaluation and what to look at, so that they can more easily justify ignoring it. Because, if it isn't their evaluation and it's imposed from the outside, they will ignore it.

Ross Conner: No. It's not that . . .

Marv Alkin: Because they . . . wouldn't then have a vested interest in it to the same extent.

Ross Conner: No. It's that they want some different ways of looking at this. They realize that they've got a way, and they think it's okay. It's the right way. It's working, but they are interested in some other ways. And then together, we develop the plan and what we want to look at.

Marv Alkin: How do they tell you they want you to develop some other ways to think about it?

[overtalk]

Milbrey McLaughlin: Dear evaluator, we don't understand what's going on here. This is something I hear a lot. I'm sure most evaluators do. Help us understand what's going on here. Or sometimes: This is how we're doing it, we know other people do it other ways, what are some of those other ways? Isn't that asking for an alternative way of looking at something?

Marv Alkin: But you see, if they know other people are doing it other ways, they already know the answer to that question. Can't you just say, Well, what other people? What are some of those other ways? Let's talk together about what might be some of the other possibilities.

Ross Conner: You could. But I think that there are cases where they don't know what is going on exactly. They just know there are other ways. They hear bits and pieces, but they haven't had a chance to think about it. They've been too busy with their own program. In some cases, they want to know, and in some cases, they think the evaluator can take the bigger view. But not for the whole term of the evaluation. This is a beginning, and then, jointly set up some important evaluation targets.[21]

Context Versus Theoretical Knowledge

Carol Weiss: Let me give you a little illustration. I give my evaluation class, year after year, a trial assignment to plan an evaluation. And after about two years of doing this, I added another piece onto this outline of what they should do. And that was to review some of the literature on previous evaluations of programs of this type. And suddenly, the evaluations have been so much smarter.[22] This past year, there was a universal primary education [UPE] program in some Asian country. And I would bet that, if they hadn't looked at previous evaluations, it would have been a very simple, you know, pre/post kind of test of achievement, attendance, graduation, and that kind of stuff. But they read some of the evaluation literature on the Third World UPE programs,[23] and suddenly they became very aware of all the complexities of trying to increase attendance in elementary grades and improving education in these cultures. And they became much more open to qualitative methods of observation, to looking at the quality of the education, what the

---

21. *Hendricks:*   I found this while evaluating Delaware's welfare training program. Delaware knew other states were doing things differently, and they even had an inkling what those different things were, but they needed someone to help them design a system that drew on other states but was tailored to Delaware.
22. *Alkin:*   Smarter! But are they better? More relevant? More likely to be used?
23. *Ellett:*   What kind of literature? Reviews of evaluation studies need not be a scientific activity.

teacher's role . . . how the teacher's role changed, whether parents were supportive or not and why that might be. They just became tuned in to the whole milieu and context of underdeveloped countries.

Marv Alkin: Well, wait a second. Was that because they were learning better how to do an evaluation? Or because they were learning more about that context? Haven't you provided them with further information on the context of the evaluation? I mean, I think an interesting experiment you might conduct one year would be to let students read an evaluation about a different context. Not about the one that they were going to do their proposal in, and see if . . .

Carol Weiss: Well, they've done that during the semester. They've done that already.

Marv Alkin: Well, but that should improve the quality of their evaluation as well.

Carol Weiss: Well, I think just understanding the context, directly, makes them more sensitive to the complexities of changing social structures and . . .

Susan Klein: So, you maybe could have gotten them to the same point by giving them some readings or having them find some readings on the context and education in that particular setting, rather than telling them to go to the evaluation studies.[24]

Carol Weiss: Well, actually, that's what they had to do pretty much because there's very little evaluation sometimes and what it was was descriptive . . . a little bit evaluative. I think the importance of evaluation for utilization is that the kinds of evaluation that they were coming up with this past year would have been much more useful to a government, a ministry of education in that country, and to the World Bank, or AID, or whoever was funding that assistance.

Susan Klein: Because it was a richer, more relevant . . .

Carol Weiss: Because it was much more relevant. And it was much more feasible as an evaluation. They didn't assume the same values, the same structures, the same achievement tests that people would normally use. They had to realize that there weren't regular achievement tests.

24. *Alkin:*   Or interview some people role-playing clients in that setting.

That there were 50 kids in one room with one teacher and six different grades. And you know, that things were complicated. And just getting more kids into the room didn't necessarily mean that you were improving education. And that some of the central processes, the political processes that were operative might even be a challenge to the social structure of the village: if kids are now going to be better educated than their parents and the village elders. An evaluator's knowing more has got to make the study both more relevant and more useful . . .[25]

. . .

Marv Alkin: But you see, you're not making a case for the evaluation being based and formulated on theory as opposed to an understanding of local context. You're making a case for a novice evaluator learning something about the situation before—in whatever way is accessible—before the evaluation goes on.

Jean King: I think I would argue that, based on what we know about use now, if there's a limited amount of time, I would much rather have the evaluator spend time trying to get to know the people and trying somehow to figure out the political setting. That will yield much more information than our trips to the library to read up on appropriate social . . .

Carol Weiss: You're setting it as a dichotomy . . .

---

25. *King:*   The question of how much "theory" an evaluator should have—and I am using the term loosely to mean a knowledge base appropriate to the program's content—may be more easily addressed by programs that use external evaluators. When an organization hires an outsider to serve as its evaluator, program people have the opportunity to buy the needed theory by hiring an individual with suitable background and expertise in the field. Whomever they hire should, to the extent possible, become familiar with the conceptual issues and programmatic solutions currently facing similar organizations.

   The importance of gaining this knowledge and awareness is equally important for the internal evaluator, who, because he or she will be part of the program for a number of years, needs to be in touch with the rest of the field. You could argue that knowing the appropriate "theory" is even more important for an internal evaluator simply because his or her organization may never have the opportunity to hire current external expertise, and it therefore becomes part of the evaluator's job to keep the program up to date conceptually. In my experience, internal evaluators have trouble doing this partly because they are typically kept busy with day-to-day evaluation activities and partly because some of the needed information is hard to come by (e.g., evaluation reports are rarely available to wide audiences). The value of informal networks across the country that keep program evaluators and staff in touch with each other is obvious.

Ross Conner: It's not that at all. I think we're talking about starting with the program and doing all of that. Then, is there a role for theory? If it comes at the wrong time or if the novice evaluator just brings in a theory and overlays that they haven't accomplished anything. That's terrible. But I think there can be a role, and it can be a useful role. It can expand the view of the evaluator and the program. It's a real multiplier in a sense. Yeah. And so it's not "either/or."

Mike Patton: I see it mostly in relation to our discussion this morning. If you're going to be speaking to a larger audience, then what else has been done is going to become important. When and how you bring it in is variable. Given Milbrey's definition of theory, I would disagree with the statement that one of the main criteria for judging whether or not an evaluation was good is its theoretical linkages, if that means the larger literature. That would not be high on my list of criteria to do an evaluation. I don't have any problem with adding it, but it would definitely not be high up, for the reason I said.[26]

Evaluator's Preconceptions

Ernie House: I think I'd agree with Mike that there's a real danger involved. I would tend to do it the way Ross and Milbrey suggest. I can look at the literature, but I believe that what often happens is that the evaluator/social scientist has these theories and eventually substitutes those for what people are really doing. Because the people themselves are not articulate about what they are doing. . . . A lot of their knowledge is tacit. We go back to this working knowledge idea again. If you say to a teacher, "What is it you're doing?" you'll get some pretty crude stuff. That doesn't mean the teacher doesn't know what she's doing. Often the evaluator researcher inadvertently brings in a whole set of variables out of the literature that presents a nice articulate picture from the researcher's point of view, but which in fact doesn't really represent the project dynamics very well.

Milbrey McLaughlin: Well, I think it's just exactly the opposite. That if you didn't look at the literature, you would read your own preconceptions into that . . .

26. *Hendricks:* As an evaluator is usually an outsider trying to function (temporarily) as an insider, isn't it almost essential that he or she use "theory" from both locations?

Ernie House: Well, that's a danger, yeah.

Milbrey McLaughlin: But if you look at the literature, you see a variety of other interpretations that are possible and, therefore, it opens you to a broader range of possibilities.

Ernie House: I think the Push-Excel evaluation provides an example of what can happen when the evaluator imposes his or her own preconceptions on the program. It wasn't so much the literature that they got their ideas from, but their own background and training. And their work in Thailand with poor people reflected their own preconceptions of what was happening, right? You know, they put that over [imposed that framework over] the Push-Excel programs, saying, Now here are the dynamics. They presented that, you know, in documents to the program people. Charlie's a very articulate guy. So these people at Push-Excel sitting around saying, This is what you're trying to do? Well, yeah, sure, I guess, I mean . . . Because he presents a nice coherent kind of framework that's got some face validity when the people at Push-Excel weren't really doing what he thought they should be doing . . . Now, that's a danger . . .

Marv Alkin: You're really presenting an unfair example. Because the distinction you make is between the evaluator who is predicating his work partially on theory that he's pulled from the literature, as opposed to the evaluator who is doing it based upon his own working knowledge and theoretical inclinations, as opposed to what Mike has depicted as a more collaborative relationship in identifying concerns out of the local context. So I think the example you gave of Charlie Murray, who I've only met once and . . .

Milbrey McLaughlin: Is he going to come to our next meeting?

Ernie House: You can see him on TV.

Marv Alkin: But I think that that doesn't really portray the dichotomous position that's been presented here. I think actually that Ernie's right. There are at least three possibilities.

Ernie House: It seems to me that we want to work all three of them . . . I can't say, Don't use the literature and don't use your "own preconceptions." But on the other hand, when the literature or your own preconceptions replace what the program people are really doing, that's the danger.

Marv Alkin: We'll work them all together in some kind of artistic fashion. I'm not sure how they should fit together. There is something to be said for testing the practitioner's view. You don't totally accept the practitioner's view at face value. You challenge it. You challenge them, because you've got some preconceptions yourself or some ideas of your own . . .

Jean King: Somebody can say, a theory.

Ernie House: Yeah. And some of it comes out of the literature as well. So we've got at least three possibilities. It seems to me those somehow have to check each other. The practitioner's is the most important . . . should be, but we often replace that with the others. Now, I'm not sure where I . . . Who's side am I on, anyway?

Marv Alkin: I think you've really opened up the question for us, as not the dichotomy that we had been talking about but as several different poles, each of which is an important element in the development of an evaluation strategy and procedure, and with all of us recognizing that each of the elements comes to play to some extent. Even though we don't like admitting that our own personal theories enter into it, they do. We all admit that. We differ in the extent to which we would focus on one or another of those poles when push comes to shove. Would you agree with that?

Ernie House: Yeah.

Carol Weiss: And it seems to me that two days in the library is not excessive. And it could be momentously revealing.

Ernie House: Yeah. In terms of the utilization question, I think it's both the opening of the eyes as one goes out to collect data and it's also the understanding of the "so whats" once one has the data. It's kind of at both ends.

Carol Weiss: And there have been some very smart people who have done some of this research before and why not stand on the shoulders of giants?

Ernie House: As Mike keeps reminding us, since the evaluator's almost always in a more powerful position in a program, the danger is that the evaluator's definition of the situation will prevail: that the evaluator's preconception will prevail. So you almost have to work against that happening, even if you want to use and need to use some of your own preconceptions and research theories.

Mike Patton: I find that the published literature—and we may be talking about different literatures and I don't know how easy it is sometimes to get at the work that's relevant to a particular area—is more research than evaluation oriented and is looking at more generic questions. It seems to me that the utilization payoff in most evaluation situations usually has to do with the nuances of the situation. The margin of utility that is contributed via general kinds of statements hasn't been high, in my experience. I don't deny that you can have them. And I don't deny that it can play an opening-up function. I'm simply placing it somewhat lower in priority. I think that there's a knee-jerk reaction about doing literature reviews that we all learned in graduate school. And I question the sanctity of that.

Carol Weiss: Well, actually, it hasn't been true of evaluation. I think you do literature reviews maybe when you write the paper for publication, but not generally before you start the evaluation. Typically there hasn't been much review of previous evaluations before you start planning the new evaluation. Each of us sort of starts, or . . . until quite recently, starts as if we had suddenly discovered a new problem.

Michael Kean: Well, there's good reason for that, though, because until recently, with the exception of large-scale evaluations, much of the existing evaluations were not published in normal, accessible kinds of channels.

Jean King: But really, they're still hard to get hold of.

Milbrey McLaughlin: Yeah. But with the Freedom of Information Act, if you have any leads at all, you can usually spring loose a whole batch of reports that the agencies had conducted earlier. And they sometimes are really helpful.[27]

Jean King: I hate to say it, but the evaluators I have known—and I admit that I come from an unusual city, a less-than-ideal situation—they aren't going to do this. No way. I mean, they just aren't going to do it. And we can say . . .

---

27. *Hendricks:*   One good way to start, and a nice political way to boot, is to ask program officials what information *they* have relied on so far. By starting at their starting point, an evaluator can understand their viewpoints and then begin to broaden.

Milbrey McLaughlin: I would respond, Their evaluations would be less useful than they might otherwise be.

Jean King: I'm not sure . . . Less useful to whom? To you?

Milbrey McLaughlin: No. To the client.

. . .

7

Other Methodology Issues

Use of an Evaluation Model

Carol Weiss: Could we get back to the notion of "studies being used" because they represent a paradigm shift? I find that really intriguing, because it seems to me that that captures a lot of the anecdotes I've been thinking of off and on, where either something that you thought wasn't working was, or because something wasn't working when you thought it was. You find an obvious inequity in something you felt was fair or something counterintuitive or paradoxical or explanatory where people have been floundering.

Mike Patton: After *Utilization-Focused Evaluation*[1] came out in '78, school evaluators and human service evaluators, often in lower levels of their organizations, wrote to me to say, not that they learned something new, but that they finally had something to call what they did. They wrote that they had felt guilty because the stuff in the textbooks, Suchman[2] and all, did not work for them. And they weren't following the classic textbook prescriptions. They appreciated *Utilization-Focused Evaluation* because they now had something to call what they did, which is the collaborative approach we've talked about. They had been going back and forth, trying to figure out exactly what it was that they were doing. Now they could go to their boards of directors and funders, and say they were doing "utilization-focused evaluation." There was now a "model" that they were following that legitimated their

---

1. Patton, M. Q. (1978). *Utilization-focused evaluation.* Beverly Hills, CA: Sage.
2. Suchman, E. (1967). *Evaluative research.* New York: Russell Sage.

work.[3] The most common letters I got were this "legitimating" of a paradigm shift. A lot of folks out there were doing some version of the collaborative approach but hadn't had something to call it. [4]

[overtalk]

Ernie House: Well, it's not just what you call it. Legitimation is what you did. You legitimated what they were doing. They could call it something else, but you made it valid. Professor Patton of the University of Minnesota has a book which calls it utilization focused. It's too bad they can't perform the same function for your skeptics at your university.

[laughter]

Mike Patton: I keep thinking Carol's going to perform that function, but it takes time . . .

[overtalk]

Mike Patton: I got a letter from a woman who had such guilt that she had not been doing it right, and was about to give it up. She really . . . she just couldn't do that other stuff. She said: "I suddenly feel that I can go on." It was incredible.

Ernie House: You didn't start a syndicated column after that? "I've had trouble with my evaluation . . . "

[laughter]

Mike Patton: Particular studies and approaches do make a personal connection with people on the firing line. They speak to people about a place that they're coming from and a place that they're going to. Clearly the timing is part of it, some kind of shift of thinking is going on from one place to another place, and what happens to appear and is understandable at that point in time will make the difference.

3. *Ellett:*   Doing utilization-focused evaluation was *legitimated* in a weak sense. A strong *legitimation* would show in what situations it has probable *benefits* (and what its probable *costs* are). The strong legitimation has yet to be done! That a lot of people are doing it doesn't legitimate it in the strong sense. (Consider all those therapists using psychotherapy. It is still an open question whether the therapy is really any good.)

4. *Patton:*   They wanted the legitimation that comes with name, and label, a published book . . .

Ernie House: There is a difference here though, I think. Part of what we're talking about is legitimating evaluation in some of these examples, and in some of them, it's not. In some of them, it's finding something new, another model. In the case of legitimating, there's some prevailing orthodoxy that says: You should not be doing this or what you're doing you should feel guilty about. And then some other "authority" comes along and says: It's okay for you to do that—you just go ahead and do it and call it this and it's quite all right. What they've done is find another authority to legitimate that.

. . .

Carol Weiss: But I think that . . . evaluation can do more than just legitimate something people already knew. It can also help to clarify and crystallize it and express sort of vague, inchoate feelings that people have and don't really understand. Once evaluation does that, it really can be very helpful.

[overtalk]

Mike Patton: I'd like to have Ernie clarify what he said earlier regarding the legitimating function of research and how that pertains to cases where the research is not congruent with working knowledge.

Ernie House: It seems to me that we're talking about what's fundamentally a legitimating function in many cases. The example you gave for your book is the best example we've had right here; that is, we're talking about a book legitimating what people are doing, legitimating something. I think that's true for Charlie Murray's book for the Reagan ministers; that's going to legitimate what they would have done anyhow.

Mike Patton: It sounds like there may be another piece here, in terms of looking at studies that seem to catch on in some way. Most of the examples we've given, it seems to me, are fairly holistic and comprehensive in what they take on. In a sense, my *Utilization-Focused Evaluation* book takes on the entire scope of evaluating. It isn't one piece of the process. With the examples you think of as facilitating a paradigm shift, they have to do with the whole of the issue. They're not just some narrow aspect of normal research, not just fine-tuning some piece of it. It is indeed constituting a system or subsystem in its wholeness and speaking to inner relationships.

Whether the research supports that or not. I mean, the research in utilization-focused evaluation is relatively weak, from the basic research point of view. But the responsiveness to it was due, at least in part, to its holistic approach.

Carol Weiss: But it resonates with a lot of people's experiences . . .

Milbrey McLaughlin: And the whole issue of getting your head around the problem. And that's what we were talking about this morning.

Routinized Data

Ernie House: I was going to raise a question and we went past it, when Ross was presenting. One of Ross's earlier points, I notice, was about working into everyday routines of the organization. But I've got one concern about that. I've been very much involved in the past several years, the past decade or so, with our university's evaluation system, which evaluates its departments. We developed a bunch of forms and so on for the department head to fill out. And that procedure became highly routinized. By the time we went around again for another evaluation (the departments are evaluated every 5 years), the department chair would manage to cover up, to answer all the questions in a very perfunctory way. The question I have, and it is a question, is when the information system, the evaluation system, becomes highly routinized, does it lose a lot of its force, so that you're not asking important questions anymore? The evaluation forms may themselves produce information that covers up questions the respondents have.

Jean King: It's the signal, the signal function. You know, you're sending the signal that everything's okay.

Ernie House: And then it becomes routine information collecting, sometimes. I'm really puzzled by that one, because I saw that happen with our system. And you almost need to come in and change it every so often, just to throw people off balance.

Ross Conner: My point, I don't think, was that the system becomes day-to-day and routinized. It's that the evaluators should become part of that system.

Ernie House: It wasn't what you said that I was responding to really. It just reminded me of that one point.

Ross Conner: I wonder if it would work if you had someone around to keep identifying those uncertainties? If, Alex, you had the resources to have people, maybe regionally, who would come around enough so they had a good pulse on what was happening and could say: Hey, I sense something different now that you people are uncertain about . . .[5]

Jean King: But how often does that happen? We're talking about these major studies. They're not regular occurrences. Once the adjustment is made and we say, Okay, we're going to set up community services for deinstitutionalized patients . . . It's another five years probably, ten years. Evaluators can't regularly inspire major changes.

Marv Alkin: I'm intrigued by Ernie's comment, in that it seems to me that it gets back to something that Milbrey was saying the other day about micros. The issue is, when the data become routinized, does it make it difficult for an evaluator to identify questions and issues which require significant data other than that which has already been routinized? Does the routinization of the information acquisition make that information bureaucratic so that attempts to gather information more in line with real questions become more difficult? [6]

Ernie House: That's exactly what has happened repeatedly in our university information system. The units respond in such a way to cover up their problems. That's exactly right. It's not my own perception; actually, the vice chancellor called it to my attention the first time. If it's powerful enough that the vice chancellor would notice it, then you know that we're talking about a major phenomenon.

Mike Patton: I think there are lots of tricks that become part of that role we're talking about, helping people interpret or make sense out of routine data. Once you've identified the problem as routinization, it becomes part of the original problem of focus; with all the data there is to look at, which things do you pay attention to? And we're evolving

---

5. *Hendricks:*   Again, does this suggest an evaluator-on-retainer approach?
6. *King:*   Ideally it would seem to me to be a function of the time available overall for data collection and analysis. Once an administrator or evaluator can assume that certain data will be collected, he might find more time actually to look at or play with the available information. In practice, however, this rarely occurs because once the acquisition "problem" has, in a sense, been solved permanently, others arise to keep the individual busy. For this reason, the great potential that management information systems offer administrators is difficult to take advantage of.

some techniques, like decision rules. I've even stooped to having betting pools on how the data will come out on a quarterly basis; everybody throws in a buck and they suddenly are interested in the outcome. They may change the variables in the pool from time to time, but if you're going to win $50 on how the result comes out, then you show up for the meeting to hear the results—"must be present to win," of course!

Milbrey McLaughlin: Do you do T-shirts, too?

Ernie House: Evaluation utilization lottery.

Marv Alkin: I was thinking of T-shirts for Mike that said, Come on into the data pool.

Mike Patton: We still have lots of room for variations on how the forecasts come in. I think it's partly a human problem of attention span, focusing on all the information that's out there, getting people to pay attention to a piece and to take it seriously. . . . And what makes it situational is the need to analyze, in each case, what the hook is. I think there always is one hook, a way to capture attention.

Ernie House: Always?

Mike Patton: Yeah, I think there is. I think there are ways of getting people's attention that will work.

Marv Alkin: That belies the comment you made earlier about there being some situations where it's not worth the evaluator's time to get the user interested.

Mike Patton: It may not be worth the time. You may not want to do it. I have founds hooks I wasn't willing to use. But I think they're there. Sometimes they're political hooks; they're power hooks; they may be ideological hooks; they may be monetary hooks; informational . . . But there are ways of trying to make it different, to get people's attention and keep it from becoming routine. It's a real challenge.

Ernie House: But when you use some of those systems, say for a university or a school district, and you try to treat everybody the same, that quickly runs to bureaucratization, routinization . . .

. . .

Secondary Use of Data

[This section continues from the discussion in Chapter 6.]

Marv Alkin: I believe that Carol and Ernie are raising sort of complementary points. We are talking about limited resources and Carol's
talking about how to have a structure that can promote the extended use
of scarce resources. What I'm hearing being said is that tertiary or
secondary use of the evaluation is still very situational. I wonder if what
Mike is talking about would apply to the examples that have been
mentioned here.

Mike Patton: Well, I think there is a continuum here of evaluative
research, with the emphasis on research versus the situational program
evaluation. Where any given evaluation is on that continuum depends
in part on who is funding something and what their expectations are.
There are clearly evaluations that get funded that are closer to the
evaluative research end of the continuum, where the purpose is to
inform public policy—to make generalizations and major comparisons.
It seems to me at the other end of the continuum there are people using
enormously scarce funds in their local program to try to do a better job.
And they are not particularly interested in having those funds used to
make broader statements. I think of the women's crisis center that I
worked with. For them to have committed the meager resources they
did to an evaluation did not leave any money to do reports that would
be widely disseminated. It did allow me to work with them on an
informal basis, to take a look at things and gather some simple data that
would improve their program. So with this broad continuum, one of the
things that needs to be clarified in the process is the extent to which the
evaluation involves a tertiary and unintended consequence kind of
ethic, and, if it does, what responsibilities are involved. I think that has
to get clarified. Who are we speaking to? And who may see this? And
then what are we going to do to meet broader needs when appropriate?

And what I try to do is to make the alternatives explicit as part of the
interaction process. One of the options is, "You folks can try to put your
program on the map, if you really think it's hot stuff and other folks
ought to know about it." That's a particular kind of evaluation; there
are some costs involved in that; there are some methodological con-

straints involved in that, because we speak better to a wider audience with certain kinds of methods rather than with other kinds of methods. And so that's one of the options. And I try to lay out those options, including: Will there be a final report? of what kind? and how much will it cost? And that's all part of the context of who they want to speak to. And then, that's their choice. That's not my choice.

. . .

Data for Multilevel Use

Milbrey McLaughlin: It's the notion of "an evaluation" that I'm beginning to resist. In framing these questions for a variety of implementers and deliverers using the new technology, you're moving away from "an evaluation" to an ongoing sort of information-informing activity. And it's not just information display at all. It's rather, moving toward a more continuous kind of evidence. [7]

Marv Alkin: When you frame questions and provide information and evidence related to those questions, that's an evaluation. At some point in the continuous flow of information a user feels that there is sufficient evidence to answer the question.

Mike Patton: I find that, to deal with the issue, one has to break it into some discrete pieces. And this notion that infiltrated the previous discussion—that the goal is "ongoing evaluation" . . . seems to me fairly mythical. "Ongoing evaluation" still needs some discrete stopping places to figure out what has happened over time. One of the things I get called on to do most often is related to this problem of people routinely getting ongoing masses of information. The sheer volumes of information make it harder for them to figure out what they know. They need focus to get a handle on the data. They need help learning how to deal with that.[8] Help may include bringing some decision rules to bear and deciding "when do we sit down and make sense out of this thing" and monitor those trends. Where there may not be a project with an end-point (and the classical endpoint) evaluation, one has to artificially

---

7. *Hendricks:*   Where's the line between "evaluation" and "monitoring"? Where's the line between "a series of evaluations" and "monitoring"?
8. *Hendricks:*   Car makers have recognized this problem and have completely replaced meters (for oil level and so on) with "idiots lights" that can be ignored until they light.

introduce something like periodic focused reviews to make the process manageable. There have to be some kinds of timeliness imposed on the data, to see how we got from here to there, and what's happened during that time. Over the course of such a process, the questions will evolve— as we figure out some things, we get on with some other things—it's ongoing in that sense, so that there's never an end; there are new questions. But each one of those new questions is a miniproject. It needs focus.

Milbrey McLaughlin: You bet. That's exactly right. Which makes a very different role for the centralized office of the evaluation. In Missouri, for example, a lot of this happens at the state department level, as I understand it. My understanding is that they have begun to train state department people to go work with school people and began to do just this sort of thing. They will come in at different points during the year with this microlevel data and begin to talk through what it means for them as a classroom decision maker. These data provide considerable information both in terms of curriculum decisions for classroom teachers and also state level data for the state decision maker. Such issues as: What about the evenness of distribution of resources? Where are problem areas at the state level?[9] This data can inform multiple levels of users.

. . .

Mike Patton: The hope you're holding forth, for data that are really relevant at different levels, is something I remain skeptical of: the hope that the same standardized data can be really useful at the teacher level, at the school level, at the district level, and at the state level. I've not seen such data yet.

Milbrey McLaughlin: People in Missouri and New York say they have state-level information that *can* help classroom-level decisions.

Mike Patton: Can! Can! But *does*?

Milbrey McLaughlin: I know about New York. I've seen people actually go out and work with classroom teachers, and I've also seen people in the state level use the data to target resources.

---

9. *Hendricks:* Too often, however, state-level managers don't look beyond the data to ask *why* resources are distributed unevenly or *why* problem areas exist.

Mike Patton: Well that certainly is one of the dreams, but I think that probably the most common complaint I run into across systems—community service, criminal justice, agricultural extension, education, across the works—is the different needs for information at levels and the incompatibility of those different needs because the questions are different.[10] I think that probably the value contexts are different. The more aggregate data for generalizations that Alex might want for state purposes is not sufficiently detailed for most classroom teachers with the 30 kids they're dealing with. It seems to me that the information needs, especially the amounts of detail needed, are fundamentally different at the different levels. The hope of bringing them together into single systems strikes me as inherently impossible. And the people who end up getting put upon are the people at the bottom, who are required to supply the information to the people on the top.

Marv Alkin: But who resist by not doing it.

Milbrey McLaughlin: Or by making it up. This will be a black decade in social science with all those dissertations that are built on made-up data.

Ernie House: I agree. We're talking about different kinds of information; we're talking about a different kind of world here. What the teacher is doing, what the practitioner in any kind of profession is doing, is very different from the kind of information that researchers and evaluators are collecting. It is only tangentially relevant to what they're doing. And there are teachers operating in one kind of day-by-day setting and people at state departments are operating in other kinds of settings. These are ways of thinking about the world, which don't match information systems. You can try to make the teachers do it, and I guess that's what we do, and I presume that's what some of these large school systems try to do: make the teachers collect test scores and try to make them use it. That hasn't been very successful.

Carol Weiss: Most practitioners feel that by spending five or six hours a day with those kids, day after day, week after week, they know those kids, and they don't need a set of data.[11]

---

10. *Hendricks:* This was (is) one of the problems with federal data systems—local staff simply don't see its value, so they give it short shrift.
11. *Ellett:* This is an interesting comment. I wonder, however, whether there is any evidence to justify their feelings of knowing.

There was a study done for parole boards a number of years ago, to show which kinds of inmates were the best risks for early parole. Parole boards need this data because they do not see their clients very often—they see them once and they have very limited information about them. The expectation was that murderers are a very good risk for parole.

Jean King: They are?

Carol Weiss: They are. They're very good risks. They don't do it again usually. You know, you kill your ex-wife and you don't go around killing lots of other people . . .

Mike Patton: Until you remarry.

Carol Weiss: But this parole board should find some of these data useful. But it turns out that even parole board members, who see an inmate for only 10 minutes at a hearing, feel that they get more from their intuition about that human being than they get from a set of data. Because the data only give them probabilities.

Milbrey McLaughlin: Yes, but Carol, I have an analogous story from a classroom. Some teachers in the Bay Area were given differential information over a three-year period on the performance of their students, given the number of curricula objectives, etc., they were surprised that there turned out to be patterns in their classrooms that they were unaware of—in terms of what kinds of kids began to respond to what kinds of things. It was a handle for them that they hadn't had before. And once they began to think about those patterns, they really saw it useful in terms of planning classroom strategies for the future.

Data for Whose Questions

Mike Patton: The analogous piece here, between those two, is: if you did the study with the parole board on *their* own parolees and their tendencies, that would have a very different impact than bringing in some national expert's piece of work on parolees. If the criminal justice folks decided that was their question, and Carol worked with them for a year, looking at the rates of their own parolees, then what they're able to do is test that data against their intuitions and begin to make some adjustments. The larger scholarly, expert piece doesn't do that for them. What you're illustrating is that when you've got people's *own* questions getting answered with some data, they'll use it.

If I didn't believe that kind of approach made a difference, I wouldn't be in the business. That's precisely where the payoff is. You get a value structure, people care about something, and you help them investigate whether or not that's the way the world really is.[12]

One of the most exciting incidents I recently had of high-level use from clearly mediocre data was a displaced homemakers program. The routine management information system stuff that they were getting, and they all hated, was the intake data. They despised it. Nobody wanted to look at or even spend time with it. To try to make it kind of interesting, we took one quarter's data, and I had them guess, before they looked at the results, how they thought it would all come out. And these were the program staff, who knew these women very well. In guessing, they were correct on the socioeconomic indicators, and how many kids the women had, and their education level, and all that . . .

The question that they were obviously very, very wrong on was the marital status of these women: divorced, separated, married, widowed. And they started talking about why was it that they knew all these other things, but this one little indicator they seemed not to know about. They had guessed that 80% of the women were divorced, and it turned out that about 60% of them were separated, but not divorced. The first reaction, of course, was not to believe the data: "There must have been a mistake here somewhere. These women are divorced. We know they're divorced. We work with them all the time."

As we talked about it, we did some interviews to try to sort it out a little bit more. It turned out that the program ethic of the staff, which was strongly oriented toward it being important to be rid of a husband who had fouled you up and get on with your life, inhibited the women in the program. The women would not tell program staff that one of the issues they were still dealing with was whether or not to cut loose from their husbands. They knew that that was not a socially desirable place to be in the program. So, although their real status was on the intake form, once in the program they never really allowed the program staff to know that they were still dealing with this fundamental issue. And so, the other immediate explanation of the staff was, well, divorce takes a long time to be finalized; this is really just a happenstance—the court hasn't approved it, but they're really divorced. That wasn't the case at all.

---

12. *Hendricks:* But sometimes an evaluator has a responsibility to *stimulate* people to care about something, in addition to addressing those cares they already have.

As a result, their program was not working well, because they were focusing entirely on job training when the major thing that 60% of the women were dealing with was what to do with their husband and their family life, and whether or not they were going to go get a job seriously and attempt to become self-supporting.

All of that information—which ended up turning the program around and changing a number of things that they were doing—all of that came out of the marriage indicator on the management information systems data that they had been ignoring for a year and a half. Through the process it became their question—because the question was, Why didn't we know that? The question was: Here was something we didn't know. Whey didn't we know that? And they got excited about figuring out how it was that they had missed it.[13] I think that evaluators have to work with people to discover questions that interest them and that they care about. That's part of the process. The trick of this business is how to get people to care about something, to have something they're interested in. It became something they were interested in once they saw there was something here that they thought they knew, but didn't know. And that was what I was searching for in their guessing. The trick was to find something that they didn't already know, that they cared about asking a question about, and that they'd investigate with me. And they couldn't avoid it: They had written their guesses down and they were obviously wrong; it wasn't just a verbal guess. It was apparent that they had missed the results. (In case I've strayed too far, let me mention that the point that I intended to speak to was the question from the previous examples of whose questions we were going to answer.)

Susan Klein: The systemic evaluation project here at CSE[14] (Leigh Burstein and Ken Sirotnik) is trying to look at that question in detail with local high schools. And they're trying to see how they can merge various data bases for use by the staff at the school. But one of the things that they've been struggling with is, What questions need to be asked about this data base? . . . As we are able to collect more and more information, how do we as evaluators help people use that information, when they haven't had the opportunity to even think of possibly knowing that it would be available? And is that information really useful?

---

13. *Patton:* My point here is that the data analysis and interpretation process (guessing the results before seeing the actual data) helped the staff pay attention and care about the results. They discovered a question, a problem in the data.
14. Center for the Study of Evaluation, University of California, Los Angeles. [*Alkin:* The study is now completed.]

. . .

Jean King: Let's extend this point a bit. Mike, what do you think about meta-analysis and the attempts at synthesizing a whole set of evaluation literature? Do you think that's worth trying to do?

Mike Patton: Meta-analysis is sort of a more statistical attempt to aggregate—combining of a number of pieces. The tradition that I'm most familiar with is the anthropological one of using qualitative data to make generalizations across cultures. And I think there's a level at which those kind of things are useful and interesting. I don't have a lot of experience with it. It is clear to the group that my belief in the possibility of generalizations at hardly any level is fairly weak. So I haven't spent a lot of time trying to do it.

Ernie House: Do you believe in any generalizations?

Mike Patton: I treat them as hypotheses that take on reality in individual situations. So generalizations are a source of hypotheses. I believe in them in that sense.

Ernie House: But even a positivist would say that there is no absolute hypothesis, so you get the next-best hypothesis you can find.

Mike Patton: But one's behavior based on generalizations varies depending on how one thinks about the meaningfulness of generalizations. For me, generalizations are a source of situational hypotheses. I think that behaviorally and stereotypically, most people do much more with generalizations than that. They start to believe that they are reality. And then that's what they aim for. I treat them as hypotheses to be tested and I tend to find more deviations from them than confirmations.

Back to meta-analysis—the level of skill involved in doing that is not unlike creating a mosaic. That strikes me as being a very artful enterprise. It's like content analysis. And one can do a synthesis and compound the error, and one can do a synthesis and compound the right findings, which is why it seems to me that the enterprise has a set of limitations and parameters. It has to do with the credibility of the person doing it, and how they go about it, and all of those kind of things that one would take into consideration in any case. So it really does depend a whole lot on those studies that are being put together, and the extent to which it makes some sense to try to aggregate them into a whole and what that might inform.

I clearly believe in institutional memory. I believe people learn things over time. I think that we can become more effective in evaluation and its utilization, so it's not that there's no memory or history or learning or any of those kinds of things going on. I epitomize the notion of . . . it may be almost teleological, that there is some kind of progress, that we learn, that we know a lot more about utilization, how to do good evaluations, how to make a difference with them, than we knew 15 years ago. That's a kind of generalization. It's a building up of knowledge.

. . .

Scope of Evaluation Reporting

Mike Patton: . . . It's not compelling to me to bring in a larger audience, unless it's negotiated up front as one of the options, which I think it ought to be.

Milbrey McLaughlin: Here's what I don't understand. I don't understand why it costs so much more, why it's so much more resource consuming. I guess if you say, one question is whether or not to write a final report at all, I can see that. But insofar as you're going to write something down, why is it so much more consuming of resources to frame an analysis in such a way that someone else can hook in?

Mike Patton: A very good question. When one is dealing with fairly situationally specific, surface uncertainties, to use some of the language of earlier in the day, a certain level of evidence is necessary for people who are in the situation to take action. If you're trying to speak to people who don't know the situation and are interested in generalizations, then a different level of evidence is necessary.

Milbrey McLaughlin: Can I stop you here? Generalizations and degrees of freedom, if you would use a nasty term, can come from theory, to use another nasty term, as well as can come from data points.

Mike Patton: All right. You follow my notion about how the level of evidence is likely to be different inside and outside?

Milbrey McLaughlin: I'm following it, but I'm also saying there's another way to treat that. Another way to treat that is not adding more data points to deal with issues of external validity but rather embedding or at least referencing a systematic kind of body of information or relationships. For instance, say a literature review that would give someone a hook into where you were, so they could begin to say, Ah, this looks like you have a case of what I have a case of. I'm not applying standards of external validity or generalization in a traditional sense. No, I'm looking for ways of building knowledge in some kind of cumulative sense.

Mike Patton: My experiences suggest to me that the more one attempts to take those things into consideration, the more the design changes and the more the data change. And I'm not . . . I'm not really arguing judgmentally that that's better or worse. I think one is likely to end up with some different kinds of evidence and different levels of evidence when either theoretical or external validity concerns enter into the picture. I find it's real clear to clients and users when you're talking with them and laying out those options to them. And they often choose those options involving speaking to a broader audience. They often prefer to do something that will hold up and be the kind of data that is needed to convince people outside of the situation. It needs to be made clear to them that different kinds of evidence speak to different people in different ways, and what the relative costs are. I find, however, as often as not, at the local level, they aren't concerned with external audiences. But as often as not, there are users who don't just want to speak to themselves and find out things for themselves. If they really would like to speak to a different group, my position is simply that that's their choice. I don't automatically presume the focus of the evaluation.

Milbrey McLaughlin: That's very interesting, though, to imagine a world of no final reports.

Mike Patton: There's lots of variation, I mean, from final reports to just writing executive summaries. The classic final report is an enormously expensive document.

Milbrey McLaughlin: Absolutely.

Mike Patton: It is the most expensive piece of the whole work. The evidence, it seems to me, is that the utilization of that, outside of Carol's students and some folks, is not terribly cost-efficient, compared to the other things one can do. For example, spending that money on some very professionally done graphs and charts for verbal presentations, which are also expensive. There are some different ways of delivering the data which involve costs that are different from what we know as our traditional research report, which is the current norm. These other approaches impact on audiences in different ways. Most of those other communication techniques are less disseminatable; they're more local.[15]

. . .

The Summary Report as an Accountability Check

Ross Conner: Mike, I like your idea about the alternative approaches, but I'm troubled a little by the idea that there isn't something there. . . . When I finish a study, I feel like I have to put something out there that Milbrey can take another look at, that you can take a look at, that Marv, Carol, that other people can look at, to test what I've done, to give me some criticism. If there's no final report, if we just have a meeting and I give the clients insights and that's it, that leaves me in a very powerful position.

Marv Alkin: Who's the client, Ross? Are your peers the client?

Ross Conner: No, the client is the person who you're giving this to, but I guess in terms of my own accountability, I want to be able to . . .

Marv Alkin: Are you looking at this in terms of a peer review process to keep you honest?

Ross Conner: Kind of, yeah, but I need some feedback. Maybe if Mike does one of these oral presentations, you'd want to have . . . invite somebody else in who . . .

Marv Alkin: But he wouldn't. And why should he necessarily do so?

Ross Conner: But part of our process, it seems to me, as evaluators, as researchers, is that we keep ourselves open to criticism. And somebody else can take a look and agree or disagree. And if we cut off that possibility . . . then we become kind of zealots, and true believers.

---

15. *Hendricks:*   There's an important trade-off many times between the permanence of a product and its impact. Final reports are very permanent but can easily be ignored; briefings usually have great impact but are transitory. An ideal communication strategy would include some of each.

Marv Alkin: No. No. Part of our responsibilities as evaluators, and as researchers, is that we keep ourselves open to criticism, right?

Ross Conner: Right.

Marv Alkin: If the criticism we're keeping ourselves open to is only peer criticism, then I'm not so sure that I would call the activity, necessarily, "evaluation."

Ross Conner: I'm not saying only peer criticism. I'm saying, if there's nothing to look at . . .

Marv Alkin: I worry about the extent to which you are going to become so involved in your evaluation, with the end result of producing a report for peer review, that you would fail to serve the evaluative needs of the situation.

Carol Weiss: But then there's the other part: that you become so committed to serve your clients that you lose sight of the canons of empirical inquiry that would satisfy your theorists.

Marv Alkin: And these are certainly two different poles.

Carol Weiss: Every evaluator has those twin responsibilities: To do a technically sound evaluation that is also responsive to the needs of the people who commissioned it. What Ross is saying is that, if there's no evidence of what you did, I mean, you could have gone in and rattled the bones and burnt the pigeon entrails and said, this is what you should do, and . . .

Review and Commentary

Part II

A number of the important comments made at the Malibu seminar are organized under the general heading of "evaluation theory." General chapter titles ("Purposes and Function," "Audience," "Role of the Evaluator," "Other Methodology Issues") provide a broad framework for categorizing the discussion. In no sense does this discussion provide a definitive statement on any of these topics as would a normal textbook. It does, however, provide the interactive insights of leading evaluation theorists related to the particular topics in question.

Purposes and Function

Ernest House perceives the prevalent view of evaluation as being akin to the model of technical rationality described by Schon. From this technical rationality point of view, he claims that the primary evaluation purpose is discovering the knowledge in the field in order to report it back to practitioners so that they might improve practice. House condemns this kind of informed technician role in which evaluators study practice. For example, thinking again of the teacher as a possible user, he notes, "Teachers know more about what they do than researchers and evaluators do." Others in the seminar group disagree with this assessment on the grounds that it is an oversimplistic representation. One also might argue that practitioners (or anyone) do not fully know or understand what it is that they do and may welcome feedback in areas of uncertainty.

Others perceive the primary purpose of evaluation to be accountability, either to those in higher administrative positions within the organization or to the public. In this instance, the notion of technical rationality is not unreasonable and, indeed, is consistent with the accountability purpose.

In further discussing the purpose of evaluation, Carol Weiss expounds on the knowledge production view of evaluation: "Consider the whole notion that evaluation generates knowledge, which is then transferred, to be utilized by practitioners, policymakers, or program directors. Underlying that is a notion that we produce knowledge, and that somebody out there in the field has the responsibility to use it . . . that he/she wants to be a good, effective person." Weiss further notes that anyone not an employee or staff member of a program unit "tends to see it that way," as do "almost all the outside contractors in evaluation." Apparently, she believes that the knowledge production view is the most prevalent evaluation conception. Although the knowledge production point of view is widespread, it is apparently far less prevalent in program evaluation. Not surprisingly, this proves to be a major point of dispute between Weiss and Patton in their "debate" in Part III.

The discussion on differences between research utilization and evaluation utilization further elaborates the knowledge production point of view. Weiss does not distinguish between research and evaluation. She views evaluation as a very sound, thoroughly systematic inquiry, supportable in making generalizations. Given such a definition, it is easier to understand some of the differences between Weiss (McLaughlin and Conner) and Patton (Alkin and King) in Part I related to utilization. If one views evaluation as very much akin to research, then responsibilities for utilization are focused more broadly—and attained best, perhaps, by proper dissemination of "research-type" data. Those with greater client orientation view utilization responsibilities differently and focus more intention on individual users.

Audience

Who is the audience for an evaluation? Clearly one's view of the purposes and functions of evaluation strongly influence definition of audience. If one views the purpose as knowledge production, audience definition is substantially broader, for then the audience consists of all those who might benefit from acquiring the knowledge. Ernest House views this stance as widely prevalent and expresses concern about those who want to produce knowledge, get it disseminated, and obtain change without due regard for the perceived reality or working knowledge of practitioners whose programs are evaluated. All participants agree that "working knowledge" (Ellett calls it beliefs and attitudes about a situation) exists in the field and must be considered.

Patton maintains that utilization-focused approach does not conflict with practitioners' working knowledge because the evaluator seeks to investigate areas of that working knowledge "that they are not sure about and want to investigate." In essence, Patton indicates a desire to "be responsive to an intended user or intended use." By this he means that the evaluation should relate to issues that users are likely to address. Weiss notes, "I wouldn't be content with what they are trying to find. I think I would want to find as much about that program as they want to know, and I want to know, and explore issues that people who have studied programs like that in the literature have raised."

Ernest House also takes exception to what he views as a narrow definition of audience. In a particularly lively exchange, he comments, "Surely you can't consider your only purpose to be meeting clients' interest. It's immoral." Patton counters that it is immoral not to serve your client well and that his sense of responsibility is to his clients as audiences—and thereby being able to take full responsibility for what they will or will not do with the evaluation. He notes, "I cannot control [be responsible for] other usages of the evaluation by other audiences."

The issue of audience also relates to resource constraint. And the extent to which the resources are constrained within a particular situation is heavily influenced by the evaluator's theoretical orientation. Under practically all circumstances, an extremely strong client orientation demands the use of available resources for satisfying client needs. In the contrary instance, a knowledge-oriented evaluator (Weiss) and a social justice-oriented evaluator (House)—if I may label them in that way—may conclude that it is not possible to do the evaluation without addressing a broader audience, but each comes to this conclusion on different grounds. Thus, despite resource constraints, Weiss and House might devote less attention to client needs in order to address the broader audience.

Role of the Evaluator

Seminar participants broadly agree that the process of framing the evaluation questions is one of the most essential aspects of evaluation. Indeed, I would maintain that *the* most important role of the evaluator is to assist in framing questions. Within that generally defined task there are differences in evaluation practice. On the one hand, some evaluators feel that it is important to "really help clients discover the questions that they have" (Patton). Others, perhaps guided by their knowledge of relevant theory, feel that the evaluator's task is one of helping to guide clients to *the* relevant questions. In part, this focus on the relevant theory-based questions is out of regard for the obligations to the broader audience, as noted in the earlier discussion.

The frequency with which questions are framed warrants attention as well. Milbrey McLaughlin, attendant to dramatically increased use of microcomputers and the consequent ready availability of data, questions their impact on the evaluator's role. In essence, participants conclude that such microcomputer data bases might lead to an interactive evaluation situation, with new questions being framed as an outgrowth of prior data analysis—all of this taking place in rather short periods of time. McLaughlin, initially hesitant to call such question-framing activities "evaluation," ultimately seems to accept that definition. Thus under changing conditions of data availability the evaluative role remains the same (assisting in question framing and aggregating and analyzing relevant data), but evaluator activities occur in a more dynamic situation and compact time frame.

The Chapter 6 discussion focuses on the role of external theory in evaluation. At issue is the relative emphasis given the clients' theory of action versus a traditional academic theory. By *traditional academic theory* we refer to either the substantive discipline field of the evaluator or the relevant theory of the program field being evaluated. On the one hand, Patton expresses greatest interest in explicating the clients' working knowledge as a theory to be tested out, expanded, rebutted, and so on. Weiss, on the other hand, feels that it is imperative to look at other theories in order to identify some of the critical variables. By way of example, McLaughlin notes that she and Berman (her coauthor), as organizational theorists, tended to define the evaluation questions "in terms of our theoretical position." The way in which a particular conceptual literature gets chosen to help define an evaluation situation causes Jean King concern. She refers to the somewhat arbitrary inclusion of various conceptual literatures as a part of particular evaluations.

For those who advocate use of external theory in evaluation, choice of theory seems to be a function of an evaluator's unique academic background and his or her particular working knowledge with respect to the program field being evaluated. Those evaluators who advocate the influential role of external theories in helping clients to frame questions justify these theories as a "basis for posing questions with respect to the client's theory." Those who do not favor the imposition of external theories from the literature would favor a situation where the client accepts the possibility of other theories and asks the evaluator to look at them as a basis for better reviewing client questions.

Other Methodology Issues

Evaluators generally want to be viewed as "doing the right thing" and to avoid professional embarrassment. Professional legitimation is a stronger influence for many evaluators than situational responsiveness. In short, most evaluators "play it safe" to avoid having their evaluations held in disrepute by colleagues. Hence they conduct evaluations based on "justifiable" or "legitimate" models (whatever those terms might mean). Of course, the "research study" claims the oldest tradition of legitimation. Thus countless evaluators recognize that they have a proper defense against potential professional attack by modeling these procedures.

The various evaluation theories are of a more recent vintage (less than 25 years old); perhaps they still require justification. Even so, there are undoubtedly adherents to the CIPP model (Stufflebeam) or to responsive evaluation (Stake) or whatever. Patton, for example, notes that evaluators in the field who had been intuitively, albeit uneasily, conducting their work in a situationally responsive manner suddenly felt "legitimated" by learning that they, in fact, adhered to his utilization-focused evaluation model. Although my earlier work concluded that most evaluators did not *feel* that they used an evaluation model (Alkin, Kosecoff, Fitzgibbon, & Seligman, 1974), most evaluators are in fact influenced by their working knowledge of an evaluation or a research model.

That most evaluators claim to follow a knowledge production or research model of evaluation is undoubtedly related to this need for professional legitimation. Many who say they embrace the views of a particular evaluation theorist may be sufficiently influenced by the threat of collegial admonition to avoid fully implementing these theories. For example, some who say that they are doing a responsive evaluation might still feel obliged to follow the tenets of a traditional research study.

Embedded within the larger general discussion of data issues is a question posed by Ernest House on the role of the evaluator when data have become routinized. A dual dilemma is posed. In one scenario, the evaluation procedures conducted routinely over long periods of time might become predictable. As a consequence, program participants and other interviewees might easily "cover up" and provide what they know to be the appropriate answers. In another instance, Patton describes the problem of maintaining user interest in routinized evaluation. As his approach is so strongly predicated on a high level of user involvement, such lack of interest would likely lead to lower levels of utilization.

No obvious solution exists for either difficulty associated with routinized data. However, in the House scenario, the problem probably calls for the evaluator making modifications in the procedures over time and being particularly attentive to confirming findings from a variety of data sources. In the latter case, Patton describes procedures to keep program personnel involved, and through that involvement to raise additional questions or areas of concern.

The issue of the audiences for evaluation has been discussed previously. What is of interest is that the choice of a user/client audience or a wider audience carries with it implications for evaluation reporting. As Patton notes, "The level of evidence is likely to be different inside and outside." Thus he poses the possibility of resource constraint dictating the inability to satisfy both audiences simultaneously. Indeed, he contends that for inside or user audiences the production of a final report is not a clear necessity. He does not discount a report as a possibility, but merely notes that it is negotiable based on what is required to satisfy client information needs.

Others in the seminar seem to be quite bothered by the deletion of a final evaluation report. In part, this corresponds to the evaluator's perspective regarding responsibility to a wider audience. Participants holding this position argue that there are means of conducting evaluations to satisfy reporting requirements to both audiences that do not appreciably increase costs. Moreover, Ross Conner cites the need for an externally distributed final report for peer review and criticism as an accountability check.

A question that may be raised in response to Conner's assertion is whether focusing on a report for peer (other evaluation professionals') criticism subverts the integrity and focus of the evaluation. I am reminded of the practice in the American Educational Research Association Division H of presenting awards in a wide variety of categories for the best evaluation studies. While I have been a recipient of a number of these awards, I am nonetheless offended by the practice. How can professional evaluators judge the quality of the evaluation study without intimate knowledge of the situational context or without an understanding of the impact of the study? Is it likely that evaluators, focusing on a potential peer review, might place greater emphasis on technical issues that may be of greater concern to professional peers as they are unfamiliar with the evaluation context? From the previous discussion, the reader can easily surmise the response of the research-oriented evaluator.

References

Alkin, M. C., Kosecoff, J., Fitzgibbon, C., & Seligman, R. (1974). *Evaluation and decision making: The Title VII experience* (CSE Monograph No. 4). Los Angeles: UCLA, Center for the Study of Evaluation.

PART III

Evaluation Theory Distinctions: Further Debate

8

Evaluation for Decisions

Is Anybody There? Does Anybody Care?

CAROL H. WEISS

As evaluators, we undertake our studies with the intention of helping decision makers make wiser decisions. We provide evidence that shows the successes and shortcomings of programs. We identify some of the factors that are associated with better and worse outcomes. And we often try to explain *how* the program works in practice and *why* it leads to the effects we observe. We expect that these data will feed into the decision-making process and influence the actions that people take at the staff level, at management levels, or in the higher reaches of policymaking.

We are often disappointed. After all the *sturm und drang* of running an evaluation, and analyzing and reporting its results, we do not see much notice taken of it. Things usually seem to go along much as they would have gone if the evaluation had never been done. What is going wrong here? And what can we do about it?

I do not always turn to economists for advice on matters like this, but I recently came across a speech made by James Buchanan, who received the Nobel Prize for Economics in 1986. On that occasion, he said that "economists should cease proffering policy advice as if they were employed by a benevolent despot, and they should look to the

AUTHOR'S NOTE: This chapter is reprinted from *Evaluation Practice*, Vol. 9, No. 1, pp. 5-19. Copyright 1988 by Sage Publications.

structure within which political decisions are made" (Buchanan, 1987). His own early work, he said, "called upon my fellow economists to postulate some model of the state, of politics, before proceeding to analyze the effects of alternative policy measures."

Evaluators have been coming to the same conclusion. A number of writers have been urging evaluators to understand the decision-making systems in organizations and the policymaking system in government if we want our evaluations to have any influence. The traditional posture of our field toward policymakers is obsolete. We have been excessively rationalistic, and we have presupposed something very much like a benevolent-despot decision maker who would listen to our results and proceed to put them into practice.

Lee Cronbach (1982) has written, "Nearly all the literature on evaluation speaks of it as an attempt to serve a decision maker" (p. 5). He says, "It is supposed that information flows to a manager or policy official who has a firm grasp on the controls. . . . Actually, however, most action is determined by a pluralistic community, not by a lone decision maker" (Cronbach et al., 1980, p. 84). That is one of the keys to understanding the patterns of utilization: Program and policy decisions are the result of multiple actions by multiple actors. So most of the advice that we have heard over the years turns out to be irrelevant, because it is geared to the unitary decision maker, the benevolent despot, who can make things happen all by himself or herself.

You've heard the advice: Identify the key decision maker (or the few key decision makers). Get them involved in planning the evaluation. Be sure the evaluation addresses the questions they raise. Limit the study to variables that they have the authority to manipulate. Communicate results early. Talk to them in person. When you write, make the report short, clear, and simple. Make explicit recommendations for improvement. Be sure that the results, and the recommendations that you draw from the results, are feasible within the constraints of their organization. And so on. Evaluators have been repeatedly advised to make themselves and their findings comfortable and "user friendly" to the key decision maker.

In some cases, the advice works. There are examples of officials who have become committed to the evaluation and have proceeded to implement changes based on evaluation findings, particularly in relatively small programs without much divergence of interests. And of course these are often good things to do in and of themselves. Talking to program managers and staff, and discussing the questions that they raise, helps to educate the evaluator about the program and the issues it faces. Maintaining an ongoing conversation with people who will shape the future of the program keeps them informed about the emerging findings. But in most cases that I know of, the influence of evaluation on program decisions has not noticeably increased. Even evaluators who have tried conscientiously to abide by the traditional advice have had indifferent success in making evaluation the basis of decisions.

Let me give you five reasons why I believe that these kinds of strictures are only partially useful in most large-scale program situations.

First of all, they assume that one or a few key people determine policy. The traditional advice fails to take account of the fact that decisions are the outcome of interests in contention. It pays insufficient attention to the political nature of program decision making. Let me quote Cronbach one more time, because I believe that this sentence of his captures a glittering truth: "What is needed [from evaluation] is information that supports negotiation rather than information calculated to point out the 'correct' decision" (Cronbach et al., 1980, p. 4). When there are multiple participants with multiple views and interests involved in decision making, there can be no single correct decision. An evaluation study that tries to provide the one best answer often winds up getting used by one side or another as ammunition in organizational contests, or it gets neglected.

A second reason that the traditional good advice has limited reach is that evaluation is never comprehensive or convincing enough to supply "*the* correct answer." There are always issues that evaluation does not address, but that decision makers have to worry about: What changes will make the program work better? How much will such changes cost? How hard will it be to implement change? Which groups will support or oppose it? What will constituents think? And so on. However good an evaluation study may be, it does not answer all questions a decision maker must consider.

The third reason that the traditional advice falls short is that many program decisions do not come about through rational decision processes. In a surprisingly large number of cases, decisions seem to "happen" without any formal decision process at all. Small steps are taken in many different offices that close off some avenues and narrow the range of available options. By a series of disjointed and amorphous accommodations, a line of action takes shape, which only in retrospect is seen to be a decision. Sometimes decisions are the side effects of other matters entirely. Sometimes the hiring of new people determines what the organization can and cannot do. Sometimes decisions are made by precedent or by improvisation. In situations like these, nobody trots out the formal decision-making paraphernalia; in fact, people are not consciously aware that they are setting precedents or taking stands. Still, a decision accretes (Weiss, 1980). When this is the case, the use of evaluation evidence is difficult. If people in the organization are not making formal choices, they do not go out and seek information—nor are they particularly responsive to information coming in. They act on the basis of what they already know—their current stock of knowledge. In order for evaluation to have an influence in these nondecision decisions, evaluation findings have to be widely diffused and accepted as part of the "taken-for-granted" assumptions that organizational actors accept.

Fourth, even when there *are* clear-cut decisions and readily identifiable decision makers, people don't always know what kind of information they need to know. I've been in situations where we tried to get people in positions of authority to describe their informational needs. It is amazing how difficult it was for them to foresee what kind of information would make a difference. They are inclined to fall back on answers that seem socially acceptable in the organization. For example, if you ask school people what kind of information they want to have in order to make a decision about curriculum or in-service training or school organization, the most common answer is "student test scores." Test scores may have nothing at all to do with the issue at hand, but educators care about student achievement, and so "test scores" is the all-purpose answer.

Finally, there are all the reasons we have known about for so long that have to do with the constellation of interests that set hard as concrete around a program. People who are involved with things as they are—including clients as well as staff and administrators—are comfortable with the status quo, and they are often wary of shaking up the system. That is one reason why the major users of evaluation usually turn out to be *not* the people affiliated with the program that is evaluated, but people at high levels or at other sites or those considering the establishment of similar programs or policies.

These, then, are some reasons why the advice about involving decision makers in evaluation and being responsive to their needs is valuable only in limited situations. Nevertheless, and this is one of the most heartening empirical findings of the last 10 years, evaluation often has considerable influence on program and policy. Consider some of the markers. Public policy discourse is permeated with references to data and findings from evaluation. Read the press releases of government agencies and the newsletters of interest groups; read the reports of congressional committees; listen to the speeches of federal, state, and even local officials. With surprising frequency, they allude to ideas that had their origins in evaluation studies. Clearly, officials believe that their case is strengthened when they have credible evaluation findings to provide a rationale. In fewer and fewer policy debates can entrants hope to prevail without good arguments, and arguments are bolstered by the respectable support of evaluation results.

How can this be? We have just been through a list of reasons why participants in decision making are not open and amenable to the findings of evaluation. How can evaluation results get around these barriers and influence policy? Well, for one thing, we have to recognize that it is not the single decision maker, the benevolent despot, who uses evaluation to improve the program. Rather, evaluation findings—and generalizations from those findings—come into currency among the many groups and interests involved in a policy domain. They infiltrate the "policy subsystem," and much of the discourse on policy and program alternatives is phrased these days in the language of social research. Participants who have no data or evidence to support their position are at risk of being brushed aside; any group whose case rests on faulty data or flawed analysis can be more easily overwhelmed. Of course, there is more to political bargaining than facts and evidence; but, where many groups vie, where power is roughly equally distributed, or where important actors have not yet taken a stand, evaluative evidence can be of significant value.

Recall, too, Cronbach's statement that evaluation is most useful when it facilitates negotiation. Evaluation that opens new facets of a situation or that discloses possible grounds for agreement can have widespread influence. For example, an evaluation of a workfare-style program suggests that work requirements both get people off welfare and give former welfare recipients the self-supporting independence that they want. Such data can rally both liberals and conservatives to support certain kinds of work requirements in the welfare program.

Let's sum up this part of the discussion. Most evaluations are undertaken in a policymaking system where authority is dispersed, multiple groups have a say, and policy is the result of conflicts and accommodations across a complex and shifting set of players. The evaluator has little chance of being a "gray eminence" standing behind *the* decision maker. But evaluation findings that become known in the larger policy community have a chance to affect the terms of the debate, the language in which it is conducted, and the ideas that are considered relevant in its resolution. Even when decisions come about through informal compromises and accommodations, without conscious activation of formal decision-making machinery, generalizations from evaluation can percolate into the stock of knowledge that participants draw upon.

Empirical research has confirmed this situation. Research on knowledge utilization has disclosed that the results of one study rarely influence the direction of the program that was evaluated. But decision makers indicate a strong belief that they are influenced by ideas and arguments that have their origins in research and evaluation. Case studies of evaluations and decisions tend to show that the generalizations and ideas that come from research and evaluation help to shape the development of policy. The phenomenon has come to be known as "enlightenment." Through diffuse processes, research concepts and ideas come into currency and have consequences for the shape of policy to come.

Decision makers tend to be interested in the topics that evaluators study, particularly if their own program is not on the block; they are interested in the general kinds of results that evaluation finds—what kinds of programs work well and what kinds of clients are most likely to fare well. They see research and evaluation as providing a backdrop of facts and ideas for keeping up with the world. Evaluation is a form of news. It is a kind of continuing education. It helps policy actors update their map of the social world (Weiss with Bucuvalas, 1980). They are likely to be more open to new information in the early phases of the policy cycle than in the later stages. Reformist governments with expansive programs are more willing to listen to evaluation than conservative governments in times of retrenchment (Tarschys, 1983). But many policy actors have a basic hospitality to the kinds of knowledge that evaluation offers.

In our Western rationalist culture, reliance on systematic fact and tested theory is seen as a proper and rational mode of behavior. Policy actors who consciously pay attention to evaluation view themselves, and are often viewed by others, as behaving rationally. It is in their interest to commission studies, call in experts, cite evaluation evidence. Such actions show their colleagues and the public that they are good decision makers, because they are doing what good decision makers do. They are abiding by the convention to study the facts (Feldman & March, 1981).

As evaluation moves into currency and becomes accepted by informed publics, it can change the premises that are taken for granted and the issues that are seen as problematic. Thus it can clarify the nature and extent of problems and their susceptibility to purposive action, and so reorder the policy agenda. It can show which kinds of actions work well and thus recast the types of alternatives that are considered as potential solutions. In these ways, evaluation serves to enlighten policy discourse (Bulmer, 1986; Kallen, Kosse, Wagenaar, Kloprogge, & Vorbeck, 1982; Organisation for Economic Cooperation and Development, 1980; Rivlin, 1971; Weiss, 1980).

How Evaluation Ideas Travel

"Enlightenment" is an engaging idea. The image of evaluation as increasing the wattage of light in the policy arena brings joy to the hearts of evaluators. But if, as we have seen, evaluation reports sent directly to policy actors do not generally bring about much change, how do these ideas travel? What communication channels bring evaluation to attention? How does evaluation have an influence?

First of all, it seems that there are certain participants in policymaking who tend to be "users" of evaluation. The personal factor—a person's interest, commitment, enthusiasm—plays a part in determining how much influence a piece of research will have (Patton, 1978). We don't yet know why some people become committed enthusiasts— no identifiable background trait or experience has yet shown to be consistently present—but we do see a number of policy actors, and a larger number of staff aides, who give evaluation a serious hearing— even go out and look for it.

Most policy actors seem to be indifferent. They are busy people, and reading reports is low on their list of activities. They tend to make do with what they already know or what people they trust tell them. Nevertheless, evaluation results still filter through. Let me mention five ways in which evaluation can come to their attention.

Staff

Probably the most immediate source of evaluation information is the policymaker's staff. Whether policymakers are bureaucrats, political appointees, legislators, or interest group leaders, they rely on staff to keep them informed. No policy actor wants to look ignorant or to be unaware of evidence that is going to be used by those with opposing views. They rely on briefings from their aides to keep abreast of the issues.

The aides in turn can look to the in-house offices of research and evaluation that exist in many government agencies and other organizations. These offices sponsor evaluation, by grant and contract, and disseminate relevant results to organizational decision makers. These offices are an institutionalized testament to the perceived importance of research and evaluation in public policymaking.

The U.S. Congress can go to the congressional support agencies—the Congressional Research Service, the Congressional Budget Office, the General Accounting Office (GAO), and Office of Technology Assessment (OTA). Whether or not members of Congress or staff seek them out, these agencies pour out a cascade of reports. GAO in particular undertakes large numbers of evaluations of government programs.

The volume of evaluation done by and for government is, despite the Reagan cutbacks, substantial. Many reports are available inside government offices, and when outside groups—such as the mass media or blue-ribbon panels—pick up the results of a government-sponsored study, its influence is likely to be magnified.

Blue-Ribbon Commissions and Panels

A second route by which evaluation reaches decision makers is through blue-ribbon commissions and panels. Presidents, Congress, and cabinet secretaries have established special commissions to examine such issues as civil disorder, AIDS, and the state of American education. Members are usually chosen to represent major segments of the society—industry, labor, government, universities, and other interests relevant to the commission's charge. Almost all commissions have professional staffs, which collect existing evidence and often undertake new research. When a commission writes its report, it relies to some degree on the nature of the research and evaluation that have been brought to light. (Some commissions are more conscientious about this than others.) Through the report, the commission gives considerable publicity not only to its conclusions but to the research and evaluation that support those conclusions (Bulmer, 1980, 1983; Komarovsky, 1975). One of the most endearing characteristics about commission reports from the standpoint of policymakers is that they represent a consensus among diverse segments of the society. Commission members have fought out their differences and resolved most of the thorny questions, sparing policymakers the task of resolving complex and often emotional issues. They can embrace the reports without fear of major opposition. Whatever their immediate effect on policy, commission reports usually add to public knowledge of the issue and of the research bias for the commission's stand.

Mass Media

The mass media are another important channel to policymakers—in fact, to all of us. Reporters on major newspapers, such as the *New York Times*, the *Wall Street Journal*, and the *Washington Post*, report significant amounts of news about research studies, statistical indicators, and evaluations (Weiss & Singer, in press). The topics that attract reporters are those already in the news, so evaluations relevant to current policy have particular appeal. Most researchers whom we interviewed in a recent study on media reporting say that stories about their work are factually accurate and give appropriate emphasis. Although they have some complaints, especially about oversimplification, they believe that readers are generally receiving an accurate impression of their work.

Policymakers pay careful attention to the media for a variety of reasons and are alerted to the evaluation findings that appear. Even though they may have their own specialized communication systems and their own staffs, they may not hear about relevant evaluation findings until they read about them in the press or see them on television. From the policymaker's perspective, media reporting of evaluation of a program in the policymaker's domain is a significant event. It is not just that *Time* magazine or the *Washington Post* gives a capsule summary of the evaluation; more important, policymakers know that the same story reaches all the other players in the policy game. They will be asked about it. They had better know about it. They can't sweep it under the rug. A zealous staffer may call around and get the original study on which the story was based. The media focus attention on the evaluations they report.

Interest Groups

From what we said earlier about the political nature of much program decision making, it should come as no surprise that another source of news about evaluation is the interest group. Many interest groups, such as professional associations, unions, and client organizations, relay evaluation data. Their interest is not disseminating knowledge. Their interest is advancing their own cases. If they find supportive information in evaluations, they make those findings part of their argument. Competing interest groups press different evidence on decision makers, and they sometimes criticize the data made available by their competitors.

Legislators, in particular, seem to be receptive to evaluation that arrives in this form, interwoven with argumentation and proposals for action. They are not particularly worried about distortion. They assume self-interest and an adversarial process, not "objectivity" or "truth." They take for granted that each side is exaggerating the strength of its case, and they assume that the facts lie somewhere between the extremes. They expect each side to point out the errors in the other side's case, and they believe they can ferret out the gist of the story.

Interestingly, they seem to be more receptive to information that comes from interest groups than they are to information that arrives under the guise of objective research. Legislators can be suspicious of academics who come bearing data. They want to know "Why are they telling me this? What's in it for them?" Interest groups they understand. They know where they are coming from and what they want. They wonder about these evaluators who claim to be impartial and objective. They wonder about the secret axes they may be grinding.

Issue Networks

Another source of evaluation information for policymakers is what Heclo (1978) has called the "issue network." Around many major issues in contention, there has grown up a set of people who have knowledge and long-term interest in shaping policy. All kinds of people are members of the network—staff of executive-branch agencies, political appointees, members of Congress and their staffs, state executives and legislators, program managers, academics, consultants, interest group representatives, and "think tank" experts. As policy on an issue develops over time, these people maintain contact with each other—serving on committees, talking on the phone, attending hearings, circulating material, and exchanging ideas. Researchers are members of many of the most active issue networks, such as those concerned with welfare reform and health-cost containment, and they become catalysts for the dissemination of research and evaluation.

Functions That Evaluation Serves

Much evaluation comes into currency through these diverse chan-nels. Policy actors in many places hear directly or obliquely about the lessons that evaluation yields. They perform their own intuitive meta-analysis as they figure out what the current state of program knowledge is.

What do they do with the information? How is evaluation translated, transmuted, or otherwise "used" in the policymaking process? Much evaluation, of course, is used peripherally or not at all. When decision makers already have considerable knowledge and experience on an issue, when they have strong ideological commitments or strong self-interest, evaluation is seen as an unnecessary frill. But on many issues the scope of problems is so complex that individuals are puzzled—and groups are at odds. They want new information, new ideas, new think-ing. Evaluation is likely to get a hearing.

There are four ways in which policy actors use information in the policy process: as warning, guidance, reconceptualization, and mobili-zation of support.

Warning

Evaluation can provide the signal that things are going wrong. If studies show that graduates of job training programs are not getting and keeping jobs, if studies show that released mental patients are not receiving community services, these are warnings that something needs to be done. If longitudinal data are available, they provide data on trends—whether conditions are getting better or worse. Sudden shifts can signal serious trouble and may be particularly potent in triggering a policy response.

Guidance

A second function that evaluation serves is guidance. It gives direc-tion for improving policies and programs. If the evaluation has com-pared several variations of a program, it can suggest which variant works better, and under what conditions. Thus some studies suggest that educating non-English-speaking students in their native language re-sults in better English proficiency in later grades, whereas "immersion" programs, in which students are dumped into English classes from the start, lead to a loss of learning in all subjects until they master English.

This kind of comparative information can be especially useful as policy guidance.

But, for all the reasons discussed earlier, program and policy people are not always docile candidates for guidance. It is much easier for evaluation to influence new programs and policies than it is for it to influence programs that are already in existence and buffered by a phalanx of supporters.

Reconceptualization

Evaluation offers another kind of contribution to policy, "reconceptualization." Studies can offer new approaches to familiar issues, new ways of thinking, new models for making sense of activities and outcomes. Evaluations can help to counteract the taken-for-granted assumptions, the musty sameness, of existing policy.

When research and evaluation offer new frames of reference, they help policymakers to reinterpret events, think critically about what happened in the past, and even reexamine past criteria for success. Recent studies of research use suggest that policy actors may welcome ideas like this—particularly if they have tried many variations of programming without success and are yearning for new directions (Caplan, 1977; Cherns, 1986; Knorr, 1977; Rich, 1977; Webber, 1987; Weiss with Bucuvalas, 1980).

Mobilization of Support

A final way in which evaluation is used is to mobilize support for program and policy proposals. Advocates can use evaluation results to help build a winning coalition. Evaluation becomes a means of persuasion. It can reinforce the conviction of the original advocates that their plan is a good one; it can stiffen the support of current allies; it can help to persuade the undecided; once in a while it can sway the beliefs of opponents, weakening their adherence to their old position. Of course, good arguments and evidence are not uniformly successful, but they are useful counters in the policy game.

Finale

Let me sum up the story. Evaluation results enter a "policy community," a set of interacting groups and institutions that push and haul their way to decisions through what Lynn (1987) calls "fluid, overlapping, and ambiguous processes" (p. 269). To gain influence, the ideas from evaluation have to come into currency and be accepted in ongoing program and policy discussion. There are many and diverse routes into the discussion: via staff, expert commissions, the media, interest groups, consultants, conferences, and hearings, among others. When the findings and the intellectual structure of evaluation begin to shape the way that decision makers think about an issue—and the elements of it that they think about—evaluation has been "used."

I have analytically distinguished four types of use to which evaluation is put: warning of problems, guidance for crafting program reforms, reconceptualization of the nature of the issue, and building coalitions of support. These categories are conceptually distinguishable, but in practice they often blur. Evaluation that signals the seriousness of a problem may also provide ideas for dealing with it and help persuade others to support the new proposal.

Evaluation has become a regular component of discussion about programs and policies. Its influence has survived the Reagan administration, budgetary cutbacks, and self-doubts in the evaluation community. Evaluators know that the purpose of their enterprise is program improvement, but I think we have come to recognize and accept the fact that evaluation does not always lead to improvements in the program under study. No matter how hard we try to be good planners, negotiators, and communicators with the stakeholders in the program, they are sometimes going to go their merry way. On the other hand, I think that we are becoming more aware that evaluation does influence decisions— often indirectly and at some distance from the original evaluation site. I think we can do more to make that happen. We are only starting to face up to the opportunities to improve the use of evaluation in the diffuse, multiparticipative bargaining processes that characterize democratic decision making. A necessary first step is to start thinking about the challenge in these larger terms.

References

Buchanan, J. J. (1987, June 12). The constitution of economic policy. *Science, 236*, 1433-1436.

Bulmer, M. (Ed.). (1980). *Social research and royal commissions.* London: Allen & Unwin.

Bulmer, M. (Ed.). (1983). Social science and policy-making: The use of research by government commissions [Special issue]. *American Behavioral Scientist, 26*(5).

Bulmer, M. (1986). *Social science and social policy.* London: Allen & Unwin.

Caplan, N. (1977). A minimal set of conditions necessary for the utilization of social science knowledge in policy formulation at the national level. In C. H. Weiss (Ed.), *Using social research in public policy making* (pp. 183-197). Lexington, MA: Lexington Books.

Cherns, A. (1986). Policy research under scrutiny. In F. Heller (Ed.), *The use and abuse of social science* (pp. 185-198). London: Sage.

Cronbach, L. J. (1982). *Designing evaluations of educational and social programs.* San Francisco: Jossey-Bass.

Cronbach, L. J., Ambron, S. R., Dornbusch, S. M., Hess, R. D., Hornik, R. C., Phillips, D. C., Walker, D. F., & Weiner, S. S. (1980). *Toward reform of program evaluation.* San Francisco: Jossey-Bass.

Feldman, M. S., & March, J. G. (1981). Information in organizations as signal and symbol. *Administrative Science Quarterly, 26,* 171-186.

Heclo, H. (1978). Issue networks and the executive establishment. In A. Kind (Ed.), *The new American political system* (pp. 87-124). Washington, DC: American Enterprise Institute.

Kallen, D. B. P., Kosse, G. B., Wagenaar, H. C., Kloprogge, J. J. J., & Vorbeck, M. (1982). *Social science research and public policy-making.* Windsor, Berks: NFER-Nelson.

Knorr, K. D. (1977). Policymakers' use of social science knowledge: Symbolic or instrumental? In C. H. Weiss (Ed.), *Using social research in public policy making* (pp. 165-182). Lexington, MA: Lexington Books.

Komarovsky, M. (Ed.). (1975). *Sociology and public policy: The case of presidential commissions.* New York: Elsevier.

Lynn, L. E., Jr. (1987). *Managing public policy.* Boston: Little, Brown.

Organisation for Economic Cooperation and Development. (1980). *The utilisation of the social sciences in policy making in the United States: Case studies.* Paris: Author.

Patton, M. Q. (1978). *Utilization-focused evaluation.* Beverly Hills, CA: Sage.

Rich, R. F. (1977). Use of social science knowledge by federal bureaucrats. In C. H. Weiss (Ed.), *Using social research in public policy making* (pp. 199-211). Lexington, MA: Lexington Books.

Rivlin, A. M. (1971). *Systematic thinking for social action.* Washington, DC: Brookings Institution.

Tarschys, D. (1983). Fluctuations in the political demand for policy analysis. In S. E. Spiro & E. Yuchtman-Yaar (Eds.), *Evaluating the welfare state.* New York: Academic Press.

Webber, D. J. (1987). Legislators' use of policy information. *American Behavioral Scientist, 30*(6), 612-661.

Weiss, C. H. (1980). Knowledge creep and decision accretion. *Knowledge: Creation, Diffusion, Utilization, 1*(3), 381-404.

Weiss, C. H., with Bucuvalas, M. J. (1980). *Social science research and decision-making.* New York: Columbia University Press.

Weiss, C. H., & Singer, E. (in press). *Reporting of social science in the national media.* New York: Russell Sage.

9

The Evaluator's Responsibility for Utilization

MICHAEL QUINN PATTON

This whole conference has, in many ways, been a celebration of utilization. Many of the sessions this week have documented that we know how to do useful evaluations and that we are doing them. I think that's what we ought to be doing and that we have a right to be proud. We have passed through our infancy, moved on through our adolescence in the last few years to mature into a profession that has something concrete, distinguishable, and needed to offer. In that we can take some pride. In that we have cause for celebration.

On such celebratory occasions, I think it's helpful to recognize our roots. Our roots include some mythology about our beginnings. Some of you have heard me refer to that mythology before or read about it in the new edition of *Utilization-Focused Evaluation* (Patton, 1986). So in the context of this celebration, let me include the ritual of taking you back to our beginnings, and, as you will recall, "In the Beginning" it was like this:

In the beginning God created the heaven and the earth.

And God saw everything that He made. "Behold," God said, "it is very good."

And the evening and the morning were the sixth day.

AUTHOR'S NOTE: This chapter is reprinted from *Evaluation Practice*, Vol. 9, No. 2, pp. 5-24. Copyright 1988 by Sage Publications.

And on the seventh day God rested from all His work. His archangel came then unto Him asking, "God, how do you know that what you have created is 'very good'? What are your criteria? On what data do you base your judgment? Aren't you a little close to the situation to make a fair and unbiased evaluation?" God thought about these questions all that day and His rest was greatly disturbed. On the eighth day God said, "Lucifer, go to hell."

Thus was evaluation born in a blaze of glory. (Patton, 1986, p. 1)

Now some would submit that it's been all downhill since that blazing beginning. But I want to suggest this morning that we have achieved a great deal, and that part of what we have achieved has come from asking the hard questions of that first mythical evaluator. How do we know what is good? What are the criteria we use to judge programs? On what data do we base our judgments? Are we too close to things to make fair judgments?

What I want to do with those questions this morning, the questions that we ask of programs, is to turn them on ourselves and ask how we know what is good about evaluation. *What are our criteria for judging our own effectiveness as evaluators?* Our answer to this question has important implications for our profession. In essence, I want us to examine our vision of who we are as evaluators, what we are as a profession, and look at what the answers tell us about our responsibilities and accountability.

A Dismal Vision

It was in this context, thinking about who we are, what we are, and what we know, that I reacted to the plenary remarks yesterday. Those of you who were here will recall that at the end of the presentation made by Carol Weiss, I stated that I would take "strong exception" to some of her remarks today. All day long thereafter, people came up to me asking what I could possibly have found objectionable in Carol's very fine presentation. I deferred their questions to this morning, but I was saddened that, with a few notable exceptions, the people with whom I talked after hearing Carol Weiss found nothing about which to be concerned in her vision of evaluation utilization, a vision that I personally found to be quite dismal, sad, and unacceptable.

Let me add quickly that I have the profoundest respect for the work that Carol Weiss has done and the knowledge she has contributed over the years. As the advance of any discipline requires open scholarly debate on issues of importance, I would hope that I hardly need to say that I meant no disrespect to Carol yesterday. I have a very deep and genuine affection for Carol Weiss. She was the editor of the very first piece I ever published in evaluation and has been an inspiration for the work on utilization that I have done over time. We had an extraordinary opportunity two years ago that was in many ways a preview of the opportunity for debate at this conference. Marv Alkin of UCLA hosted a three-day meeting at a university retreat on the beach of Malibu with Ernie House, Jean King, Ross Conner, Carol Weiss, myself, and several others. We spent three days talking to each other outside the public limelight about our opinions on the state of the art of evaluation utilization. We had a long time to discuss our respective views and to understand each other. Thus I was especially surprised yesterday by Carol's report on the dismal state of evaluation utilization, even though she limited her comments to large-scale policy-oriented evaluations. Because of the high esteem in which Carol Weiss is justifiably held by our profession, I feel compelled to offer both contrasting conclusions on the actual impacts of evaluations and a dramatically different vision of what can be—and I believe should be—our collective vision of evaluation use. So I want to spend a few minutes reacting to the vision that you heard yesterday before I go on to share with you my own vision.

Those of you who were here will recall that she began by taking exception to the popular advice we've all heard about how one might go about increasing the use of evaluation. . . .

Following these observations she gave five reasons why "these kinds of structures are only partially useful in most large-scale program situations" and five ways in which evaluation can come to the attention of policy actors. She then concluded with her vision of evaluation utilization:

> Let me sum up the story. Evaluation results enter a "policy community," a set of interacting groups and institutions that push and haul their way to decisions through what Lynn (1987) calls "fluid, overlapping, and ambiguous processes" (p. 269). To gain influence, the ideas from evaluation have to come into currency and be accepted in ongoing program and policy discussion. There are many and diverse routes into the discussion: via staff, expert commissions, the media, interest groups, consultants, conferences, and hearings, among others. When the findings and the intellectual structure of evaluation begin to shape the way that decision makers think about an issue—and the elements of it that they think about—evaluation has been "used."

Evaluators know that the purpose of their enterprise is program improvement, but I think we have come to recognize and accept the fact that evaluation does not always lead to improvements in the program under study. No matter how hard we try to be good planners, negotiators, and communicators with the stakeholders in the program, they are sometimes going to go their merry way. On the other hand, I think that we are becoming more aware that evaluation does influence decisions—often indirectly and at some distance from the original site. I think we can do more to make that happen.

The overall impression Carol Weiss left on me in her speech was that working carefully and strategically with intended users of evaluations has had "indifferent success," that specific evaluation contributions to program improvement are rare, and that our best hope is indirect influence "at some distance from the original site." For national *policy research* these conclusions may have merit, but *for program evaluation we have had much success, and can and should do better.* I take strong exception to the assertion that evaluators who have followed conscientiously and skillfully the advice to work with intended users to achieve evaluation use have had "indifferent success." I believe there is substantial evidence to the contrary, enough to indicate that cases of high-level targeted utilization are far from exceptions. It's simply not true that the advice Weiss questions about how to achieve higher levels of use has had indifferent success. It's important to know that it's not true because there is substantial evidence that the people who have followed that advice, and *have developed skills in implementing that advice,* have been well served by that advice and have served well their clients: specific program decision makers and stakeholders.

I speak not only of my own experiences, which include large-scale, broad-based evaluations as well as small, local ones, but of the evidence from others engaged in this kind of evaluation. This conference has presented a tremendous amount of evidence demonstrating evaluation use. The work that GAO is doing in large-scale evaluation efforts is basically guided by careful, committed attention to use. There is very distinguished work on high-utilization evaluations being done in a unit that is not well known, but that I have had the opportunity to get to know, namely, the internal evaluation unit of the FBI. This unit conducts nationwide program evaluations of large scale. They aim for and achieve very direct, immediate results. They are consistently achieving very high levels of evaluation use for program improvement and decision making by being utilization focused. The distinguished work of Marv Alkin, including his presentations at this conference, constitutes evidence of dramatic, immediate impact on decisions and program improvements (see, e.g., Alkin, 1987a, 1987b). The work of Bill Cooley using client-oriented and decision-oriented evaluation in large urban school districts shows how evaluation can contribute to ongoing program improvements with clear and dramatic impact on a large city school system. A forthcoming issue of *New Directions in Program Evaluation* will feature client perspectives on evaluation. Edited by Jeri Nowakowski, that volume will discuss examples of the high impact of evaluations when oriented toward the information needs of specific clientele. Those clientele need not be singular and they need not be benevolent dictators. They can be multiple, and the impacts on them can be dramatic. The Caribbean Agricultural Extension Project evaluation is one such example, an evaluation of a project aimed at agricultural development in seven Caribbean countries, an evaluation that directly and importantly affected a $5 million funding decision. At a more local level, my colleagues in Minnesota, including distinguished work at the county level by Joan Velasquez and her staff, have presented evidence at this conference documenting the direct and immediate utilization of their work.

I can *without difficulty* name at least 25, probably 50, practitioners of evaluation who are making a good living following utilization-focused evaluation advice. They are serving clients well and are having a dramatic impact on programs and decisions.

Neither Carol Weiss nor I have had the time in these plenary presentations to present conclusive evidence in support of our respective points of view. Nor would the evidence be definitive. There are differences of definition, nuances of meaning, and subtle variations in emphasis that separate our perspectives. What we are really dealing with are impressions. My impressions, then, are that a significant number of evaluators and evaluation units are making substantial, documented contributions to program improvement and decision making. Thus our perceptions vary substantially on the current impact of evaluation professional practice. What about our visions of what should be and what is possible?

Even if the statements about "indifferent success" were true, which I assert they are not, the Weiss alternative of what we can hope for is one of limited vision that I find quite dismal. It is a vision of indirect influence at some distance from the original site, usually at a time much later than the completion of the evaluation, through enlightenment of a fluid, overlapping, ambiguous policy community. Again, this may be an appropriate way of thinking about national policy research, but not program evaluation. I suggest that the Weiss vision of use lacks accountability, and is absolutely *not* marketable to potential and actual purchasers of evaluation services. Such a vision of use would be unacceptable for both internal and external contractors, that is, those who must make themselves valuable to supervisors in the organizations that employ them and those who must produce something of value under contract to clients. Marketability is, I believe, a reasonable criterion against which to judge a vision of utilization—and the Weiss vision, in my judgment, is not marketable.

Alternative Visions

What we have, then, are alternative visions, paradigms, or world-views concerning how we go about our business, what we can promise, what we are accountable for, and what we should realistically hope to achieve. Weiss laid out before us four possible uses of evaluation: warnings, guidance, reconceptualization, and mobilizing support for vested interests. Notably missing from that list is directly influencing change, directly affecting decisions, immediate program improvement, and follow-through on specific recommendations for improvement. My vision includes, indeed emphasizes, such uses.

Now it is true that in my own research on how knowledge gets used, I have found, as Carol Weiss and others studying knowledge utilization have found, that there have seldom been, in the past, direct and immediate uses of policy evaluation results for making major decisions. Such findings about knowledge use are an important context for this debate. It makes sense that policy research would be used in more diffuse and less direct ways than program evaluation. What many of you have understood is that Weiss and I may really be talking about different kinds and levels of practice. Carol Weiss is a skilled and important contributor through policy research. But I don't think her vision is sufficient for program evaluation, so I want to share with you a vision of what program evaluation can be when it is accountable, utilization-focused, and salable—a vision of which we can be proud and one that we can deliver.

A Utilization-Focused Vision of Accountability

First, I want to point to a couple of examples that come out of this conference that point to the potential for evaluation accountability and impact. One of the most dramatic is the GAO work that was described briefly in the opening plenary presentation. Lois-Ellin Datta gave additional details in a session sponsored by the AEA Topical Interest Group on Utilizing Evaluations. GAO in one year produced 290 reports with 1,134 recommendations. A recent study was conducted on the impact of those recommendations. They monitored the recommendations for 18 months to find out what happened to them. They found that 80% of the recommendations were accepted by the agencies to which they were directed. That is clear, dramatic use of evaluation findings. Indeed, I understand from senior GAO colleagues that their performance evaluations are tied to the utilization of their findings and they are accountable for that use.

The FBI evaluation unit, headed by Deputy Assistant Director Richard Sonnichsen, has a similar system. They follow up all of their reports within six months to find out what has happened to the recommendations. On an annual basis they publish a report on the evaluation unit, a report card on what has happened to their recommendations. In this way they are accountable for evaluation use. Their data on adoption of and follow-through on recommendations is impressive. From 1980 to 1985 they conducted 37 evaluations of major FBI programs, producing 342 recommendations; 82% of the recommendations were approved by senior administrators and 90% of those approved were fully implemented (Sonnichsen, 1987).

Marv Alkin does evaluation work with the community colleges in California. The state office of the Extended Opportunity Programs and Services operates in over 100 community colleges and annually publishes a list of all the recommendations made for all the community colleges, including what has happened to those recommendations.

These examples paint a picture of a profession that is prepared to do what we have demanded of programs—to be accountable. Think about what we as evaluators demand of a program. We go into a program knowing up front that its goals are likely to be vague, nonmeasurable, conflicting, multiple, and difficult to prioritize. The program staff may tell us that what we have to understand is that their impacts will be realized only years from now, that the goals are very difficult to measure, and that they are operating in indirect and multiple ways to make a difference. Do we accept these problems as a basis for avoiding program accountability? Absolutely not! And yet we are now turning around under the Weiss policy research paradigm and saying that the best we can offer are vague, indirect impacts down the road somewhere.

I'm suggesting that we apply to our own professional practice the same demands we make on programs. Moreover, whether we apply those standards or not, it is clear that the funding community and program people are going to apply those criteria to us. *We have to be accountable*. We have to have something concrete to offer. And I believe we do, that we are making a difference with our findings.

The Standards

Part of my vision comes from the standards. Both the Joint Committee standards and the former ERS standards make it clear that our worth is to be judged by use. Evaluations are to help improve programs, help make programs more effective, and provide information for decision making. That is use. That is our accountability.

Intended Use by Intended Users

Let me define what I mean by *utilization from an accountability perspective*. Many of you familiar with the first edition of *Utilization-Focused Evaluation* (Patton, 1978) know that a weakness of that book was my failure ever really to define utilization. The second edition corrects that deficiency (Patton, 1986). By *utilization* I mean *intended use by intended users*. If you think about it this sounds an awfully lot like a program-type goal for an evaluation. Intended use for intended users. It is results oriented. It means that we negotiate up front with intended users what an evaluation ought to achieve to make its benefits worth its costs. Then we are expected to deliver on that, or to be judged as not having met our goal for use.

Being results oriented is popular now in management, it's popular in program development, and it ought to be an idea that we incorporate, and I think we are incorporating, in evaluation.

Let me give you a metaphor for what we're talking about. This year's AEA president, Bob Covert, told me that this summer he was in Minnesota doing some fishing. He was out in one of our rural communities where there are real fisherpersons who take their fishing very, very seriously. Those of you who have ever tuned in to National Pubic Radio to hear the good ole days of Lake Wobegon know that Minnesotans take their fishing very seriously. And they knew that this moonshiner from Virginia was not a fisherman. It was written all over him that he was not a fisherman. It didn't matter to these Minnesotans if he had the best, most technically sophisticated fishing pole and went out in the best boat on the water and fished for hours. It didn't even matter if he caught a whole boatload of "garbage fish," which is what we call everything except a few special fish in Minnesota. Catching garbage fish does not make you a fisherman. A fisherman is not a fisherman because he has great equipment. He is not a fisherman because he sits on the water catching garbage fish. Nor would he be a fisherman because he had a whole fleet of boats or because he had developed an entire institution devoted to fishing and published journals on fishing and sent people out on boats with nets and poles to do fishing. *A fisherman is a fisherman if he catches the desired fish.*

Now Bob tells me he was the object of a lot of jest from the locals the first couple of days he was there. But one night he and his family went out with some advice about where they might have a little better luck and in the course of the evening they caught a seven-pound walleyed pike, which is the "primo" fish in Minnesota. They took that walleye back to the place where the locals were hanging out and showed it off. At that point, and only at that point, the locals were prepared to say that the moonshiner from Virginia had become a fisherman.

You see where the fishing metaphor takes us. It is not enough that we have methods, that we have the trappings of doing evaluation, that we have institutions, that we write about it, and that we publish it. I'm suggesting that you are not a program evaluator until you catch the desired fish—which is getting your results used, that is, intended use by intended users.

Now that may appear scary for those of you who have not been dealing seriously with utilization accountability. But the good news is we know how to achieve high levels of use and, as the examples I cited illustrate, many are doing it. Attaining accountable levels of use comes from our knowledge of how to work with programs, and that knowledge includes dealing with intended users and primary stakeholders in whatever ways they have to be dealt with, to help train them as information users, and working with them on a mutual commitment to the use of both the evaluation process and its findings. It comes from skillfully and responsively following the kind of advice nicely summarized by Weiss yesterday and quoted earlier in this speech.

What I want to do in the time remaining is discuss some of the strategies I've found helpful in delivering on the accountability promise of intended use by intended users.

Overcoming Staff Fear

Sometimes increasing use involves overcoming fear. What I'm referring to is a situation that I often encounter with a program staff who I have good reason to believe are likely to be hostile toward and/or fearful of evaluation. Fear is a very real thing in what we do. (You may experience some of that fear yourself as you think about what it means for you to be evaluated on the basis of what you do as an evaluator, to be held accountable for use along the lines delineated above.) One of the things I like to do is deal with that fear of evaluation up front. I assemble the primary users, administrative representatives, funding representatives, staff representatives, and client representatives for an initial session where we talk about what the evaluation process is going to mean, and begin to engender a commitment to use. This gives me an opportunity to interact with them about their image of evaluation and evaluators, and I find it is a critical discussion in order to understand their perspectives.

During such a discussion we have the opportunity and responsibility to take control of the image we project of evaluation. Every time we do an evaluation we are projecting an image of the profession. Each of you represents the profession and is projecting an image of the profession and what we have to offer. We establish who we are in what we do and in the results that we achieve. So one approach that allows us to increase use is to create from the very beginning of an evaluation process a positive expectancy that *this evaluation is going to be useful.* Such positive expectancy about utility may well require a departure from staff members' past experiences with evaluation, so they may be skeptical, and they have a right to be skeptical until we have delivered otherwise. But it is important that we create in ourselves and in them a positive, accountable expectancy that evaluation ought to be and indeed can be useful.

Asking the Right Questions

A second consideration as we engage in this dialogue with intended users is asking the right questions. That takes a lot of skill. Whether we are talking about doing evaluability assessment, which is one way of helping to understand what's possible in an evaluation, or interacting with one stakeholder or multiple stakeholders, asking the right questions, I think, includes asking about intended use for intended users and how one would know if that occurred. What would it mean for a specific evaluation to be useful in improving the program and improving decision making about the program in that particular context?

Learning to ask questions and really listening to what clients say is a critical skill. Jeri Nowakowski was telling me about her edited overview of the forthcoming *New Directions* volume devoted to clients' perspectives. She said that if she had to reduce it to a single bottom line it would be that the most effective evaluator-client relationships have been when evaluators have really listened to their clientele and worked with them to facilitate use.

I do interview training in which asking the right questions is a major consideration for consulting and data collection. Asking good questions is not always easy. One of the ways I like to train interviewers to ask good questions is to have them interview children. The marvelous thing about interviewing children is that they haven't learned all the niceties of how to pretend that your question isn't dumb when it is. Children tend to answer whatever you ask, which can be quite embarrassing.

One of the first evaluations I ever did involved open-education programs in North Dakota. The open-education advocates claimed that learning was great fun for students because they made the children the center of learning. They even suggested that learning was so much fun that the kids just didn't bother with things like recess because going outside to play wasn't any better than what went on in the classroom, so children just continued at what they were doing in the classroom. Therefore, we included in our interviews with children a question about what they did during recess.

About my third or fourth interview, I was interviewing a little first-grade girl, and I came to this question five to ten minutes into the interview. I asked her, "What do you do during recess?" She replied, "I go outside and play on the swings on the playground." I said, "Why do you go outside?" She looked at me quizzically and answered, "Because that's where the swings are." And I could tell that she knew she had one of those adults on her hands who did not quite understand how things operate, that if you want to swing on the swings you have to go outside where the swings are. So she very patiently explained the nature of the world to me, then we were able to get on with the business at hand.

There are times when we have to ask what appear to be dumb questions. Peter Drucker, the management consultant, says that's what he does. He meets with corporate boards and begins by asking, "What business are you in?" He reports that they are often annoyed, if they haven't been warned, because they figure he hasn't done his homework. "How can this expensive consultant show up and ask us what business we're in?" Drucker then proceeds to work with them for what often turns into days, helping them to figure out what their business *really* is, because they typically don't know. And finding that out makes a difference to that business.

That's a lot of what we're doing: asking the questions to help programs figure out what they're really doing, how they would know if they did it so that they can do it better. Both we and they can be accountable in that process.

Being Situationally Responsive as an Expert Evaluator

Related to asking the right questions is learning how to be situationally responsive and learning how to recognize variations in situations and people so that you can gear your process to them. Expert evaluators are sophisticated at situation recognition. Sharing expertise is one of the purposes of this AEA meeting. I want to devote a couple of minutes to a vision of what it would mean to be an expert evaluator, to reflect on what you can accomplish through expertise. The context for this reflection is clear recognition that expertise does not happen overnight and it's not just a result of training. Expertise comes from miles of evaluation work, but it's worth knowing what those miles can yield if you're willing to work at becoming an expert evaluator. In holding out a vision of expertise, I want to turn to some other fields that have looked in greater depth at what expertise means and think about the implications for evaluation.

I found an interesting article that reported on studies of expertise in various games—world-class games, the top of the field. Let me read an excerpt from Etheredge's (1979) work on expertise. He says:

> It takes at least 15 years of hard work for even the most talented individuals to become world class chess masters: what they seem to learn is a repertoire for recognizing types of situations or scripts or intuitive sensibilities and understandings about how these situations will largely unfold. Simon estimates a differential repertoire of 50,000 situation recognitions at the world class chess level. There is also some increase in overall long-range strategic planning ability—beginners typically are hard pressed to go beyond one move deep; world class players often anticipate 3 or sometimes 5 future moves in calculating alternative reactions to their moves. (p. 40)

I suggest there's a parallel here to anticipating utilization and knowing how to bring it about.

> Data from experienced and highly successful chess players, poker players, tennis players and other professionals suggest the theory that one further learning from experience is the capacity to diagnose not just specific game situations but to model "psyche out" different opponents. (Etheredge, 1979, p. 40)

Etheredge also reports that it is likely that experienced players have developed more efficient scanning and the ability to discard unnecessary information and have a ballpark sense, which seems like an intuitive but is really a practiced sense, of where to devote attention. You will be hard pressed, in my mind, to find a better statement of what evaluation expertise involves than that statement: situation recognition and responsiveness, anticipation, and being able to analyze people—knowing where, when, and how to focus attention.

Becoming an expert involves miles of practice. Let me share with you what that level of commitment may mean. One of the remembrances of my high school years was Bob Richards coming to town on a motivational tour for young people. Bob Richards was the Olympic decathlon champion, and he described how Olympic champions train. As a young man who was trying to get in touch with what the world of work was going to be like, I remember being impressed with the work and commitment involved. He described what would now be called the "no pain, no gain" principle. The climax of his stories was the conclusion that if you want to become expert at something, if you want to become a world-class player, put 10,000 hours into it. His estimate of what it took to reach the Olympic level of competition was 10,000 hours of concentrated work, just to be able to compete.

To those of you who are just beginning your work, I want to urge you not to be discouraged by some of the early difficulties, but to realize that when you walk those many evaluation miles, working at and reflecting on utilization, you can become an expert in delivering on the promise of evaluation: intended use for intended users, making a difference in programs and program decision making.

Reflection and Evaluation

A commitment to expert-level work includes reflecting on our own practice, applying our evaluation skills to what we do as the GAO is doing, as the FBI evaluation unit is doing, as many internal evaluators are called on to do. It means taking the time to follow up our own work and find out what worked and what didn't work, and to do formative evaluation of our own processes to learn from what we do.

It is sad that we apply so little of our own evaluation skills to our own practice. Fritz Steele, who is a consultant to consultants, calls this "the action-reflection dilemma." He says action for consultants usually involves helping clients take time for reflection. But when does the consultant take time for reflection and processing personal experiences? This action versus processing dilemma results, Steele (1975) believes, from "the emotional seductiveness of the action side of the coin. There is always the temptation to move on to some new action without fully processing what occurred in a finished project, getting feedback from clients, reviewing notes, and discussing the experience analytically with colleagues. Taking the time to evaluate an evaluation process, to review a consulting experience, or follow-up utilization of a study's findings are ways to continue learning" (p. 19). To learn from your learning is part of the commitment to being a skilled professional, and it is part of what this forum, the AEA meetings and the American Evaluation Association, is meant to facilitate. It is an important part of why we are here, to learn from each other and to learn from reflection on our own processes.

Being an Advocate for Evaluation

A final hope that I would leave with you as part of this discussion of vision and responsibility is that we ought to be advocates for evaluation. We can and ought to be advocates for evaluation based on the knowledge that we have a quality product and process that can improve programs.

I want to use a metaphor here that may not be altogether comfortable given our research orientation and some of the ways that we think about ourselves. When I look for ways of increasing my expertise, I look for ideas wherever I can get them. I try to draw on a number of different fields and the understandings that people have developed in fields that are older than ours. One such field I have found intriguing is sales. There has been a tremendous amount of research on what makes someone an effective salesperson. A lot of sales training is motivational hype, but I've been listening to tapes and reading what the top salespeople have to say about effectiveness, and I think there may be some lessons for us there. I have time to mention only two of them.

One lesson comes from a seeming consensus in the sales literature that a prerequisite of being an effective salesperson is having a quality product that inspires confidence and commitment. I hope that it is evident to you from my remarks today that I believe with deep conviction in evaluation as both a useful process and product for program improvement. When I talk with program people, I can tell them with conviction that evaluation can make a difference to their program. I can assure them that a utilization-focused evaluation process undertaken with deliberation and seriousness can make a difference in what they do. I believe that. I believe there's evidence for that assertion, including evidence from these meetings, so I can "sell" evaluation and its utility.

However, a quality product seems not to be enough. Skill in selling is needed to communicate the product's virtues. One sales skill that I find particularly intriguing is apparently a real problem for salespeople in that it is one of the things that they must work and work and work on to master. The challenge this skill carries for salespeople provides, I think, an interesting analogy to our own difficulties in selling evaluation. With regard to this skill, I want to quote one of the supposedly top of the top salespeople, one of the real hypesters in this field, but also a man who has some real knowledge about selling and has the numbers to back up his claims—one Zig Ziglar. Let me tell you what Zig Ziglar said in a recent national newsletter for salespeople. He was asked about tips for increasing sales and he said that perhaps the area of greatest weakness among most salespeople is "the closing"—how to actually bring a sale to a close. He cites research showing that 63% of all sales interviews end with the salesperson not specifically asking for the order. He then goes on to note that Dr. Herb True of Notre Dame found that 46% of the salesmen he interviewed ask for an order only once, then quit; 24% ask for the order twice; 14% ask for the order three times; and 12% give up after the fourth attempt. *Yet his research on effective sales shows that 60% of all sales are made after the fifth closing attempt* (Ziglar, 1987, p. 6).

Now, those of you who, with mild manner, suggest one time to a potential user that maybe there's something important to be done with the evaluation see the implication of the sales comparison. "Closing" evaluation use, like closing a sale, is something you work at. Having the closing in mind is having a clear vision of what it means to use an evaluation, and then pursuing that use, not once, not twice, not three times, not four times, but pursuing that use as long as it takes to deliver on your accountability, thereby achieving intended use by intended users.

One of the ways you do that is to understand the closing *from the beginning*, to negotiate a shared understanding of what it's going to mean to close the evaluation, that is, to achieve use. You need to communicate at every step in the evaluation your commitment to utility.

One of the ways that I'll communicate that commitment to use during early negotiations is to ask if they expect a final report. This question seems to get people's attention. "Will you want a final report?"

They look at me and they say, "Come again?"

And I say, "Do you want a final report?"

They say, "Well of course, that's why we're doing this, to get a report."

And I respond, "No, we're doing this to get you information to improve your programming and decision making. A final written report is one way of communicating the information we get. But there's substantial evidence now that it is not always the most effective way. It is very costly to write final reports. There are other ways of dealing with this information. So, let's talk about what you can buy in terms of utilization, which is what we're really trying to get here. Not a report, but utilization. Let's talk about the most effective ways to get use and see if a final, written, costly report is the way to do that."

I find a lot of times that this is the point where they finally start to understand that what I'm talking about is something different from just producing a thick evaluation report so that they can file it under "has been evaluated." The point is to take use seriously from the very beginning.

A Mission and a Vision

I think, then, that we have before us in the evaluation standards, in the work of this meeting, and in the examples I have cited—we have before us a vision of a positive, proactive approach to utilization-focused evaluation that makes a difference and is accountable. The evaluation process makes a difference as people go through it. The evaluation results make a difference as they are used in intended ways by intended users.

The new mission of the American Evaluation Association includes increasing evaluation use and promoting evaluation as a profession. To promote evaluation as a profession, I submit to you, we need a vision of our profession as making a difference, not in some vague future, distant from the original site of the evaluation, but in the more immediate sense of achieving intended uses (evaluations goals) so that people know what they're paying for.

My vision is of an evaluation profession delivering on a promise of intended uses by intended users—and documenting through utilization follow-up studies the difference evaluation has made. Such a profession would be confident in its product and processes, sufficiently confident to "sell" evaluation (or at least promote it enthusiastically). Such a profession would make a demonstrable difference to the quality of programs evaluated, and thereby to the quality of the lives of clients served by those programs.

Such a profession, I believe, now exists. My vision is not of a distant future, but a description of what I believe now exists in much evaluation practice. That's why I invited you today to join me in celebrating evaluation.

References

Alkin, M. (1987a, October). *EOPS operational program review.* Paper presented at the annual meetings of the American Evaluation Association, Boston.

Alkin, M. (1987b, October). *Utilizing evaluations.* Paper presented at the annual meetings of the American Evaluation Association, Boston.

Cooley, W., & Bickel, W. (1986). *Decision-oriented educational research.* Boston: Kluwer Nijhoff.

Datta, L.-E. (1987, October). *Utilizing evaluation: The case of GAO.* Paper presented at the annual meetings of the American Evaluation Association, Boston.

Etheredge, L. S. (1979). Government learning: An overview. In S. Long (Ed.), *Handbook of political behavior.* New York: Plenum. (Pages cited in text refer to prepublication monograph.)

Patton, M. Q. (1978). *Utilization-focused evaluation.* Beverly Hills, CA: Sage.

Patton, M. Q. (1986). *Utilization-focused evaluation* (2nd ed.). Beverly Hills, CA: Sage.

Patton, M. Q. (1987). *Creative evaluation* (rev. ed.). Newbury Park, CA: Sage.

Sonnichsen, R. C. (1987, October). *Advocacy evaluation: A strategy for organizational improvement.* Paper presented at the annual meetings of the American Evaluation Association, Boston.

Steele, F. (1975). *Consulting for organizational change.* Amherst: University of Massachusetts Press.

Velasquez, J. (1987, October). *Managing evaluation systems over the long haul.* Paper presented at the annual meetings of the American Evaluation Association, Boston.

Weiss, C. H. (1987, October 16). *Evaluation for decisions: Is anybody there? Does anybody care?* Plenary presentation at the annual meetings of the American Evaluation Association, Boston.

Ziglar, Z. (1987, July/August). Closing skills. *Personal Selling Power 7,* p. 6.

10

How Primary is Your Identity as an Evaluator?

MICHAEL QUINN PATTON

The October 1987 issue of *Evaluation Review* had as its lead article the results of a study that is of considerable importance to evaluators interested in understanding the internal dynamics of our profession. Shadish and Epstein (1987) have published a study based on a stratified random sampling of the membership directories of the Evaluation Network and the Evaluation Research Society, the two organizations now merged in the American Evaluation Association. The study took place just as the merger was happening in 1986.

The first finding that stood out to me concerned professional identity. They found that 31% of the respondents would personally describe their *primary* professional identity as that of "evaluator" (p. 560).

This is a dramatic finding, and I suspect that more current data would show an even larger primary identity as "evaluator" among AEA members. Unfortunately, we have difficulty tracking this pattern because evaluators, until recently, have not recognized this possibility. At least I take that to be the explanation for what has been the format of the data collected with the membership application for the American Evaluation Association. We discovered in reviewing the application form this year that the background question about primary discipline listed some 15 alternatives—*but did not include evaluation as a choice!* I am pleased

AUTHOR'S NOTE: This chapter is reprinted from *Evaluation Practice*, Vol. 9, No. 2, pp. 87-92. Copyright 1988 by Sage Publications.

to say that we have corrected that oversight, but it reveals the roots of evaluation as historically and traditionally a secondary professional activity within one's primary discipline or specialization. . . .

In celebrating the increase in the number of members who take their primary identity from evaluation, I in no way mean to denigrate our colleagues for whom evaluation is a secondary or tertiary identity. I bring the matter up at all only because of its implications for the profession and because one's identity may affect one's view of evaluation and how one engages in the professional practice of evaluation.

Evaluation Identity and Professional Practice Orientation

Shadish and Epstein surveyed evaluators about a variety of issues, including methods preferences, approaches used, purposes given priority, organizational settings in which evaluations are conducted, and theoretical influences on practice. They found that responses clustered around two contrasting views of evaluation: "academic versus service evaluators" (p. 587). (They empirically found four possible types, but conceptually the four reduced primarily to two.) "Academic evaluators" tend to emphasize the research purposes of evaluation, traditional standards of methodological rigor, summative outcome studies, and contributions to social science theory. "Service evaluators" tend to emphasize serving stakeholders' needs, program improvement, qualitative methods, and assisting with program decisions.

Shadish and Epstein conclude:

> The general discrepancy between service-oriented and academically oriented evaluators now seems warranted on both theoretical and empirical grounds. (p. 587)

In addition, Shadish and Epstein report that evaluators whose *primary* professional identity is evaluation are more likely to manifest the service/stakeholder orientation, with an emphasis on formative evaluation and improved program decision making. Those who did not identify primarily as evaluators (but rather as sociologists, psychologists, educators, or other) were significantly more likely to be engaged in academic evaluative research emphasizing research outcomes and summative judgments (p. 581).

I read the Shadish and Epstein article soon after the October 1987 AEA national meetings in Boston. It helped me understand some of what transpired there. This issue of *Evaluation Practice* begins with the plenary remarks I made at the Boston meeting. In those remarks I contrasted my vision of evaluation utilization and our responsibility for use with the goals for the profession articulated by Carol Weiss (1988) on the previous day. Many people have since suggested to me that Weiss and I are simply operating in different arenas, that her remarks were addressed toward summative policy evaluation at the national level, while mine were aimed at a more narrowly defined version of formative program evaluation. While it does appear that we typically operate in different arenas and are involved in evaluation in different ways, I believed then, as I do now, that we have fundamentally different views of evaluation as a field of professional practice. Carol Weiss has an academic-research perspective on evaluation. I take an action research and stakeholder-oriented approach—what I've called "utilization-focused evaluation" (Patton, 1986).

We now have empirical verification from Shadish and Epstein that the field is very much split along precisely these lines. What inadvertently turned out to be a debate between Carol Weiss and myself could not have been more timely or more representative of varying perspectives among the membership.

Respecting Diversity

I love a good paradigms debate. What we have here are the makings of a good paradigms debate to replace the withering—and withered—qualitative-versus-quantitative debate. (See Patton, 1986, pp. 209-213, for ten reasons the qualitative-quantitative debate is history.) There are a number of dimensions to these contrasting paradigms of professional practice: service versus judgment; process versus outcomes; action versus truth; even the old qualitative-versus-quantitative debate may be resurrected here given the tendencies and patterns reported by Shadish and Epstein.

Yet, while the Shadish and Epstein article confirms the reality and importance of diversity among evaluators, diversity that may be of paradigmatic magnitude, the authors also point out the dangers of such divisions. It is on those dangers I want to focus, particularly as a context for my plenary remarks elsewhere in this volume.

Shadish and Epstein close their article with a concern that while AEA's membership diversity can help make the field unique and exciting, it also has the potential for increasing tensions between applied and academic interests, "tensions that arise because of the different demands and reward structures under which the two groups often operate" (p. 587). They go on to note that such tensions could lead to "polarization'" and they cite as evidence the debate within psychology between practicing versus academic clinical psychologists, which has led to a major schism in the profession, with some members calling for reorganization of the American Psychological Association or for a totally new organization. They conclude:

> To the extent that the underlying causes are similar—and there are indeed some important relevant similarities in the political and economic characteristics of the two professions—the lesson to evaluation is clear. Program evaluation must continue its efforts to accommodate diverse interests in the same profession, as it has recently done so well with the merger between the Evaluation Research Society and the Evaluation Network. Indeed, some have recently argued that we need to reach out even further to join our efforts with those of such colleagues as policy analysts. . . . Such reaching out is not easy, of course, for it requires a good deal of flexibility and new learning. In the long run, however, evaluation will not be well served by parochialism of any kind—in patterns of practice or anything else. (p. 588)

Supporting Diversity

I want to go on record as supporting, indeed advocating and working for, membership diversity in AEA. I think it is important for me to clarify my position in this regard because it would be possible to construe my plenary remarks from the Boston meetings as advocating only one view of evaluation practice, what Shadish and Epstein call the "service-oriented" approach. In my enthusiasm for holding forth a service-oriented, utilization-focused vision of professional evaluation practice, I may have appeared intolerant of those who do not share that view or engage in that practice. That was not my intent. My intent was to facilitate open discussion and debate about alternative visions of evaluation practice.

. . .

References

Patton, M. Q. (1986). *Utilization-focused evaluation* (2nd ed.). Beverly Hills, CA: Sage.
Shadish, W. R., Jr., & Epstein, R. (1987). Patterns of program evaluation practice among members of the Evaluation Research Society and Evaluation Network. *Evaluation Review, 11*, 555-590.
Weiss, C. H. (1988). Evaluation for decisions: Is anybody there? Does anybody care? *Evaluation Practice, 9*, 5-21.

11

If Program Decisions Hinged
Only on Information

A Response to Patton

CAROL H. WEISS

This is the third part of a miniseries on the use of evaluation. For those of you who missed the earlier episodes, I'll start with a brief recap. You can also enjoy the drama and beauty of this episode without worrying about what went before.

I gave a speech at the American Evaluation Association in October 1987, which also appeared in the February 1988 issue of *Evaluation Practice*. The paper discussed obstacles to the use of evaluation results, channels by which the obstacles are circumvented and the results come into currency, and the functions that evaluations serve. I intended to illustrate the many and varied ways in which evaluation results influence programming even when program decision makers do not implement results immediately and directly. Compared to much that has been—and is being—written about the sorry fate of evaluations, I intended it to be a beacon of hope.

Although I thought it was an upbeat talk, Michael Q. Patton, who spoke at AEA the following day and whose speech was published in the

AUTHOR'S NOTE: This chapter is reprinted from *Evaluation Practice*, Vol. 9, No. 2, pp. 87-92. Copyright 1988 by Sage Publications.

May 1988 issue of *Evaluation Practice*, took exception to it. He especially disagreed with two points I had made. First, he disagreed with my statement that evaluators have had "indifferent success in making evaluation the basis of decisions." He said that success was much greater than I had indicated. Second, he believed that my vision for the future was "dismal." He quoted my statement:

> Evaluators know that the purpose of their enterprise is program improvement, but I think we have come to recognize and accept the fact that evaluation does not always lead to improvements in the program under study. No matter how hard we try to be good planners, negotiators, and communicators with the stakeholders in the program, they are sometimes going to go their merry way. On the other hand, I think we are becoming more aware that evaluations do influence decisions—often indirectly and at some distance from the original site. I think we can do more to make that happen.

Mike found that aspiration paltry and uninspiring. He counterposed his own vision for evaluation use: intended use by intended users to improve programs directly.

In his President's Corner article in the same issue, Mike elevated these differences into a "paradigms debate." Throwing in a few more dimensions (e.g., service versus judgment, process versus outcomes), he observed that he and I were spokespersons for differing paradigms of what evaluation does and what it should aspire to be. I don't agree with the positions he ascribes to me, and, even in the abstract, I don't see the differences as being as stark as he claims they are. But perhaps I shouldn't object too loudly. Mike's formulation gives our interchanges a stature that, if we are canny, we can parlay into a textbook for the next generation of evaluators, an international conference, or a multibuck research grant to collect empirical data on the competing claims. What I would like to do here is point out what I see as the strengths and weaknesses in Mike's arguments and examine the evidence on which his claims and mine are based. Then I'll elucidate the implications of the two positions. Since Mike and I have respect and affection for each other, we can conduct this exchange with good humor and in a mutual search for understanding.

Convergences and Divergences

I like a lot of Mike's AEA address. In his charming anecdotal style, he captures our attention and lifts our spirits. Evaluation is important, he says; it is useful; it makes a difference in the world. Evaluators: Believe in your profession, gain experience and learn to practice it well, and stand behind (be accountable for) your work. That is a stimulating and encouraging message. Periodically we all need to renew our confidence that what we do makes a contribution to the betterment of the world. I also agree that the way we make our contribution as evaluators is by convincing and/or persuading program and policy people to use the evidence we collect as a guide to better programs.

Here are the points on which we differ.

Indifferent Success

I said that we have had indifferent success in this venture, in "making evaluation the basis of decisions." Mike claims that he can "*without difficulty* name at least 25, probably 50 practitioners of evaluation" who "are having a dramatic impact on programs and policies" (his italics).

I am delighted that Mike can think of 25 to 50 evaluators who are having an impact (out of how many? 100? 200?); Leviton and Boruch (1984) provide evidence that many evaluations lead to program change. But these statements do not refute my point. Program/policy people do not routinely use evaluation "as the basis of decisions." Note that I didn't say the record of evaluation was bad; I said "indifferent," which according to my old Webster's Collegiate means "neither good nor bad, large nor small, desirable nor undesirable, etc." What I wanted to convey—and still do—is that even when evaluators try to follow utilization-focused prescriptions, their influence is okay, fair, about the midpoint on the rating scale.

I think that evaluators can do better than they are doing to encourage attention to their findings, and I think they should. But overall, I doubt that we can ever persuade stakeholders to make evaluation results the overriding consideration in program decisions. For one thing, program people know a lot more about their programs than simply the things the evaluator tells them. They have firsthand experience in the operating organization; they know the site, the clients, the staff, the problems, the budgets, the conflicting directives from sponsors and funders, the state of relationships with other organizations that refer clients or receive clients, the history, the complaints and kudos, and the prospects for the future. Evaluators can tell them many things, but, as Gilsinan and Volpe (1986) write, "the evaluation researcher is faced with perhaps a single opportunity to design and implement . . . a study under less than ideal conditions" (p. 182). The evaluation study cannot cover all aspects of the program, and it can never be the only basis on which decisions are made. To ask program managers and planners to embrace evaluation findings fully is to ask them to bracket their years of experience and direct immersion in the daily world of the program, and in effect to abdicate their responsibility in favor of an evaluator who inevitably has only a partial view of their dilemmas. I doubt that Mike meant to imply such a course. He was taking issue with the affect, the emotional loading, in my statement rather than the literal words ("making evaluation the basis of decisions") themselves.

What evaluators should aspire to achieve in the area of utilization is influence, not the status of philosopher-kings whose dictates determine program futures. It is presumptuous to think that one evaluation study, no matter how conscientiously done, should be the major basis for changes in program. (I won't even mention the evaluation studies that are done at mediocre levels of competence or less.) Evaluation is better advised to add to understanding about the program, to illuminate the range of options and likely effects. In essence, evaluation should be continuing education for program managers, planners, and policymakers.

The Ubiquitousness of Program Politics

Even when we talk about *influence* on programming, there are important reasons why program people don't always pay close attention to evaluation results. They have many interests in their program over and above carrying out the prescribed process and achieving the prescribed results. They want to have a satisfactory work life, get along with their colleagues, gain recognition and respect, see their organization grow in prestige and financial solvency, maybe outdo a competing agency or faction, have a chance for advancement, do work that is esteemed by members of their profession, observe valued rituals, and have fun. When evaluators' results and recommendations put values such as these in jeopardy, program people sometimes give precedence to their own interests.

Self-interest, organizational protection, the quest for advantage—these elements are noticeably absent from the Patton world. In a manuscript about the use of evaluations that is 25 typed pages long, Mike Patton never mentions the word *politics*. In his world everybody behaves rationally. Not only are the program and policy people all rational, ready to base their decisions on the best available evidence if the evaluator is persuasive and persistent enough, they are also altruistic in motive. They want, above all, to improve their program to serve the best interests of the clientele. They don't seem to be concerned about drains on the budget, finding qualified staff, extra work, disturbing ongoing relationships with other agencies, possible negative feedback from community groups or the press, getting the grant renewed, satisfying the curmudgeons on the board, or any of the concerns that exercise the program people I have dealt with. His stakeholder groups are ready to utilize evaluations if the evaluator makes a good enough case. They don't worry about scarce resources or their programs' reputations or their own advancement or avoidance of unpleasant tasks. His policy people aren't worrying about the next election, or getting larger appropriations, or "getting along by going along" with influential legislators or administrators.

According to Patton, all the evaluator has to do is tell them the facts and point out the "right" course of action. Granted, the evaluator may have to say it many times and in many different ways, having to be a salesman, a charmer, a person with great interpersonal skills. The evaluator has to believe in the potency of the product he or she is selling, Mike says, and learn the techniques of salesmanship. But with enough attention to early contacts, practitioner involvement, client participation in the evaluation, and good dissemination, the evaluator will have dramatic impact on the decisions of the rational and high-minded managers and policymakers.

Let me tell you about some evaluations that I have been involved with.

(1) I directed an evaluation of a federally financed program in a social action agency. Shortly after the evaluation study was reported, the federal grant ended. No other local agency had the resources to pick up the program (even though it had been quite successful). The staff of the sponsoring unit in Washington who should have been interested in the findings were swamped with reports and worried about their own futures. Utilization: zilch.

(2) A million-dollar evaluation on which I served as consultant came up with a considerable amount of useful information about process and outcomes. It showed that the program was having modest success in improving medical practice in some areas, less success in other areas, and it pointed to strategies that were affecting program effectiveness. Just as the work was finishing up, a new person was appointed to head the parent agency, and his priorities did not include the program under study. The director of the program was encouraged to leave, and the program was relegated to peripheral status in the agency. All the evidence of success and important recommendations about directions for improvement found their way into professional publications, from whence perhaps they may rise someday to affect the next reincarnation of the program.

(3) An evaluation study of a program in a small agency was initiated because there was a strong difference of opinion among the staff about the value of devoting substantial resources to this one program at the expense of other programs that the agency was running or wanted to run. When the evaluation was reported, supporters of the program latched onto the findings that were positive; opponents flaunted the findings that were negative. The argument within the agency continued to rage much as before, but each side now quoted evaluative evidence to justify its case.

(4) Another evaluation study found that one mode of programming was having significantly better effects than other modes, and the evaluator recommended expansion of the effective strategies. However, this type of programming was also considerably more staff-intensive, and costs of operation were almost one-third higher than the usual costs. Expanding the more effective strategy would also entail cutting back on the number of people who could be served, with all the negative publicity such a decision would entail. So the agency decided to proceed much as before, promising to make minor adjustments toward the better mode of service as the budget allowed.

Every evaluator I know has had experiences like these. Not all the time, of course, or they would all have fled the field or become confirmed cynics, but often enough that they recognize the scenario. The Patton doctrine of accountability would say that the evaluators were responsible for these failings. Somehow, if they had really been on the ball, they could have either foreseen or alleviated the hostile pressures. I wish I knew how.

Understanding How Organizations Work

People who study organizations are thoroughly familiar with the propensity of agency staff to act nonrationally. In fact, few scholars of organizations any longer believe that organizations make decisions by the rational route: defining a problem, searching for alternative solutions, calculating the advantages and disadvantages of each solution, and choosing the most satisfactory alternative on the basis of the evidence. The rational model of decision making sets high store by using information, such as evaluation conclusions, in selecting a course of action. But students of organizations—whether in sociology, psychology, management, public policy, or elsewhere—see little of this type of behavior when they go out and study organizations. Rather, they see organizations acting according to bureaucratic rules and standard operating procedures, or through organizational politics (with factions or subunits vying for advantage), or through "garbage-can" processes (where a decision is the almost-chance confluence of the streams of participants, problems, solutions, and choice opportunities that are flowing through the organization at the moment), or acting first and crafting explanations of their actions afterward, retrospectively labeling them "decisions."

Let me call in some of the big guns to illustrate current thinking in the organizational literature. Pfeffer (1981) writes:

> It is not much of an exaggeration to claim that power and its effects are omnipresent in organizational decisions. Power affects the allocation of resources both across departments and across personnel categories. . . . Power has effects on the structure that emerges in the organization, including its information system. (pp. 231-232)

Brunsson (1985) reviews the experience of a number of organizations and concludes that "organizations have two problems: to choose the right thing to do, and to get it done" (p. 27). These two tasks call for different procedures, and the requirements are often in conflict. He writes that decision making that would include taking all the available data into account is irrational as far as taking action is concerned, because review of all the pros and cons lowers people's motivations and commitment to act. He concludes that "irrational decision-making and narrow prejudicial ideologies are necessary for any viable organization" (p. 31).

In his classic study, *Essence of Decision*, Allison (1971) writes about analysts. Substitute the word *evaluator* and hear what he says:

> "Solutions" to strategic problems are not discovered by detached analysts focusing coolly on *the* strategic problem. The problems for players are both narrower and broader than *the* strategic problem. Each player focuses not on the total strategic problem but rather on the decision that must be made today or tomorrow. Each decision has important consequences not only for the strategic problem but for each player's stakes. Thus the gaps between what the player is focusing on (the problem he is solving) and what a strategic analyst focuses on is often very wide. (p. 175)

> Each player pulls and hauls with the power at his discretion for outcomes that will advance his conception of national, organizational, group, and personal interests. (p. 171)

Mintzberg (1983) writes about the major shift that has taken place in management theory in the last generation. He characterizes it as a complete about-face, "from the notion of given organizational goals to that of fluid power in and around the organization with no set goals, from an organization devoid of influencers to one in which virtually everyone is an influencer, from the view of the organization as society's instrument to that of it as a political arena" (p. 8).

Organizational scholars are almost unanimous in recognizing that organizational members are intent on more than the welfare of the people whom they serve. Organization members use a decision situation for a large number of purposes, which, according to March and Olsen (1976, pp. 11-12) include

- an occasion for executing standard operating procedures, and fulfilling role-expectations, duties, or earlier commitments
- an occasion for defining virtue and truth, during which the organization discovers or interprets what has happened to it, what it has been doing, what it is doing, what it is going to do, and what justifies its actions
- an occasion for distributing glory or blame for what has happened in the organization, and thus an occasion for exercising, challenging, or reaffirming friendship or trust relationships, antagonisms, power or status relationships
- an occasion for expressing and discovering "self-interest" and "group interest," for socialization, and for recruiting (to organizational positions or to informal groups)

- an occasion for having a good time, for enjoying the pleasures connected to taking part in a choice situation

As part of the decision-making process, organizations may well look to evaluation evidence to help them figure out what they have been doing and what they should do in the future, but obviously there are a lot of other things going on.

Reliability of the Evidence

On what does Mike base his belief that the level of use of evaluations is high? Mostly on the basis of evaluators' accounts of their own success. As evaluators, we have all come into programs in which staff tell us how successful they are being. We take these accounts with a grain of salt and subject them to empirical test. As the director of a mental health program told me long ago: The job of a program practitioner is to believe; the job of an evaluator is to doubt. As *practitioners* of evaluation, it is important for us to believe in the worth of the enterprise and to downplay the cases of shortfall. But as *evaluators*, we are obligated to examine the evidence.

Mike's evidence comes largely from papers that evaluators have written for professional audiences about their successes in utilization. Most of us can write papers like that, too, if we want to display the sunny side of the story. It is part of the truth, but by no means the whole truth.

Another type of evidence that Mike cites is follow-ups by evaluation units of the fate of their recommendations. For example, units in the General Accounting Office and the Federal Bureau of Investigation have counted up the number of their recommendations that have been accepted and implemented, and the rates are high. Having once engaged in an exercise of that sort myself, I view the data with respect, but with some skepticism. In one case, I remember, we tracked the uses made of a study that made five recommendations. One recommendation was for a major overhaul of the program, and the other four referred to making improvements in record keeping, budgeting procedures, accounting practices, and reporting. The agency implemented four of the five recommendations (take a wild guess about which ones). Its utilization score was 80%!

I'm always a bit uneasy about taking recommendations as the unit of utilization anyway. To the best of my knowledge, we haven't looked very closely at where evaluators' recommendations come from. Some recommendations may be well grounded in data, and others may be flights of fancy from people without much expertise in program planning or operation. Let me share a few hunches about the sources of recommendations. It is a diversion from the main theme of this article, but it might inspire some of you to make a careful study of the subject.

In the best cases, recommendations emerge directly from the data. There is good evidence that one practice in the program is superior to other program practice. For example, if students who spend more time on the learning task tend to learn more, the evaluator is well justified in recommending more time on the task. More commonly, I imagine, recommendations represent a leap from the data. They may derive from professional standards or guidelines. For example, when a program is not particularly successful, and the evaluator knows that it is not abiding by "approved practice" in the field or in the practice profession, the evaluator recommends approved practice. Sometimes, recommendations seem to be made because what the program is doing doesn't work very well, and the evaluator assumes that doing the opposite would be better. For example, if the unsuccessful program is using group counseling, the evaluator may recommend individual counseling; if the unsuccessful program relies on incentives to individual workers, the evaluator may recommend group incentives.

In some cases, evaluators have expert knowledge of the program field. They have studied many programs in compensatory education or physical rehabilitation or foster care, and (with or without professional training) they have built up a repertoire of knowledge. Their recommendations derive from this body of expertise. More often, I suspect, evaluators rely on logical thinking. They try to figure out what it would take to make a program work better. They implicitly develop a logical model of the program in their mind, fixing gaps and inconsistencies that they see in the program, and base their recommendations on their layperson's understanding.

It is not unknown for evaluators to spend so much time on data collection and analysis that they have very little time at the end to figure out the implications of their data. With two weeks left before the report is due, they scramble to find something reasonable to recommend. The cogency of their recommendations will depend heavily on how well informed they are about the field, about other programs and prior evaluations, and about individual and collective behavior. For the people in the program who are the intended users of the findings and recommendations, taking evaluators' recommendations seriously can be either a brilliant stroke or a massive exercise in futility. I'm more comfortable with the idea of their taking evaluation results seriously. Program managers and practitioners may know better than the evaluator what implications to draw from the evidence and which directions are likely to be the most fruitful—which is a good point to get back to the main line of this argument.

In all, I think that the degree to which agencies make direct use of evaluation results is—if you don't like the word *indifferent*—not bad, fair, a sometime thing. If the evidence shows them something that needs fixing and a way to do it, they will often try to do it. If the evidence helps them do what they want to do anyway, they will use it. If it provides one more piece of the puzzle of agency action, it will take its place in the collage. If it is out of whack with what they believe and know, or believe they know, they may think about it and file it away for further consideration later. Mike Patton and his students (1977) did one empirical study of the utilization of evaluations, and here's what they found:

> We found that evaluation research *is used* by decision makers but not in the clear-cut and organization-shaking way that social scientists sometimes believe research should be used. The problem we have come to feel may well lie more in many social scientists' overly grand expectations about their own importance to policy decisions than in the intransigence of federal bureaucrats. (p. 144)

> Thus, none of the impacts described was of the type where new findings from an evaluation led directly and immediately to the making of major, concrete program decisions. *The more typical impact was one where the evaluation findings provided additional pieces of information in the difficult puzzle of program action, thereby permitting some reduction in the uncertainty within which any federal decisionmaker inevitably operates.* (p. 145)

> Occasionally a major study emerges with great impact. But most applied research can be expected to have no more than a small and momentary effect on the operations of a given program. (pp. 148-149)

When Patton based his conclusions on empirical study of the extent of utilization, he came out with a bit more jaundiced account than I have given. Of course, that was a dozen years ago, and evaluators—with Mike's help—may have learned a good deal since then about increasing utilization. But I think that the general patterns persist. Too many other considerations intrude on program decisions and operations to allow evaluation results to carry the day. And, I would add, that is often all to the good. Evaluation studies should add to the depth of understanding about programs, but we should not expect evaluations to supplant all the other knowledge and values that democratic societies employ to make social choices. As Cronbach et al. (1980) wrote:

> An evaluation of a particular program is only an episode in the continuing evolution of thought about a problem area. . . . The better and more widely the workings of social programs are understood, the more rapidly policy will evolve and the more the programs will contribute to a better quality of life. . . . The evaluators' professional conclusions cannot substitute for the political process. . . . What is needed is information that supports negotiation rather than information calculated to point out the "correct" decision. (pp. 2-4)

Mike was very candid about his reasons for becoming incensed at my modest (meager?) reading of utilization success. Evaluators are not in a good position to market their wares if they cannot promise significant impact. He said in his AEA remarks:

> The Weiss vision of use lacks accountability, and is absolutely *not* marketable to potential and actual purchasers of evaluation services. Such a vision of use would be unacceptable for both internal and external contractors, that is, those who must make themselves valuable to supervisors in the organizations that employ them and those who must produce something of value under contract to clients.

So, there's the rub. If we acknowledge that evaluation doesn't routinely lead to program improvement, we risk the loss of clients. Mike repeats that "the Weiss vision, in my judgment, is not marketable." Even if it is true, the implication is that we shouldn't say so publicly—or we undermine our ability to generate business.

This is the part of the case that troubles me most. Mike believes in evaluation that is "accountable, utilization-focused, and salable," but there seems to be more emphasis on its salability than on its integrity. I think it is wrong to mislead clients and potential clients about what evaluation can offer them. It can do much, but it can't promise, let alone guarantee, direct program improvement. I think it is wrong to mislead evaluators about what they should expect of themselves. They can increase the quality and quantity of information and ideas available to program people, but they should not hold themselves responsible if other contingencies—for good or ill—outweigh the power of the evidence. To expect that evaluation results will be intentionally used by intended users in the form that evaluators advocate is to set all of us up for frustration.

Competing Paradigms

Drawing on a study by Shadish and Epstein (1987), Mike suggests that there are two kinds of evaluators: those who are interested in working with clients to maximize the use of their results and those who are "academic" in orientation and care little about use. He implies that I am of the latter variety. In his President's Corner article, he gracefully urges that the American Evaluation Association should embrace all its children, no matter how misguided their ideas may be, but it is obvious that he hopes "academic" evaluators will sit downwind of him.

It's true that I teach in a university, but I am as committed to the use of evaluation results as any person alive. (As a precondition, I am also committed to improving the methodological quality of evaluations, both quantitatively and qualitatively, so that they have something valid to say.) In the putative paradigms that contrast judgment versus service, outcomes versus process, truth versus action, and quantitative versus qualitative, I am hopelessly at sea. I am interested in service and don't eschew judgment; I study process and outcomes; I use quantitative and qualitative methods; I believe that truth helps to foster action. (My research has shown that agency people are more likely to use research when they are convinced it is accurate and they won't be shot down if they rely on its evidence; Weiss with Bucuvalas, 1980.) Tempting as it is to divide all manner of human behavior into dualistic categories (good/bad, yin/yang, rational/political, academic/caring), a liberating slogan for the 1990s might be "Challenge all typologies!"

A Vision for the Future

Here are some things that I hope Patton and I can agree about. Let us all strive to improve the quality of our evaluations. First, let us try to ask the right questions—the key questions—the pregnant questions—questions that have important implications for the future of programming. Then let us use designs that are appropriate to the questions we raise, not forgetting that qualitative evaluation requires careful design as well. Let us work to hone our methodological skills, our working-with-people skills, our understanding-of-program-life skills, our capacity to understand and interpret what we find. From the very beginning, let us work to encourage the *evaluative cast of mind* among policy and program planners, so that they are skeptical of the received wisdom and the latest fads and ready to examine the assumptions on which programs are based. Finally, let us begin the evaluation with dissemination in mind and be sure we continually diffuse the evidence we assemble to all the people who have a say about program futures.

But let us not expect to run the program world from behind our notebooks and computers. And let us not expect that good skill and goodwill are going to rid this fallible world of self-interest, apathy, search for agency aggrandizement and political advantage, or random events. If evaluators judged themselves and their performance solely against the criterion of rational and noble program decisions, that would lead to dismal news indeed.

I still believe in the longer run. Now it is perfectly true, as John Maynard Keynes has said, that in the long run we are all dead. I don't mean *that* long a run. But in the space of two, three, five, or eight years, many of the results of social research come into currency and overtake formerly taken-for-granted assumptions. Rossi (1987) recently wrote:

> In the short term, good social research will often be greeted as a betrayal of one or another side to a particular controversy [and rejected]. . . . It is important to keep in mind that in the long term, good research will often, if not always, be assimilated into conventional wisdom. (p. 79)

In my experience, that is true about evaluation results. And just as scientific research is being translated into practical technology more rapidly now than it was in the past, so too do good evaluation findings more rapidly influence program design. The influence may be blocked at the site that was studied, because managers and sponsors, staff and clients, all have interests and beliefs tied up in one way or another with things as they are. But down the road at the next program, in programs just starting up, in the state capital, in the foundation office, and maybe soon again in Washington, evaluations influence how people think about programming and the kinds of programs they are ready to support.

References

Allison, G. T. (1971). *Essence of decision: Explaining the Cuban missile crisis*. Boston: Little, Brown.

Brunsson, N. (1985). *The irrational organization*. New York: John Wiley.

Cronbach, L. J., Ambron, S. R., Dornbusch, S. M., Hess, R. D., Hornik, R. C., Phillips, D. C., Walker, D. F., & Weiner, S. S. (1980). *Toward reform of program evaluation*. San Francisco: Jossey-Bass.

Gilsinan, J. F., & Volpe, L. C. (1986). Do not cry wolf until you are sure. *Evaluation Studies Review Annual, 11*, 175-187.

Leviton, L. C., & Boruch, R. F. (1984). Contributions of evaluation to education programs and policy. *Evaluation Studies Review Annual, 9*, 597-632.

March, J. G., & Olsen, J. P. (1976). *Ambiguity and choice in organizations*. Bergen, Norway: Universitetforlaget.

Mintzberg, H. (1983). *Power in and around organizations*. Englewood Cliffs, NJ: Prentice-Hall.

Patton, M. Q., Grimes, P. S., Guthrie, K., Brennan, N., French, B., & Blyth, D. (1977) In search of impact. In C. H. Weiss (Ed.), *Using social research in public policy making* (pp. 141-164). Lexington, MA: Lexington Books.

Pfeffer, J. (1981). *Power in organizations*. Boston: Pitman.

Rossi, P. H. (1987). No good applied social research goes unpunished. *Society, 25*(1), 74-79.

Shadish, W. R., Jr., & Epstein, R. (1987). Patterns of program evaluation practice among members of the Evaluation Research Society and Evaluation Network. *Evaluation Review, 11*, 555-590.

Weiss, C. H., with Bucuvalas, M. J. (1980). *Social science research and decision-making*. New York: Columbia University Press.

Review and Commentary

Part III

Part III presents a set of papers written by Michael Patton and Carol Weiss. These papers bear on the topic of evaluation theory and expand on the interchange of the Malibu meeting. The first of these, Chapter 8, is a paper that was originally presented as Carol Weiss's plenary address to the 1988 annual meeting of the American Evaluation Association (AEA). Her topic was "Evaluation for Decisions: Is Anybody There? Does Anybody Care?" Her paper addressed the major theme of the AEA meeting, "evaluation utilization." Reading this chapter, one readily notes many of the discussion areas prompted within the Malibu seminar and addressed in earlier sections. Michael Patton, scheduled to address the AEA annual meeting the next day, took great exception to a number of points made by Weiss; his speech on that subject appears as Chapter 9. Furthermore, Patton, noting the differences in their views, subsequently produced an article (Chapter 10) in which he described a recent research paper by Shadish and Epstein (1987) and referred to his and Weiss's differences as a "paradigms debate." Finally, Weiss responded to the Patton papers (Chapter 11). All of these chapters as presented are excerpted from articles in *Evaluation Practice*.

This review and commentary attempts to provide some perspective on the Weiss/Patton debate. Part of the commentary may be gleaned from the reading of the articles themselves and noting their relationship to the themes discussed in Parts I and II. Other insights I may have acquired from my friendship with both of the "debaters" and my role in providing advice and feedback on various of the rebuttals. My speculations about their motivations, reactions, and so on are not necessarily accurate—they are simply my best guesses about what was going on, and why.

Unfortunately, the presentation mode of Part III—as opposed to the more interactive style of the seminar—forced a debate to occur. Because of the format, Weiss and Patton were forced into a more formal style of presentation. Thus both felt the need to make their cases totally and fully, and in the process some overgeneralizations of each other's views appear. Each of the debate participants also felt the necessity to pick on some minor points of semantics. Indeed, the format forced the perception of great differences and antagonism to each other's views, which was not the case. Patton and Weiss find a great deal to agree upon:

- Both agree there is evidence of *both* success and shortcomings in the conduct of evaluation.
- Both have general understanding of and agreement on the kinds of factors necessary for obtaining utilization.
- Both recognize that evaluation operates within a political context.
- Both recognize that a potential decision maker/user does not operate with a clean slate and has a "working knowledge."
- Both agree that a "decision" is not the only evidence of evaluation impact.
- Both agree that there are a number of instances where evaluations "lead to decisions"—especially if one views program modifications and changes in attitudes about a program as "decisions."

However, Weiss and Patton also find a number of areas to disagree on. The forceful debate seems to be prompted largely by each one's surprise that the other did not understand his or her views. Apparently the Malibu seminar left them both with the feeling that they better understood each other's views.

Now, let us examine some of the disagreement. Patton spoke with me at the AEA meeting and was dismayed about Carol's paper; Carol shared her rebuttal paper with me and asked for comments—she did not understand why Michael was reacting (overreacting?) to her paper. Patton in his article expresses shock that Weiss should cite "indifferent success in making evaluation the basis for discussions." What is *indifferent*? Patton undoubtedly viewed the word critically, as meaning a "lack" of success, while Weiss viewed it as "okay, fair, about the midpoint of the rating scale." Thus a part of the jousting relates to the semantic overtones of the word *indifferent*.

When Weiss referred to indifferent success *"as the basis for decisions,"* her context was a situation where stakeholders would make the evaluation results "the overriding concern in program decisions." She simply has difficulty in finding situations where it is the *overriding* concern. Patton, on the other hand, views evaluation's role as having influence—perhaps even major influence—for intended users. Clearly, by these terms, evaluation is a basis for decisions. Would he expect it usually to be *the* overriding consideration? I doubt it. But perhaps he is offended by the term *basis for decisions* and he and Weiss, again, disagree based upon semantic interpretations of such terms. A large part of the issue is the difference in focus. When Patton focuses on intended use by intended users, he can easily conceive of evaluation being the basis for decisions—if the evaluator selects programs and users carefully enough and does an expert enough user-oriented evaluation.

Despite the implication in Weiss's statement that Patton seems to operate in a manner oblivious to program politics and organizational workings, clearly Patton knows better than to assume that there are no contextual influences, no working knowledge of individual users, and the like. Indeed, he discussed these issues and acknowledged them in the Malibu discussion. "Indifferent" is derived from different assumptions of what each means by "basis for decisions" and by who the users are.

Beyond these semantic differences the debate goes deeper. Whether the success is "indifferent" or not (whatever the meaning), Patton apparently does not believe that Weiss is fully aware of the extent of utilization success. He argues that he can "without difficulty name at least 25, probably 50 practitioners of evaluation who are having dramatic impact on programs and policy." It is clear from Weiss's ridicule of this statement that Patton and Weiss are talking from two different frames of reference. The communication problem is exacerbated by Patton having provided these numbers, which seems to imply (at least to Weiss's mind) that this is his representation of evaluation's total impact. To this she retorts, "Out of how many? 100? 200?"

Indeed, this discussion takes us away from the main point, namely, that across the spectrum of evaluation there are a large number of individual evaluators whose work has a dramatic impact on programs and policy. I would guess that the number of evaluators having impact yearly to be in the thousands, and the total number of evaluators to be in the tens of thousands (and these might be gross underestimates). The logic seems reasonable to me that the numbers one comes up with are partially related to one's view of what an evaluation is. Let me elaborate. There were more than 15,000 school districts in the country in 1987-88 (National Education Association, 1988) and I would imagine that each has *at least* two evaluations done per year (federal Title I Program, bilingual education programs, court-ordered integration programs, state-funded programs, and so on). Add to this list a comparable number of local social welfare, mental health, and criminal justice programs. And what about other county programs? Statewide programs? Community colleges? Colleges and universities? Foundation-supported programs? Finally, we add the federal programs that Weiss is most accustomed to working with.

Now we begin to see part of the problem. Weiss clearly focuses on a more limited pool of evaluations, evaluations that for the most part are directed at large agencies, legislatures, and Congress. Indeed, at a number of points in her chapters she refers to legislatures and the way in which they operate as a basis for deriding the relationship between evaluation and decision making. These evaluations have high levels of visibility, multiple constituencies and advocates, and the like. Decisions in these kind of instances, as Weiss (1980) has so nicely documented in her own research, tend to a far greater extent to "accrete." Smaller, local-program-oriented evaluations typically are less politically "loaded" and thus are less visible; there are fewer people involved in program decisions. Very frequently they do not involve "funding/no funding" decisions. "Decisions" might be made about modifications of the staff development component in a school district integration program. Or, as a consequence of an evaluation, the statewide Chancellor's Office for Community Colleges might decide to conduct a workshop to improve data management procedures within community colleges; or the same agency might work with the legislature in implementing a bill to require that directors of a specially funded program at colleges be employed full-time.

There are a variety of primary users who might be the targets of evaluations and might be in positions to make "decisions." In some instances "decisions" are made by school superintendents or assistant superintendents, or school boards who review the evaluation report and, based upon one, several, or many of the recommendations, make decisions specifically related to that program. In other instances, program directors who are not threatened by job extinction may have initiated the evaluation study and may simply want to improve their programs. There are countless instances of evaluations having direct impact in which some sort of decision is made. Nor do these direct-impact decisions need to rely on evaluation information as the sole source of input.

Another Weiss statement provides a further point of conflict. She notes that "even when evaluators try to follow utilization-focused prescriptions" they fail to have influence. There is a seeming incongruity here. While Weiss presents a list of procedures ("advice" she calls it) for evaluators to follow, she apparently discounts the value of such advice because it is geared to the notion of the "unitary decision maker." Thus one has the impression that Weiss has not really been exposed to very many situations in which evaluators *really* try to follow utilization-focused prescriptions.

Indeed, the broader issue is whether a research-oriented evaluator (or, in Shadish & Epstein's terms, an "academic evaluator") can really follow a utilization-focused prescription. While both Patton and Weiss might note the advice of identifying the key decision maker (or the few key decision makers), clearly, as we have seen from the discussion—both in the papers in this section and in Parts I and II—they would do it in quite different ways. And I believe that Patton would be quite unwilling to accept Weiss's process of defining decision makers as being sufficiently interactive to be in conformance with his utilization-focused prescriptions. While Weiss would maintain that identifying the decision maker is important, she defines the process more narrowly than does Patton and simply is not committed to that as one of the primary modus operandi of conducting an evaluation. A similar conclusion can be drawn about the other items of advice mentioned by Weiss:

- Get decision makers involved in planning the evaluation.
- Be sure the evaluation addresses the questions the decision makers raise.
- Limit the study to variables that the decision makers have the authority to manipulate.
- Communicate results early.

Furthermore, the added utilization-focused prescriptions that Patton provides in Chapter 10, such as intended use by intended users, overcoming staff fears, being situationally responsive as an expert evaluator, and being an advocate for evaluation, are not likely to be embraced by Weiss.

In summary, it appears that some of the differences between the Weiss and Patton positions are clearly associated with program level, as was noted in the discussion presented in Parts I and II—different vantage points, if you will. However, Patton maintains that it is more than the level involved, that instead it is a "paradigms debate"—that "academic evaluators" and "service evaluators" differ on the purposes given priority, on methods, on preferences, and so on. And he believes that these differences reflect the disagreements that he and Weiss are having. While Weiss rejects the notion of paradigmatic differences, she nonetheless makes the ultimate admission of the academic evaluator: "Making the evaluation studies available in the literature is a given . . . you don't take on a study unless you are going to publish it" (see the section headed "Defining Misuse" in Chapter 13). Weiss's rejection of paradigmatic differences seems primarily to be a reaction to the way in which the issue was phrased by Patton, who appears to be "intolerant of those who do not share . . . [that view or engage in that practice]." While indicating that such was not his intent, Patton nonetheless appears to offend Weiss on this point. The extent to which those paradigms are different because of the relative acceptability of each in the evaluation arenas in which Patton and Weiss most typically operate is an unresolved issue.

So, what can we say about the paradigms debate? First, I would concur that indeed Patton and Weiss are operating with different paradigms of evaluation. Weiss aligns more with the academic-oriented view of evaluation and Patton with the client-oriented view. These orientations, or paradigms, are possibly more suited for use at particular levels of evaluation (program versus policy), but either paradigm might be employed at any level.

Weiss and Patton are not the sole proponents of their respective paradigms. Each has a great number of paradigm-mates, and there are substantial disagreements among those who share the same general paradigm. Indeed, differences in theoretical views about evaluation might be so great that the somewhat simplistic two-paradigm model does not do the field justice. On this matter, the reader is referred to a study by Janice Williams (1989) in which she empirically examines evaluation theoretic differences of major evaluation writers.

References

National Education Association. (1988). *Estimates of school statistics: 1987-88*. West Haven, CT: Author.

Shadish, W. R., Jr., & Epstein, R. (1987). Patterns of program evaluation practice among members of the Evaluation Research Society and Evaluation Network. *Evaluation Review, 11*, 555-590.

Weiss, C. H. (1980). Knowledge creep and decision accretion. *Knowledge: Creation, Diffusion, Utilization, 1*(3), 381-404.

Williams, J. E. (1989). A numerically developed taxonomy of evaluation theory and practice. *Evaluation Review, 13*(1), 18-31.

PART IV

Politics and Ethics

Participant Introductory Comments

Participants

Marvin Alkin: Evaluators work within a political system. There is no denying this or pretending otherwise. We cannot retreat to the sanctity of the research world. While I do not advocate that evaluators actively engage in the political battles, neither is the evaluator role passive with respect to the political context. The evaluator must conduct his/her work with knowledge of the actors, agendas, conflicting value systems, etc. The evaluator's work should provide visibility to political conflicts and make reliable and valid data available pertaining to these issues. . . . High ethical standards are requisite for credibility and future effectiveness.

Ross Conner: Political and ethical considerations are always present in an evaluation setting and are also in flux. Rather than meaningful, and creative work if the evaluator can seize them.

Ernest House: There are limits on the uses of evaluation information. Evaluators cannot do simply whatever the sponsor of the evaluation, usually a government official, wants them to do. Evaluations must serve the interests not only of the sponsor but of the larger society, and of various groups within society, particularly those most affected by the program or policy under review. Hence evaluation is political and ethical, as well as technical. As a social practice it entails an inescapable ethic of public responsibility, and this responsibility extends well beyond the immediate client, if indeed once conceives of the sponsor of the evaluation as the client.

Michael Kean: I do not believe that there are any ethical issues in evaluative implementation, per se. The basic ethical principles apply.

233

As such, there are no issues. Data should never be changed and should be fully and honestly reported. During 8 years as executive director of the Office of Research and Evaluation of the School District of Philadelphia, I bore ultimate responsibility for over 1,200 separate and discrete evaluations. On only two instances was I ever approached to change (i.e., falsify) data. As I said, there is no issue. Were I pressed by my organizational superior to change data (and I never was), my response would be a simple but direct no. I would also hasten to remind the requester that if I were willing to lie for him, how would he ever know whether I was lying to him?

Jean King: Evaluation and politics are inevitably linked, and the field has happily advanced to a point where this is accepted. The classic expectation on the part of evaluators that decision makers would calmly review evaluation results, then follow the recommendations given, is, we now recognize, unrealistic on several counts: Results are often inconclusive or contradictory; the study may itself be flawed; other events may influence future actions; and so on. However, the *potential* for generating information renders the evaluation process powerful because people need information to help them make decisions—and to rationalize those they want to make. Evaluation can help in both cases, but it can never overshadow the larger human process at work in organizations.

What matters finally both in the conduct of evaluations and the use of their results are two conditions: (1) the presence of one or more individuals who care about the process and want to do something with the results; and (2) a political environment that will allow that to happen. The ethics of the people who care about the evaluation—and this includes the evaluators—will directly affect the entire process; if they choose to subvert the evaluation to their own ends, the enterprise will be suspect and unavoidably flawed, although no one may ever know. The evaluation setting has an equally powerful effect. Evaluation information may have little influence in a charged political environment where people are jockeying for power and act in ways they believe will promote or at least protect their own position.

Evaluation and ethical issues go hand in hand because of the inevitable values questions that the process raises. What *are* appropriate standards of conduct for program evaluators? Are they fixed, or is there such a thing as "situational" ethics? The questions we must ultimately ask ourselves include the following:

- Who decides what we evaluate?
- To whose issues will we respond in an evaluation?
- Who determines access to people?
- Who owns and controls the results of our efforts?
- Is it incumbent on us as evaluators to speak for those of little power?
- To whom, finally, do we report?

While we can posit ethical principles for evaluation in the abstract, ongoing practice may routinely challenge these.[1]

Susan Klein: There are many important political and ethical issues related to the use of evaluation. (1) As with any area of disciplined inquiry, it is important for evaluators to share their biases, criteria, standards, and methods publicly so that the user will be able to take these into account. (2) Attention to equity is both an important political and ethical issue in evaluation use. This means that care should be taken to describe whether or not the program, product, practice, or policy has a differential impact on females, males, members of minority groups, the limited English proficient, persons with low income, etc. It is equally important to make an affirmative effort to help members of the less information-privileged groups obtain evaluation information about the best available choices in a way that they can use the information. (3) Often when users seek evaluation information, they ask for the solutions. The information providers are rarely prepared to respond to such a request, or else they answer from a list of options limited by factors other than quality. Sometimes these lists are limited to solutions produced by their own organization, by schools in their state, or, in the case of the National Diffusion Network, federally-sponsored exemplary programs. Politically and ethically we need to develop fair, public procedures to make it easy for users to select among the best options. (4) Another important political issue is to provide funding to conduct additional research on evaluation use and to implement the ideas presented above in as comprehensive a way as possible.

---

1. I am reminded here of the example often used in discussing Kohlberg's stages of moral development, in which an honest man is led to steal an expensive drug for the higher good of saving his spouse's life. In ongoing evaluation practice, the "higher good" may suggest activities that could concern the people paying for evaluations, and evaluators may confront ethical dilemmas in which someone—perhaps themselves—must lose.

Alex Law: I believe that every evaluation is a political act, political in the sense that there is a continuing competition for stakes among the clients of an evaluation. These stakes could be financial, power, turf, or authorization to act. Clearly in this ambiance there is the potential for misuse. The credible evaluator has high ethical standards. The fact that evaluations are performed in a political environment should not be viewed as a negative. Indeed the need for information by the clients places the evaluator in a unique and often powerful position. The ethics of the evaluator provide a guard against misuse.

Milbrey McLaughlin: Ethical dilemmas feature in almost every evaluation because evaluation involves people, their efforts, aspirations, and self-interests, and because evaluation inherently is a political act. Ethical behavior demands honesty on the part of the evaluator about self-interest or conflict of interest. It requires evaluator sensitivity to unintended but harmful side effects of evaluation, perspective on the program or system that includes all relevant stakeholders, awareness of possible misuse or abuse of evaluation findings, and scrupulous care to honor promises of confidentiality and performance. However, deciding what constitutes ethical behavior often necessitates creative problem solving as the dilemmas arise about how to meet simultaneously the interests of individuals, organizations, the larger society, as well as the profession. Unfortunately, beginning evaluators are seldom told that the quality and value of their evaluation efforts often will rely as much on their skill in resolving ethical dilemmas as on their technical expertise.

Michael Patton: The power of evaluation derives from its reduction of uncertainty for and facilitation of effective action by evaluation users. Issues of power and ethics then revolve around the following: Whose questions get answered in the evaluation? Who are the primary intended users? Who has first access to findings? How will findings be shared, in what ways, to whom, for what purposes, when? What are intended uses determined by which intended users? What is the evaluator's relationship to evaluation users? These are the fundamental issues of the evaluation and all of these issues involve political and ethical considerations. In utilization-focused evaluation, the evaluator's first obligation is to primary intended users. These primary intended users are the clients the evaluator serves.

Carol Weiss: For a lot of people, politics is a dirty word, and one of the early aims of evaluation research was to "take the politics out of decision making." It was expected that good data would provide the basis for rational choice, and decisions made on the basis of evaluative evidence would avoid the bargaining and deals of politics. That hope turned out to be not only futile but fundamentally misguided.

Politics is the system we have for allocating values. In our society it is the core of democratic decision making. Evaluation of any programs that cost money and allocate valued services cannot escape becoming involved in politics. Political considerations intrude in three major ways. First, the policies and programs with which evaluation deals are the creatures of political decisions. They were proposed, defined, debated, enacted, and funded through political processes, and in implementation they remain subject to pressures—both supportive and hostile—that arise out of the play of politics.

Second, because evaluation is undertaken to feed into decision making, its reports enter the political arena. There evaluative evidence of program process and program outcomes has to compete for attention with other factors that carry weight in the political process. Evaluation reports will be embraced or attacked, cited or ignored, partly on the basis of whether they support people's existing positions and whether they deal with issues that *matter* to important groups. Third, evaluation itself has a political stance. By its very nature, it makes implicit political statements about a range of issues, such as the vulnerability of some programs to evaluative review while other programs roll along unexamined, the legitimacy of official program goals as the criteria for evaluation, and the right of evaluation funders to decide evaluation standards. The political proclivity of evaluation is basically reformist, looking toward modest change rather than fundamental restructuring.

If evaluators expect their work to have influence on future programs and policies, they have to recognize that they are political actors. The need is not to avoid politics but to understand it, and to contribute to the wisdom and judgment with which political outcomes are realized.

Discussants

Frederick Ellett, Jr.:   As evaluation activities take place in a given social-political context, the evaluator has certain ethical, legal, and political responsibilities. As an evaluator, he/she is subject to the standard professional code of ethics. This code includes the *strong presumption* that the evaluator will obey the law and will honor the explicit and implicit contract with client. But this is only a strong presumption; it can be overridden by countervailing ethical reasons. Although a person has taken on the *role* of evaluator a person *cannot* thereby *abdicate* his/her appropriate ethical responsibilities. Of course, what the evaluator's appropriate ethical responsibilities are will depend on the specific social-political context. (It is quite unlikely that the evaluator's ethical responsibilities are exclusively limited to serving the client's interests; it is equally unlikely that the evaluator's ethical responsibilities are always and exclusively linked to the concerns of a particular, disadvantaged group.) Given that there is an ethical responsibility that a person make a reasonable effort to consider the consequences of his/her actions, an evaluator, too, has a similar responsibility to consider the social-political consequences of the evaluation activities.

Michael Hendricks: Some evaluators believe that evaluation is a *research* activity. I disagree. Evaluation is very definitely a *political* activity, even though it happens to be a research-oriented one. If you doubt this, listen in the next time an agency head decides what programs to evaluate. The trick for evaluators is to use this political orientation in our favor, not against us, and this *can* be done. After all, politics creates some powerful incentives for commissioning and listening to evaluations.

12

Ethical Issues

Some Political Realities

Marv Alkin: I'm going to push the group to another level here . . . I'd like you to think about what is it that we need to learn about the nature of knowledge-producing activities, about the nature of evaluation, that we don't already know? And what are the ways in which it might be most feasible to go about obtaining those understandings?

Alex Law: Let me try a couple of ideas here. In the past year or so, I've been struck with what I call the "informal" aspects of information, as opposed to a formal structure. For years, my division has been separate from the programmatic branch and has been at the center of varying degrees of knowledge.

Jean King: What divisions are you affiliated with?

Alex Law: Division of Program Evaluation and Research of the California Department of Education. Over time I've become convinced that the evaluators who are working on various programmatic projects know more about these programs than the program people who are actually involved in them. They have a broader overview of what's going on. The evaluators make more intelligent commentary on them. Through the position of the director, I've been increasingly able to communicate this directly to the superintendent, and we get more direct action that way. Ross, let me give an analogue of your proposal. We have a bilingual program. We have been evaluating the bejesus out of the bilingual program forever. And it's like the delinquent problem. No matter what you do, it doesn't work on some global aggregate scale. So the program people run up to Canada and learn all about what's happening in Canada. The question is not whether there's going to be a bilingual program. There is going to be a bilingual program. That's political imperative. You're not going to get around that. The real question is what format is that program going to take. And it's increasingly clear to me that evaluation can shed precious little light on what an effective format would be in a unique school situation. We have to fall back and reconceptualize what we're talking about now. External commentary: We'll go through the literature, go through this intellectual exercise of questionable merit and come up with various lists of what should be done. I know that won't work, and the people who've been involved know that that won't work, but we're recycling the process anyway.

Susan Klein: Why? Why are you going to recycle it? Why can't there be institutional learning?

Alex Law: In programs like migrant and bilingual and special education, there is precious little institutional memory of what has gone before. It becomes almost an ad hominem type of phenomenon. The last person with credibility is the one who says, this is the way to go. It takes about 18 months to two years to recycle and find out that was no different than what we've been doing for so many years. If we're going to continue to throw money at the bilingual program, people are going to continue to evaluate, and they're going to continue to find that on an aggregate scale, it's not effective. But I have to go back to what you're saying: There are unique cases in which bilingual programs are incredibly effective. Where we do find they are effective, we find the people who are implementing the programs are doing what they know works and in most cases are avoiding state guidelines.[1]

[laughter]

Alex Law: We live this, I think, forever and ever. So here is again an ethical dilemma for the evaluator: Do you blow the whistle? No, you don't.

. . .

1. *Hendricks:*   I'm struck by how much of the discussion has focused on summative versus formative evaluation strategies. By and large, administrators are less interested in report cards than they are in being helped to improve.

Evaluation Responsibility for Misuse

Carol Weiss: Well, I guess the thing that I'm still surprised at is that, in a country of 220 million people, the population of a thousand evaluators, two thousand evaluators . . .

_____: Oh come on, at least 4500 . . .

Carol Weiss: You feel you can still make a difference by working for one project at a time with one set of clients, and be thankful for the very . . .

Mike Patton: You've hit on a really important, basic philosophical piece with me. And I made my peace with that as a Peace Corps volunteer, who went to save Upper Volta, and ended up being glad to have touched a couple villages. I made my peace with the kind of impact I was going to have then, and gave up saving Upper Volta. I haven't tried to replicate those initial misconceptions since. It has something to do with my personal notion of responsibility, about what I can and do take responsibility for.

Carol Weiss: No, I understand your feelings about responsibility. I think perhaps if you were being misquoted seriously in, say, the Health Care Financing Administration, that you would feel impelled to go and correct their misconceptions. But you're not responsible for use beyond your immediate . . .

Mike Patton: Certainly if I thought they were going to make some big decision that I was being misquoted about, I honestly wouldn't ignore that. But I don't track it. There are people who worry about getting a word out of sync in a paper, and they'll write in a letter and correct that. I don't have that compulsivity about the thing. And the more I'm misquoted, the less I worry about it. And it seems the longer your stuff is around, the more it gets misquoted. So it's harder to stay on top of the distortions.

. . .

[overtalk]

Mike Patton: That example's a nice one, because bringing in the larger audience would have created confidentiality problems for some of those groups, that would have involved risks for them. Well, telling that story even, certainly putting it in print, doesn't make that program look real good from their point of view.

Carol Weiss: Well, who knows what program it is?

Mike Patton: You can find out. I don't know. It's not compelling to me to bring in a larger audience, unless it's negotiated up front as one of the options, which I think it ought to be.

. . .

Unintended Use by Unintended Users

Milbrey McLaughlin: But Marv, how do you then integrate the point that Carol made earlier this afternoon, that not all use is the result of a one-to-one relationship between evaluator and evaluatee?

Marv Alkin: I think one of the important points that's emerged out of our discussions this afternoon—and indeed your own studies support this—is that there is a need for those who are doing the evaluation to communicate at an early stage and not be in a situation where they have to say: We've got this report—what are we going to do to link? So I guess I'm not terribly persuaded by the applicability of that model.

Mike Patton: I can share with you how I think about this issue because I raised it in a paper I wrote, a question about a hierarchy of utilization. In my own mind, there is one. And I think that my first responsibility, in the kind of work I do, is intended use for intended users. And that's what I call primary utilization. There is, beyond that, an ethic under which we operate for dissemination, for which I take no responsibility except to do it. That is, to make the information that comes out of an evaluation that is intended use for intended users available to a wider audience.[2] But typically, what unknown people do with that and how they use it is not something I take responsibility for. I think it's interesting to trace how dissemination affects people and what kind of things they pick up and what they respond to and what they don't respond to, but I don't take primary responsibility for what they do. In fact, I assume and expect that, in the dissemination process, the product will be abused and misunderstood and misused and will end up in places

2. *Hendricks:*   Sometimes I deliberately *avoid* dissemination to anyone other than the intended user. Does Michael see this as unethical?

I never imagined, in different kinds of ways. I don't try to track that, and I've stopped losing sleep about it. What I do take responsibility for is intended use for intended users. Very heavy responsibility. And I focus my efforts on making that process successful. And the rest I leave more to serendipity.

Carol Weiss: Well, that's fine as far as responsibility's concerned. As far as importance is concerned, I don't think that's that. I think some of the most important effects of an evaluation have been unintended use by unintended users. I don't care whether you take responsibility or not.

Marv Alkin: If you're not going to take responsibility, then why are you worried about it? Beyond saying that you're going to disseminate and get the information out, if you have no sense of responsibility for what happens to it, then how much more are you going to do?

Carol Weiss: I think the question becomes, very interestingly: To what extent is the quality of the information as research primary, because it's going to flow in all kinds of channels that you may never even know about and have consequences that you never even suspected? Or is responsiveness to a particular set of individuals with whom you are working paramount, because that's where you feel your responsibility lies? And I guess I come out on the other side of the question from Mike. It seems to me that it's more important to have sound, well-documented, carefully conceptualized information available, because it's going to be, or it may very well be, picked up by people in all kinds of places I don't even know about—let alone anticipate. And may have really significant kinds of effects.[3] I think, for example, about the research on early childhood cognitive development that was done in the late 50s and early 60s, that was taken up by people involved in early childhood education and then the Head Start program. And people who were doing that early research never thought about programming. They were just studying kids' cognitive development. And if they had been cutting corners and being responsive and only looking at things in terms of the theoretical understandings and assumptions of their clients, they would have ignored lots and lots of things that turned out to be highly significant in the development of early childhood education. So I think I come out now very differently from where I was ten years ago, thinking it's

3. *Ellett:* But isn't planning for such things difficult or impossible? If they just happen by chance, the utilization-focused evaluation (UFE) has no influence. Weiss is really saying the UFE should *try to fix things* so that this occurs more often (and not by mere chance).

better to do careful, sound, critical research and thinking problems through as deeply and as thoughtfully as possible, because God knows who's going to pick it up and what consequences that evaluation is going to have.

. . .

The Morality of Attending to Client Concerns

Mike Patton: Well, you see, if my client is the person who is making the decision about those two program choices, then that's where I would begin. It's a specific level of decision making. My client could be a congressman/woman who wants to decide policy for the whole country, and that would lead me to a different set of questions, on a higher level, but the process would be the same, user oriented, client oriented.

. . .

Ernie House: Well, how far would you pursue this orientation? Surely, you can't consider your only purpose to be meeting your client's interests?

Mike Patton: Tell me why I can't.

Ernie House: Why? It's an immoral position.[4]

Mike Patton: I could argue it's immoral to take anything else into account when that's the person who supposedly . . .

Ernie House: You can't. You can't. It would be a long argument which you'll lose.

Mike Patton: Go for it.

Ernie House: There are too many counterexamples. For example, who has the money to purchase evaluation? The most proper people in society. You serve only the most proper people in society? You wouldn't condone that.[5]

---

4. *Ellett:*   I believe House overstates it. Surely Patton's position seems unjustifiable, unreasonable, and *perhaps* immoral.
5. *Ellett:*   I believe House has brought up some very important issues on these pages. He has raised the issue of social justice. Is this a legitimate standard for UFE? House is also facing up to some of our problems in a supposedly democratic society. This is extremely relevant. UFE can't go on in a vacuum!

Mike Patton: That's not my experience.

Ernie House: That's usually the way it is . . .

Mike Patton: That's not part of the theory, to me, in terms of the way I work . . .

Ernie House: That may not be what you think your experience is, but that would be empirically demonstrable somehow. Well, take medical care. If the doctor is only concerned with a particular patient and not concerned with the distribution of his or her services across the society as a whole . . .

Mike Patton: Which does seem to be the dominant motif, does it not?

Ernie House: Absolutely. Would you approve of that? Medicine for the richest? Surely, you can't condone that kind of position.

Mike Patton: But you're attaching clientele to the monetary system. I do evaluations where there's no money involved, and I have clients whose interests I . . .

Ernie House: Well, you may. But it's not really separate from the monetary system, you see. It can't be. It's not separate from the power system. Not in this society. You must ignore the entire structure of the society in order to believe that. And you don't.

Mike Patton: What I am talking about, in terms of my personal responsibility, is . . .[6]

Ernie House: That's what I'm talking about.

Mike Patton: . . . is this set of people that I can work with, who will be different from case to case. What I take immediate responsibility for is what they do, the things that I do with them. I recognize that there's a broader set of things that are going to happen, but I don't take responsibility for what happens with those broader set of things.

Ernie House: Well, you must. Then . . .

Mike Patton: Because I can't . . . It's not my . . .

---

6. *Ellett:*   But the issue is not what Patton is "willing" to take on. We're talking about the legitimate responsibilities of a UFE!

Ernie House: Then you are immoral. Right? You'll back off that position. You cannot possibly justify that position. You don't hold that position. I mean, you say it, but you can't hold it.

Mike Patton: My sense of responsibility . . . What I mean by that is that I take action and try to control what goes on. When results get into the dissemination network, and I lose control over that, I also don't take responsibility for it. That's what I mean.

Ernie House: Well, yeah, I understand. . . . Yeah, maybe we're arguing a little bit at cross-purposes, but at other times, you do worry about the distribution of your services.

Mike Patton: Yeah, I've stopped answering distortions of my work.

Ernie House: Yeah, well, I'm not talking about distortions.

Mike Patton: That's what I'm talking about.

Ernie House: But see, you have to have a concern beyond the immediate welfare of the immediate client. I believe you do that.

Mike Patton: I think I build that larger concern that you're talking about into my interactions with that client. But the person I'm directly and immediately taking responsibility for bringing that to bear on is that client. There is a moral concern. There is a moral and value context that I bring to bear in that interaction. But I don't take responsibility for what goes on outside that interaction.[7]

Ernie House: But we have to.

Mike Patton: I take responsibility for bringing that in.

Ernie House: You have to do it sometime. You may not do it right then, working with that client. But you have to show concern for the rest of society. You can't just sell your services to whoever can purchase those services. That would be an immoral position.

Mike Patton: I resist confusing the monetary issue with the approach that we're talking about. They seem to me to be separate issues.

---

7. *Patton:*   There is an exception that may help clarify my position. One of the options I present to clients is to speak to a broader audience. If that's what the client wants, I'll help him or her do it. But if the client wants an idiosyncratic, nongeneralizable study, I'll also do that, and then I wouldn't worry about the larger dissemination audience.

Ernie House: You have to be concerned with the monetary and the power issues sometime or other, at some point . . .

Mike Patton: Yeah. That's right, but . . .

Ross Conner: You probably also pick and choose your clients, right?

Mike Patton: That's right.

Ross Conner: My concern would be with the student who picks up, say, *Utilization-Focused Evaluation*, reads it, believes it, goes out ready to do it, and then they're willing to work with anybody. And maybe they don't have the luxury of picking and choosing who they work with. Would this fit in with what you're saying?

Ernie House: It's easy to construct preposterous examples. Some guy has a concentration camp and comes to you and says, "Look . . . "

Marv Alkin: Why don't you give us a real-world example, so we don't look preposterous? Give us a real-world example of how you work with a client, but still show an expression of concern for interest groups beyond the client.

Ernie House: If you do a Follow Through evaluation, or whatever kind of evaluation you do, sometime or other, I say that you should be concerned about the interests of the less advantaged people in society.[8]

Marv Alkin: And Mike has said he can't.

Ernie House: I think he does. That's not the same as the situation where the person who can afford the evaluation comes to you and says, Here's what I want you to do. And you work only with that person, serve that person's needs. That's not saying what I just said.

Mike Patton: No. And I've resisted tying it to the monetary relationship. I said I would take responsibility for intended use for intended users. There can be a broad range of types of people within any particular evaluation problem, as one runs through the stakeholder laundry list and it shakes out. Whoever is in a task force or whoever I'm dealing with, at some point, they become the intended group. They are the ones who are going to use this thing and who I aim my efforts at. And what I'm saying is that I take primary responsibility for working with that set of people on the evaluation. We build in some things that

8. *Ellett:*   Here House reflects his John Rawlsian view of justice. Perhaps what he has in mind is that the UFE should foster such dissemination.

they're going to do with it, but nevertheless, there are some limits to it. We also attempt to package it and disseminate it in ways that other people can pick it up and use it, because that's part of the ethical context within which it is done. But that is a secondary effect. It is a luxury. One of the things that I regularly ask people now, quite seriously, in the evaluation consulting enterprise, is whether or not there's a need for a final report in this evaluation. Now, our scientific canon would say that, of course, there has to be a final report, because that's the disseminatable document. But my situational responsiveness is such that I don't find the need for a final report.[9] I don't have sufficient commitment, even to the dissemination process, that I would ask people to spend that five grand that it takes to produce that, when we might well spend that five grand better on the immediate information that's needed for the situation. There's a cost involved in meeting the larger dissemination function. A high cost in a lot of cases.

Carol Weiss: How about a journal article?

Mike Patton: Well, the journal article usually presupposes sufficient monographic reporting of the data that people can get more methodological detail. But I would be very reluctant to ask people to pay for the cost of producing an article that I was going to publish. I often do that on my own time, but that's part of the negotiation. The issue is how much it's worth paying the cost of that larger dissemination function versus the other potential uses of that money and time and effort for elaborating the information needs of the situation. And by raising the question of whether or not we need a final report, or even a written report of any kind, the real merit of such a product can be evaluated and costs can be attached to it. This should really be looked at because we know that a great deal of utilization occurs informally and verbally and in the process of the thing. There are a number of situations in which I now work that do not involve a report.

Ernie House: Which almost ensures that there won't be the kind of indirect use by unanticipated users that Carol's talking about.

Mike Patton: Well, it'll be difficult. It doesn't ensure that this type of use won't happen. But it will be more by word of mouth and it will spread.

9. *Hendricks:*   In my own work, I find a rough draft report to be much more powerful than the final report. In fact, I often include sections in the draft that I have no intention of leaving in the final, just so I can make points I feel are needed.

Ross Conner: Well, that's risky business, because what gets remembered may not be the exact words of what you meant . . .

Mike Patton: Well, what gets quoted and often misquoted out of the reports is just as bad.

Ross Conner: Yeah. That's true.

Ernie House: I think the issue of unintended use is a difficult one. It's easy to think of misuse. For example, to what degree is Coleman responsible for the misuse of those studies? He does them in such a way that he lays himself open to people picking up on and generalizing far beyond probably what they should.[10]

Mike Patton: But the evaluator's ability to respond to that stuff is very difficult when it gets widespread. Two issues of *Evaluation Review* came out within the last year that quoted me as representing the position that utilization is direct immediate use on major decisions. They did this because there's a quote in *Utilization-Focused Evaluation* that says, "The dominant view in evaluation has been that utilization is direct immediate impact on major decisions." And the whole thrust of the book is to argue that that's not what it's about, that much important use is incremental, conceptual, and formative. And two articles attribute that narrower position to me. I just stopped answering them.

Ernie House: I can see why you stopped writing things down.

[laughter]

Mike Patton: But the same thing happens with specific evaluations. Part of the empowerment process that I want to convey to the people I work with is that they take responsibility for the indirect use because I'm typically not working in a substantive area where I have a long-term commitment. That's part of the difference between the specialist and the generalist. And that may be a difference which determines how much one looks at the unintended use. But I really work to empower people who do have that disciplinary or professional commitment. And I look to make them the disseminators and the people who are going to look after the unintended use, and answer the distortions, and follow this thing through, and champion it. And I want to provide them with the set of skills to do that, rather than doing that myself. Then they take

10. *Ellett:* I think House is arguing that the real merit must be seen to involve social values and consequences beyond Patton's client!

the responsibility. In fact, there's a whole shifting of responsibility in this collaborative mode, where it is less the evaluator's responsibility and more the stakeholders' and users' responsibility, not only the immediate action, but for the secondary use, tertiary use, and on down the road. And I leave them to track it, and lose track of the thing altogether myself. And they've done that.[11]

Ernie House: Well, you've probably . . . I think that's where you bring your notion of justice and ethics in. You're still talking about empowerment.

Mike Patton: So I sneak some morality back in.

Ernie House: Well, no . . .

[laughter and overtalk]

. . .

Ethical Dilemmas

Mike Patton: What I've had problems with are some ethical dilemmas of a different sort that I think border on misutilization. I'm not sure what to call them; I struggle with them. As I was telling some of the folks the first day, qualitative mucking about in programs often turns up things about the program that you weren't looking for that are criminal or unethical. These are things that we have to deal with. That's not the intended use of the intended users; that is finding out things we never wanted to know and wish we didn't know after we found out, that we then have to deal with. I've had a lot of those kinds of problems, and I've dealt with them in different ways.[12]

The other issue that has come to me more recently is protection of human subjects. I think in qualitative methods, it arises somewhat differently, because the prior checks are harder to maintain. And that is the presumed right of the researcher to go in and ask people questions about almost anything that they want to ask them about, without careful

11. *Hendricks:*   I think Patton's point about specialists versus generalists is important. Generalists may feel more loyalty to the entire field. Obviously, some of each kind of loyalty would be ideal.

12. *Hendricks:*   What should an evaluator do if she discovers criminal activity in a program? Is there an obligation to report? To whom? Or is there an obligation for confidentiality? I feel that, at a minimum, she's obligated to report it to the client, whether or not the client wants to hear about it.

consideration of what that does to people. There's considerable training and forethought one has to have to really deal seriously with protection of human subjects. As a very recent example, we were doing interviews with farm families in northeastern Minnesota. I had known about some of the farm stress and the normal family stresses one would expect. We were asking what seemed on the surface like straightforward questions about what farm families wanted to have happen to their farm and what they wanted to have happen to their youth. But what became clear to me in the course of those interviews was that for a number of those couples, those questions were so painful and so basic that they had put them aside for the last 10 or 15 years of their marriage. And then suddenly, we show up and introduce those questions back into the relationship, and it was clear that, in the classic anthropological dilemma, we had changed that system in ways that I wasn't sure we had a right to, in retrospect. We had introduced some new dynamics, simply through the interviewing. I always knew people were changed as a result of good qualitative interviews—most of that positive—and believed that self-reflection was probably good and you took those kinds of risks. But I have now become more conscious of how the interviewing process can affect the people involved.

I guess part of the ethical dilemma of studying misutilization is that you're going to make people conscious of things that, psychodynamically, they'd just as soon not deal with. And I worry a little bit about my rights to go in and introduce some of these questions. I think that part of the research ethic has been that people are put on earth, by God, for us to study. And we can do anything, can ask them whatever we want to, and it's all in the name of truth and it all shakes out in the end. Anthropologists have probably dealt with the effects of research on the local setting more than anybody else. Although researchers don't come up against it quite as often or dramatically, evaluators find that they're really having effects on people's lives and jobs and futures and program services. And it's obvious that our ethical fine-tuning is weak, in comparison to the kind of problems we're encountering. Misutilization is partly a surrogate for that whole set of ethical issues that we've not addressed very well in our training. There is very little in the literature that speaks directly to the practical side of dealing with these issues. The standards begin to do that, but they do it in a pontifical kind of way that isn't as real as the nuts-and-bolts experiences that people are running into—that I'm running into. They involve the whole range of political pressures, as well as these ethical concerns about what kinds of rights do I have to ask certain kinds of questions. And my handle around that, I guess, is the utilization handle, trying to be as clear as we can be that the potential good and benefit that comes out of the data merits the potential risks, which is the human subjects solution. But I think we need to be much more deliberate in our thinking about these issues before we go into these families and start asking them our questions. We need to consider the potential risks and how much we are likely to learn that we can really use, and how much they need to know about it up front to do it.

Alex Law: I have the same problem to a different degree. Evaluators very often find out more than they really want to know. The question is, What do you do with that? I've had fortunately few but outstanding issues where you find people do illegal things. And my solution was to go to the person and say, "Don't do that." Now, did I have a right to do that? I mean, this has been troubling me for some time. Or should I just publish it, and say, "This person should be punished."

Mike Patton: Do you run into cases where they are doing things that are illegal, but in your value system, in the best interests of the clients?

Alex Law: No, this is in their own self-interest.

Mike Patton: Well, I've run into some of those.

Carol Weiss: My class got into a discussion recently about whether evaluators should agree not to make public any information to the detriment of the client that they find out from evaluating a program. For example, if you learn during an interview that one of the participants has committed a crime—as Mike was saying the other day, robbed a local 7-11 store—you tend to think that that's confidential information; you don't release it. But if you find out that the administrator of a program was misappropriating the funds, somehow that doesn't fall under the same confidentiality restrictions. And I said, No, I don't think it does, because we're studying the program and that is a direct programmatic weakening. And yet, I find myself very uncomfortable with this as a solution . . .[13]

13. *Ellett:* Look. These are complicated issues. No one can say that a reasonable way of handling them is easy to find. Indeed, there may be many reasonable ways to go. But the logical point is that in a democratic society (committed to rational policy and so on) the evaluator has to be concerned about these issues and seriously consider what his responsibilities are. In this sense, I disagree with Patton and side with House. Weiss's hesitancy shows that she recognizes the serious moral force of the issue.

Milbrey McLaughlin: Well, yeah. In the years that I was at Rand, I mean, I could have blown many districts out of the water. My resolution has been, if it's not related directly to my sets of questions . . .

Carol Weiss: That you don't say anything . . .

Milbrey McLaughlin: I mean, it's hard. I mean, it was information that came my way by virtue of having built trust and such, and . . .

Mike Patton: Under some interpretations, though, you're an accessory.

Milbrey McLaughlin: That's right. I even got subpoenaed once, and I still didn't tell. But hell, it's . . . because you have made an implicit contract with the respondent, and in something like that . . . I mean, the ground rules should be clear about what the public data are.

Marv Alkin: I believe we may now have shifted the topic to misevaluation?

Milbrey McLaughlin: To utilization dilemmas.

Carol Weiss: To ethical dilemmas.

Milbrey McLaughlin: Well, there's a whole ethical side to utilization. I mean, there truly is.

Marv Alkin: Well, we're not talking about bad evaluations or even the quality of evaluations, but misevaluation—the way in which the evaluator deals with different data sets that he acquires during the course of the evaluation.

. . .

Alex Law: I don't want to turn this into a confessional . . .

Carol Weiss: We love it, Alex.

Alex Law: A number of years ago, well . . . there's a tribe of Indians in California, they're desperately poor, and essentially unemployed. And a well-intentioned senator from up there managed to give them some funds. But you couldn't just give them money; you had to do it for some overriding reason. So they conceived of an employment program for the parents in the schools, and the only way the Republicans would vote for that was if they had an evaluation that showed that this so-called program was effective. Now, the stark fact is that the parents were illiterate, and there was no way they could have acted as reading aides for the students, which is what the program was supposed to do. So, here I am to evaluate a nonprogram. And how do you do this? Well, it turned out that this tribe had a tradition of oral history. And they found that having parents in the classroom was a way to carry on their oral history. So the real emphasis of the evaluation was the transmission of their oral history. The evaluation became a tool for accomplishing a social good.

Carol Weiss: Well, you see, that's why I think misuse is a difficult concept to get my head around anyway, because when you start taking into account the larger social good, it becomes very hard to make judgments about the immediate use or misuse of evaluation. People do rather strange and wondrous things, because there is a larger social good involved.[14]

14. *Alkin:*   Or, they *perceive* a larger social good based on their values.

13

Evaluation Misuse

Misuse: Some General Issues

Jean King: I want to add another anecdote, because one thing that we have not touched on here are the dangers of misuse and abuse. Consider a program like Title I (now Chapter 1) that may have its own evaluation staff, and these people are not very well trained. And yet the results of their studies—and I use that term very loosely—they do these fancy designs, they think, and they go out and collect some data and plug it into a computer and get some fancy numbers out, and they act on those in the directions that the data suggests. And it's very, to me, frightening to watch.[1] Because everybody's happy. The process is working. The director says, I got to study this.[2] That's not good. It's fine when everything's working right. But when there's a problem with the system, there is the potential for misuse or use of bad data. We haven't talked about that. Nor have we talked about the political process. The point is that, in some systems, Title I may have its own evaluation staff, because they refuse to work with the R&E[3] office. They simply will not do it, for very political and personal reasons.

. . .

Mike Patton: One of the kinds of scenarios that seems to accompany utilization is the confirmatory scenario, where somebody sort of vali-

---

1. *Ellett:* Why is it frightening? Because most of these "studies" are pure misinformation!!
2. *Hendricks:* Note how often the group uses anecdotes to make points. Yet if administrators discussed a program this way, would we castigate them as "unscientific"?
3. Research and Evaluation.

dates at the right time the paradigm shift and gives that credence in a research mode.

. . .

Jean King: The problem oftentimes is the political setting. People simply can't act. I don't know how we deal with that. But then it goes back to trying to understand the evaluator and the user. But what do you do in those situations?

Ernie House: I don't know. In some ways it's so different from some of the other things we were talking about at a different level. You have a set of policymakers here, let's say, the president and his henchmen who have a certain mentality and way they view the world. You get a study that fits into that mentality. It's consistent with the framework that they employ, and there's a sense in which there's a receptivity there already. And we also have people in social science who are willing to provide that, to meet that market. They take social science data, and even if it doesn't fit, they fix it up in such a way that it will meet the needs of those powerful decision makers.[4] Which may be one of the saddest things you can say about the social sciences. Now here we get information which is usable, right? But what do you say about the integrity of a discipline that supplies this kind of information? This is the other end of the utilization thing. Maybe some stuff shouldn't be utilized, which is your point. We're talking about misuse here. And don't we have any kinds of standards to oppose misuse of some of these data? I'd say that's as much a problem for us as lack of use.

[overtalk]

Mike Patton: You have to separate the value piece, where people use data within a value context, from the more overt conscious abuse that you're talking about. It seems to me that supply-side economics is an example of manipulating some data, in terms of value structure, to try to make sense out of a particular approach.[5] None of those are going to hold up in their pure form, on either side, whether Keynesian or

4. *Hendricks:* Politicians, whether Republican or Democrat, will *always* use data for their own purposes. To pretend otherwise is to miss an opportunity to understand their world.
5. *Ellett:* "Unconscious abuse" is almost as bad as "conscious abuse." Note: It is not abusing the information. What is being *abused* here is the commitment to *rational* thinking and *rational* policymaking. I think all members of this group are committed to these values.

supply-side or something else. The same thing is going to be true on the social side. And a lot of these critical studies seem to represent paradigm shifts, coming at points where the old stuff has begun to deteriorate. Whatever the dominant or multiple paradigms are, they aren't working all that well. And the world is ready for some new hope, some new piece of something. That has a confirmatory element in it.

There's a good example of a social action paradigm shift which has just come out in the criminal justice area in Minneapolis, having to do with arrests in domestic abuse cases. It's gotten widespread attention. They did an important piece of research on the consequences of arresting the perpetrator in domestic abuse incidents where the conventional wisdom had been: The woman will get more beat up, if you arrest the abuser. When he goes back home, he's really going to hurt her badly and it's going to aggravate the situation. Under this approach all the police would do is stop the immediate abuse and leave the situation alone—at most making a social work referral. It was clear that that wasn't solving the problem. They were ready for some major new approach to the problem, so they introduced an experiment in a couple of places, Minneapolis being one, where they started arresting abusers, no matter what. The word was out. The police had to arrest in every domestic call, and those people convicted had to spend time in jail. The research followed up what happened, and the results showed actual declines in incidents of reported domestic violence among that group where they did the arrest. Those arrested didn't go back and beat up the person who called the police. The women felt suddenly that they had some protection. And it did the things that people were afraid to hope it might have done. Now, police departments all over the place are adopting this approach. It's an imperfect, flawed study, it's a small sample, but it's getting incredible attention. Ted Koppel featured it on *Nightline*.[6]

Marv Alkin: The context for use is an important factor in whether evaluation gets used.

Mike Patton: But people were ready for some change, and when they're ready, when the old paradigm of intervention isn't working, people will grasp for anything that holds hope of working.

. . .

6. *Ellett:* This is the evaluation study of the real-life experiment that is useful for *rational policy*.

Instances of Evaluation Misuse

Jean King: I think we have to plumb the variable of misuse. I vowed to talk about that since before I came. Let's take a situation, where we have people who are going to use the evaluation for personal gain. You know, they hire Patton. They bring him down, and say, Okay, here's what I need. And so, he's agreed to take this contract for a reason we don't know. What do you do in that case where a person—forget peer review—is going to take what you do, your information, and construe it for his own purposes? I mean, I've watched that happen all the time. Do other people have that experience also, or is it just . . .

Ernie House: Superintendents do that all the time. If the information's good, they take credit for it . . .

Jean King: And if it's bad, they'll pick the right pieces out and have that written up in the big chart with 4×8 display. You know what our responsibility as evaluators is in that situation? To see to it that bad information's not used, or that good information is not misused? How do we help the client that we're not paid by, but who may be harmed by the misuse of this information?

Ernie House: I think we have a responsibility.

Jean King: I do, too, but I don't know what to do about that. I can give you a great example of the only evaluation I was almost fired from and I wish I had been. It was for these people who were running an adolescent after-school center. And so I wrote a report that was, I thought, rather positive, and they hit the roof because this was going to their funding agency. And they just said that they weren't sending it in. Then, without my permission, they rewrote it, put my name on it, and sent it in.

Ernie House: You have an obligation to write the agency and tell them what's what.

Jean King: That's what happened, and that's why I was almost fired and wish I had been. But I mean, there I was, saying you can't do this . . . and they did it.

Ernie House: They cannot take your findings and distort them. That's not part of our ethics of evaluation.

Carol Weiss: But to stop it. How do you stop it?

Ernie House: That's more of a practical issue. You may never be able to stop it. They may have done this without her finding out about it.

Carol Weiss: Well, this is an obvious case, but take the covert case where the superintendent releases part of the report, but not the part of the report that reflects poorly on the district. What would you do?[7]

Ernie House: It depends on the situation. There are any number of things that could be done. It's more of an ethical issue that you really should take some kind of action when somebody distorts your findings that way.

Michael Kean: I'll give you one example of what we used to do in Philadelphia, because I think it was sort of unusual. We averaged well over a hundred program evaluations a year, which required final reports and everything else. And we negotiated up front that the final reports were in the public domain. Now, the superintendent and the Office of Informational Services, if they chose to issue a press release on selected parts of a report, could do that. But the media in the city knew that they could come to me and get the entire final report and that, if they so chose, I would sit down and go through the final results one by one, good, bad, and indifferent. And maybe that kept the superintendent "honest." Throughout all of those, almost a thousand evaluation reports, I only had two instances where anybody came to me and even hinted that I change findings. In one instance, it was the superintendent's assistant, and I simply went right to the superintendent and told him. He wouldn't believe it and essentially said, No, you must have misunderstood him and there shouldn't be any change. Well, it wasn't pressed. In the other instance, it was a program director in special education that did much of what you just said your adolescent after-school center folks did, Jean. And I went and said directly, this has happened. And he removed her from the project. He probably was afraid of us because he knew that we had a lot of information and that ultimately, the press would come and get those data. I think once you compromise yourself, then that's it forever. That worked for 8 years and over a thousand evaluations.

Ernie House: In our society, when we say, I'm doing an evaluation of something, there are certain kinds of norms that are implicit. It doesn't

---

7. *Hendricks:* This is also, in my opinion, a much more likely scenario. Administrators rarely (in spite of this glaring example) risk such obvious deceptions, but they often pick and choose information to highlight.

make any difference what your agreement is. There are certain norms that are implicit. One of those norms is that the report be honest. To make an agreement with somebody to do an evaluation and then say, I'm going to write an untrue report, is a contradiction of the very contract that the person accepts. It's understood in the society itself, that evaluations will be truthful. And so we really don't have much choice in that matter.[8]

Carol Weiss: If people can't trust evaluations, then why do they need evaluators? They can send out their aides and . . .

Susan Klein: We have a little bit of a related problem with the Joint Dissemination Review Panel submissions. Early on, we changed the rubric from requiring that submissions demonstrate that they met their objectives, because the objectives or the goals were always so grandiose that there was no way that programs could meet their goals. So instead, we changed it to say that they should make claims and provide evidence for the particular claims that they made. Okay. That solved a lot of problems, because we focused on specific things that were good. But one of the problems that still remains is, of course, they only make positive claims. Never do they say that the program didn't work in this particular kind of situation. And also, when they provide their evidence to support their claims, they may not be reporting the full amount of information they have. They just skip the cases that didn't work out. So in our last state of the panel meeting, we were wondering how we could get programs to really tell us what worked and what didn't work.

. . .

Carol Weiss: Well, I'll give you a partial, oblique answer. I was talking to a journalist a few weeks ago, asking her what it was about certain research studies that made her trust the data. And one thing she said was, well, if it comes from a reputable research organization. And another was if they presented some evidence that ran counter to their hypotheses, some exceptions, some qualifications of their major findings, something they expected that didn't quite work. This added to the credibility of the research.

Marv Alkin: Accept only "lukewarm findings."

8. *Hendricks:* I believe reality is slightly more complicated than Ernie's comment might suggest. Otherwise, why do we ask for comments on draft reports, if not to check our own possibilities for error?

Jean King: Knowing that now, every report I write will have this.

Carol Weiss: She said if people are honest enough to tell you that some things they expected didn't work out, then you trust the things that did work out a lot more.

Alex Law: But that's fudgeable, too. That reminds me of a real estate story of people who bought these clunkers. And people said, these real estate people seemed so honest. They led us into the basement; they pointed to the holes in the pipes—keeping our eyes away from the holes in the roof!

[laughter]

Carol Weiss: But I think I might turn back a couple of those joint submission review panel justifications, and say, Wasn't there anything that didn't work, that wasn't positive? You know, what you have presented is so unlikely, tell us the rest of the story.

Alex Law: The only two examples of misuse that occurred in my tenure came not from state activities, but from certain contract activities. Everything we do has intense public scrutiny, from the beginning to the end, because we not only have open access, but we have control agencies who are watching us. The watchers are very diligent. But watchers aren't functioning when we have contract evaluations. And when the contract evaluations are clunkers, then the scrutiny comes after the fact. That causes a great deal of trouble.

Carol Weiss: Was the perception that the evaluation was wrong or that people misused it?

Alex Law: It was interpreted as being manipulated, because the report went through an editorial process between the time when it was seen by our staff and when it was presented to the legislative committee.

Ernie House: Evaluation has become so important that all kinds of agencies of any size have evaluation units within them, such as California state agencies. And it's pretty clear, I think, when you have an evaluation agency inside a big bureaucracy, a lot of pressure can be brought to bear on the evaluation to produce certain kinds of evidence.[9]

9. *Hendricks:* This raises an important point about the actual organizational location of "internal" evaluators. They need to be close enough to the action to stay active with current (and future) plans, but they also need to be shielded somehow from undue pressures.

And reports are taken and edited and tampered with in various ways by those people higher in the organization. This is one of the things that bothers me most about misuse, and I'm not very clear what to do about it. Most of the ethics that we have involve contractual relationships, but here you've got evaluators within the organization. What can they do, what can they say, when the superintendent or the assistant superintendent takes the information and says, "Let's take this negative stuff out and write it this way rather than that way." I think that's a very difficult problem and one that's pervasive.

Marv Alkin: It's drawing close to 10:00 p.m., so if you don't mind . . . I hate to curtail this, but if you don't mind, why don't we return to this topic tomorrow.

Ross Conner: I've got an answer for you.

Marv Alkin: We'll start tomorrow with your answer—it will provide a good way to get started.

Standards to Curb Misevaluation/Misuse

Marv Alkin: Okay. Ross was going to start us off this morning by helping us out with misuse, and I think you said you had a good example.

Milbrey McLaughlin: He said he had the answer.

Marv Alkin: Oh, the answer. Who wants a story if we get an answer?

Ross Conner: Ernie's comments centered around what we can do about the pressure that is brought to bear on in-house evaluation units by their parent organizations, and how much of that constitutes misuse. Right?

Ernie House: Right.

Ross Conner: My partial solution to that, to be more humble, had to do with the structure that I was proposing. That was one of the things that I was responding to in the Washington case, that an outside influence was needed to keep some checks. A separate institute could serve this function by working with the in-house evaluation unit. I think it's the way it ought to be. You have to be close enough to the program, to have those roots, as Alex was talking about. But you also need the outhouse, if you will, to provide an independent check, a balance for some of the pressures that might go on inside.

Ernie House: We don't really have any kind of effective monitoring now of evaluation. It's not like reviewing journal articles where people can look at them and critique them. And that's not terribly effective either sometimes, but we don't have anything like that in evaluations. Only the big evaluations ever come under some kind of critical review. Maybe this idea of an external institute is a possibility. It might be one way to go.

Carol Weiss: Well, there's been the standard setting exercise that several of the associations engaged in,[10] and the codes of ethics.

Ernie House: I don't think those really have much bearing on the problem. Not that I dislike the standards, but they're not enforced in any way.

Carol Weiss: No, they're not. And they're not even well known. You couldn't enforce them, but I think it would be a great help if people who are in evaluation knew and subscribed to a clear code of ethics. Then they could stand up to their superiors and say, But look, the code of ethics of my professional association says I can't do that. That at least would provide some leverage.

Ernie House: I think you're right, and I think it is a real problem, particularly in all these methodological disputes we get into all the time about what constitutes good evaluation. On the other hand, I'm not sure how else to police the profession. There are an awful lot of bad things going on out there in the name of evaluation. I've seen people present themselves as evaluators without following any kind of reasonable standards. So I think there is a problem. I wouldn't want some kind of police force policing all these evaluations and trying to review them all.

Alex Law: There's a real problem with this methodological review. In many cases, you get into academic quibbles, which don't make a bit of difference. Somebody's riding a horse and says, "You used analysis of variance and that's clearly the wrong thing to do, therefore the whole evaluation is flawed." This is said to a naive group and this naive group is going to say to the evaluator, "You didn't know how to do it." The

10. Joint Committee on Standards for Educational Evaluation. (1981). *Standards for evaluations of educational programs, projects and materials.* New York: McGraw-Hill.

evaluator may in fact have been using a sound methodological approach. There has to be some leavening of the process. I don't know
how it occurs.

Michael Kean: We tried a couple of approaches back in Philly, one of
which worked and one of which had tremendous potential to do so but
never got off the ground. The first approach involved one staff member
who acted as sort of a meta-evaluator. This individual, who happened
to be extremely knowledgeable in methodology and design, reviewed
the evaluations, both in their planning stage, in process, and at the end,
and evaluated how well they were put together and how well they were
conducted.[11] Now if there was some chicanery or something going on,
then I realized that he might not be the most objective person to
intervene. But we weren't concerned that somebody was cheating; it
was really a matter of, "Are we using the best approach to evaluate the
program?"[12]

Marv Alkin: Did he review both internal and external evaluations?

Michael Kean: We worked with virtually no external evaluators, almost entirely internal.

Marv Alkin: And did you use other staff in this? Did they analyze the
documents or did he go and . . .

Michael Kean: Oh, no. He did the whole thing. He had free rein. And
it was very useful. I think it really improved our product and our
process. And this went on for a number of years, and then somebody
came up with the idea—this was the second approach I mentioned
earlier that really was never approved—that, Gee, if it's working this
well for us internally, why can't we form a network of large city school
systems that also have decent-sized evaluation offices to do the same
thing? But instead of having a single, internal evaluator doing it, why
not use a small team—an Alex Law and person X from New York and
person Y from Chicago—to come in and spend a week in our district.
And it would be sort of a cooperative thing. And we actually worked
the whole thing out, where nobody would get paid to participate. The
person would be on leave from their district, but in return, that district
would receive similar services from some other people. Ultimately, the

11. *Ellett:*   The key to defending any empirical methodology: that it gives sound and
reliable statements about what is probably the case.
12. *Hendricks:*   GAO uses this technique to review the progress of evaluations within
its Program Evaluation and Methodology Division.

problem was that there were some travel and subsistence costs, and some districts said, We can't pay that. And it was a back-and-forth kind of thing that never got off the ground. But I'm convinced that something like that would be very, very useful. It would be sort of internal, within family, but not so embedded within a single district. Just because we were doing it one way in Philly didn't mean that it was the best way to do it.

Marv Alkin: What were the primary guidelines and purposes for that evaluation auditor? Was he looking for and being concerned about the technical quality of the evaluation, or was he primarily being concerned about the data collection, or the use or misuse of findings?

Michael Kean: Less use and misuse than the first two, Marv. Mainly because he functioned mostly . . .

Marv Alkin: Relevance? What about relevance?

Michael Kean: Yes. Relevance. Absolutely.

Marv Alkin: But, was it relevance in terms of the perceptions of the people who were the primary decision audiences or users?

Michael Kean: If the primary client for the evaluation was the director of program X, he would spend time with that program director, discussing how the evaluation was developed, and did the evaluator spend time with you, and do you fully understand exactly the kind of information that is going to be provided, and is that information useful, and why is it useful, and how are you going to use it? Now we did not, in fact, go back to that person after the evaluation was completed, to find out the extent of use. We did go back to make sure that what the client got was what he or she expected to get, but we did not go back and say, three months later or six months later, Did you actually use it?

Marv Alkin: I would anticipate that in that kind of a setup, you would like to see that auditor conduct interviews with people representative of various other constituencies . . .

Ernie House: Well, ideally, ideally. But I think the main idea is that there be some kind of overview. That your work isn't purely private. That's the basic idea. I don't think I'd want really hard-and-fast rules and standards applied, because there's so much disagreement in the field as to what the proper methodology is. But I think the fact that somebody's going to look at your work and say, Well, you know, you really did something pretty outrageous here you shouldn't have done, is the fundamental idea, however that might be exercised.

Alex Law: We have two levels of checking. One is an internal, methodological check, which frankly doesn't work very well because sometimes it gets heated and emotional. Someone else has to arbitrate what is the best, and this is usually during the design phase. The other part of the internal check would be some commentary on the analysis. The second and more valuable check—and this is external—is to ask the cognizant program manager to nominate two program people to do a review of the first draft of the report, to point out any factual errors that may be in there. They can change only factual errors. You may have done a big one. This check has helped a lot, because it gives program people a chance to make commentary to you. And often, we will include this commentary in the report, as an elaboration.

Ross Conner: I found that to work well, too. I typically give the first draft of an evaluation I do to the program people, let them look over the entire thing, and ask them to write a commentary, which I then put in with the report. I don't change any of theirs. They can make comments on mine, and I agree to put footnotes in at any points that they feel strongly about, but I have the final say on whether I'll change my own piece. And that's worked out very well. They've got their page or two or however much they want to give on their view.

Jean King: We're talking here about the evaluation process, not the use process, and we certainly have to do this. I mean, if the evaluation process itself is flawed, then it may be better if the evaluation findings are not used. One has to think about this. But I'm also wondering . . .

Mike Patton: That's not even the whole process. I mean, you're only talking about the data accuracy.

Jean King: That's right. And we're also assuming some kind of report. What do we do with Patton, who's coming . . .

Mike Patton: Can't get the goods on me.

Jean King: Can't get the goods on him. He talks a good line, so if we said that . . .

Ernie House: I think we're going to have to wire him.

[laughter]

Ross Conner: Michael [Kean], how did your school district evaluators accept this independent person?

Michael Kean: It worked fine, because he was really one of them. He came from their ranks. He wasn't viewed as an outsider and he was . . .

Alex Law: He was on the take.

Michael Kean: Well, no, I was on the take. He wasn't on the take. I don't mean to say that it was one huge, happy family without any problems. He was one of the more knowledgeable, more senior staff in terms of the number of years he had been doing evaluation. And this was in the mid-70s, when, if you'd been involved in evaluation for any time, you were pretty much an expert. I mean, hell, I'd been involved in evaluation since 1967 at that point, and I was considered a grand old man. But he knew his way. He was very good, and he also . . . I hate to keep going back to things like personality and approach and things, but he just . . . he was very even-tempered. The kind of person that you really trust. Really, I'm very serious about that. He was a very non-threatening guy and could tell you very directly that you've got some problems here, let me tell you where I see some problems, without really getting the person tremendously defensive or anything of the sort. So it worked very well. He had a fairly high level of respect among his colleagues to begin with. It probably would not have worked if he had been viewed as a person coming in to clean up a shop.

Misuse: Further Examples

Alex Law: We're skirting the problem of a client's misuse of an evaluation. Once the evaluation is out of the shop . . .

Mike Patton: I'm not sure we know very much about that. It seems to me, we're at the point with misutilization where we were when Carol first raised the question of utilization. We don't really know much about the dimensions of it or how it occurs. How can we propose solutions to things that we don't really know very much about? On the more blatant, legalistic, purely ethical side, you're coming up with fairly classical, legalistic controls. But this . . . the whole nature of the misutilization animal is one that I don't feel I know very much about. And what I suggested in the paper was that, misutilization seemed to me like a whole different phenomenon than utilization. Or at least it's an empirical question, whether or not there's some crossover.

I don't think we can apply what we know about utilization directly to misutilization. I don't know that there's very much literature that speaks to misuse, in any empirical sense. It seems to me the methods for studying misuse are going to have to be different than the methods for studying utilization. It's a subject in our current political environment which takes on particular importance, because it seems to me that the symbolism of the current incumbent of the presidency [Reagan] is that one doesn't need to speak with accuracy or guardedness; that values are more important than facts.

The misutilization problem is not a static one. It's a dynamic one. I suspect the dimensions and the nature of it are changing with the information revolution. And we need to get in and get a handle on that. I don't have a lot of empirical questions remaining—with the exception of some possible fine-tuning and things—about the utilization piece, but I'm wide open on misutilization. I really don't feel I've got a handle on that one at all.[13]

Alex Law: Would you characterize selective reporting of results by the client as misutilization?

Mike Patton: I would think, in some kind of typology and continuum, that that would certainly be a piece of it. And it seems to me that there are at least two kinds of misuse: conscious and unconscious. I mean, a lot of what I encounter is not deliberate misutilization. It is people thinking they're doing it appropriately, by whatever set of standards—that's the standards problem. Some of it is blatant. I've not looked at it systematically or tried to think it through inductively, with an empirical base.

Carol Weiss: Well, there is information from public opinion research and the whole tradition of studying and coping with misreporting of public opinion survey data.

Mike Patton: In the media, largely?

---

13. *Hendricks:* One useful approach to defining misutilization might be to create a laundry list of possible examples and see whether there's any consensus among evaluators. I predict very little consensus, for one person's misutilization could easily be another person's utilization.

Carol Weiss: Well, partly in the media. Some of it involves candidates, advertisers, surveys done for commercial firms, public officials. And AAPOR, which is the American Association of Public Opinion Research, has been in existence since 1936. It has a code of ethics and a standards committee that examines cases of misreporting, selective reporting, and misleading selective reporting. They actually get in touch with offending parties and hold hearings. So there is . . . if you want to take that as an analogy, there is a body of experience that's not so distant from the evaluation experience, that we could probably learn a lot from.

Milbrey McLaughlin: Michael, the reference that you triggered was Ralf Dahrendorf's book, *Homo Sociologicus.*[14] Have any of you seen that? It was one of the things that saved my life when I first came to Rand. The theme of the book is talking about man as being from the social sciences, sociology, and how there's an essence of any individual which makes him ultimately not modelable, in an economic sense. But he has a chapter that talks about the responsibility of researchers vis-à-vis misuse; that because of the fluid, dynamic nature of people and institutions, it's often difficult to anticipate the use that your evaluation or your research might have. But as a researcher in a particular setting, one can be quite clear about some of the potential misuse at the time that research is done. You can be clear about what this research does not say, in a way you can't be clear about what it does say. So he's arguing that it's attendant upon the researcher in a research report to . . . not to sketch possible uses, but to sketch possible abuses and things that this report is not saying and will not say. Which is something we don't often do.

Ernie House: Last November, I was serving as an expert witness in a trial in Missoula, Montana, where the school board had decided that it would evaluate the teachers, and so it fired a teacher with 13 years of teaching experience. She took a leave of absence, and when she came back to the district, they subjected her to entry-level interviews. The director of personnel had had some evaluation training and decided that he knew how to construct a set of interviews that would detect a poor teacher. They turned out to be a rather rigorous set of interviews, a rather grueling set. And they put this woman through these, which made a real wreck out of her. And they dismissed her for being incompetent on the basis of the interviews. And she had 13 years of experience.

14. Dahrendorf, R. (1971). *Homo sociologicus: Ein versuch zur geschicte, bedeutung und kritik der kategorie der sozialen rolle.* Opladen: Westdeutscher Verlag.

Marv Alkin: Dismissal based on the interviews?

Ernie House: Just on the interviews. Now she had 13 years of teaching experience, and the highest ratings in the district. According to Montana law, she could appeal this. The lawyer of the Montana Education Association took on her defense, and so we had a two-day hearing and I was an expert witness in the trial—that could be classified as misuse. I testified for the defense because although I didn't know whether this woman was really a good teacher or not, I didn't think they should have used the evaluation quite the way they used it. I'm not opposed to teacher evaluation at all. I'm for teacher evaluation, but what they did doesn't really constitute proper use. These people were quite well intentioned, I think. They're really trying to improve teaching in the district and make it more rigorous and all that sort of stuff. I think the director of personnel had just enough evaluation experience to think that he knew what he was doing, but . . . I mean, it is a tricky situation. I think that's misuse with good intent. I believe that the people were sincere, even though wrongheaded in the way they went about dismissing this teacher.

Michael Kean: We seem to be skirting around the definitional issue. I don't know if we want to really deal with it. . . . I was going to raise another question: Would you consider failure to use, misuse? The old notion of, if you're not part of the solution, you're part of the problem. If you simply, not out of malice, but, here's the information and well, that's nice, we'll put that report on the shelf. And they never get around to using it. Is failure to use, misuse?

Carol Weiss: Not by Mike's terms. He says they're independent dimensions. So nonuse is part of the use dimension, but it's not misuse.

Jean King: Well, it's misuse if you do it on purpose. In other words, if it says the program is no good and it's bilingual ed—and you're going to support bilingual ed no matter what—then . . .

Mike Patton: Yeah, if you took steps to squash it, I mean, made sure it didn't get out, interfered with the normal nonuse process, then . . .

Jean King: Active nonuse, right?

Mike Patton: But I guess I would entertain that malicious nonuse was indeed misutilization.

Jean King: Unless it's a lousy report. A lousy evaluation . .

Alex Law: Then it's appropriate nonuse.

Carol Weiss: But you see, that gets very, very subjective. We could take one instance and we would all disagree about whether it was malicious. Whether it was appropriate. Or whether it was even nonuse.

Marv Alkin: There's another element in this, if you think about use—appropriate, inappropriate, whatever. A lot of what we're talking about is use of some written evaluation product. What about those many instances where all kinds of uses have been made of processes, of the evaluator as a resource, long before the report is written? I think we have to think about those kinds of issues, too. It's again what Mike was talking about yesterday. Sometimes there are many reasons for one not to write a report, or if the report is written, one of the reasons to put it on the shelf is because many of the important intended uses of the evaluation have already taken place, before the report is written up.

Carol Weiss: Well, that's true at GAO, for example, where the GAO people go out and they look at a program. They talk to people in the department about what they're finding. If the people agree that, Yes, this seems to be terrible, they immediately institute some changes. And by the time the report is written and goes through all the review and whatnot, changes have been made. And the agency's response in the back of the report frequently has a whole long section that says, We did numbers 1, 3, 7, 11, 12, 13—those are already in place.

Alex Law: I have an interesting problem: About a year ago, I was asked to start reporting achievement scores by ethnic category within schools. And I said, the potential for abuse is high. And I pled the case and I won.

Mike Patton: This would be school-level data, not individual-level data?

Alex Law: School-level data prevailed the first year, but the issue was reopened and I've just lost. The plea is made that minority communities really need this information. So it was reported, in this instance, to the press. What is the responsibility of an evaluator in a situation like this? I'm predicting social mischief.

Ernie House: You make the best arguments that you can, that's all you can do.

Mike Patton: Well, you could mobilize opposition, if you felt strongly about it.

Ernie House: I think he has limited options.

Mike Patton: If a prestigious group like this passed a resolution, certainly that would carry the day . . .

[laughter]

Susan Klein: No, but I think that, seriously, there may be certain kinds of misuse that you have in mind. If you really identified those clearly and figured out some ways to prevent them by deriving additional information or warnings or guidance . . .

Alex Law: An interesting anecdote came about when we were involved with the tests. I, among others, didn't feel comfortable with the way the item bias screening was going, so I went out to the schools to get empirical data. We never reported it, but used it for a statistical review of the items. The schools, of course, knew that we were collecting additional information, and one school district said, I want the results by ethnic classification from school districts C and B, who are next door to me, because I want to prove to the public that I'm doing a better job of teaching Blacks than they are. That was their explicit goal in this. Now, if the demographic characteristics of A are hugely different than B and C, then they're going to win, blow them away. It has nothing to do with their instructional program; it has everything to do with the parents of these kids. And this is the kind of issue that I can foresee.

Michael Kean: You're all familiar with what happens when the local media gets hold of test scores . . . no matter how hard you work, the chances are at best 50/50 that you're going to get a really objective story or an educational editor that really understands what scores mean. In some cases, one can be somewhat creatively obfuscative in dealing with this, but you can't always win. One of the things that we avoided doing every year was to publish test scores in any kind of order, other than alphabetical.[15] And the education writers for our three newspapers at the time would always yell and scream and say, "You are going to ruin my entire weekend and I'll have to take the scores and go through all

---

15. *Hendricks:* This raises an interesting question: whether an evaluator has an obligation sometimes to *confuse* issues, to prevent a client from taking action prematurely or inappropriately. I once suggested that one might follow this path, but my audience clearly disagreed.

this. Won't you do this?" And I'd say, "I know exactly what you are going to do with them, and I'm not going to be party to that." But they would always take them and change them around. They did some really hideous things, too, and then at one point, I figured maybe I should just do the ranking for them, because at least they wouldn't screw up the ranking.

Political Nature of Evaluation and Misuse

Alex Law: Well, getting back to the issue. I'm going to argue that evaluation is a political event, and as long as it's a political event, you're going to have some mischief attached to it. I mean, that's the sense that I have. There's something that goes far beyond the control of anything a responsible evaluator can do. Once a report is given to the client where does your responsibility end?

Jean King: There are problems even before the report is written—and now I'm thinking of internal evaluators and in-house evaluators who have been there for 20 years and want to keep their jobs. They've got their draft, and they take it to their boss who says, Well, you know, this paragraph is out and let's rewrite this. What does that person do? Now we would say, Fight it. My professional standards say you can't do that. But do you want to lose your job over this evaluation? I mean, that possibility really exists, and I empathize with that person greatly. I'd like to say, Yeah, fight and lose your job. But then, on the other hand . . .

Ernie House: Yeah. That's the kind of problem I mentioned last night, because I happen to be working with some organizations where that's happening. Particularly when the evaluation unit is inside. And that's what Ross was responding to today. When the evaluation unit is inside a big bureaucracy, or maybe a small bureaucracy, pressures are brought to bear. And these people are not only evaluators, they're bureaucrats, so pressures are brought to bear upon them.

Jean King: And they can fire a bunch of them, but they'll just keep going until they find the people who will change it and feel comfortable changing it and . . .

Mike Patton: There is another side to that . . . It was really interesting at a recent American Public Welfare Association meeting in Washington. They had several state welfare directors and program people on the panel. And the question was put to them—and these were some of the better administrators, I suspect—but the question was put to them, Had they ever squashed negative evaluation reports? And one man had a particularly interesting perspective. He said the hardest decisions he had to make and the greatest risk to his career involved squashing bad, negative evaluation reports, because those get leaked to the press. And the fact that he squashed the report and refused to release it had all the wrong implications. The report was terrible. It was inappropriately done. It was an external evaluation in this case. When it got to him, the evaluator had overstepped bounds and not done what he'd been asked to. They hadn't monitored it. The data collection was bad. And he decided that the report should not be released. But in so doing, the word got to the press, and he took incredible heat for having squashed a bad report and not being able to explain the nuances of that. As far as the press was concerned, the thing ought to be public, even if it was bad and, of course, the press was totally unsympathetic with his attempt to keep bad information, damaging information, out of the information mainstream.

Marv Alkin: So that was appropriate nonuse that looked like malicious nonuse.

Mike Patton: That's right. And the rest of the panel started telling examples. It turned out they all had stories like that, where the difficulty for them was not trying to manipulate good data for bad purposes. Their more common experience, from the administrative point of view, was trying to deal with the problem of bad data having been created. Which is like Alex's data, in a way. Alex is trying to squash evaluation data, in a sense. He's trying to keep information from doing damage.

Carol Weiss: Then there are codes of withholding evaluation data for humanitarian motives. I'm familiar with an evaluation of a welfare program which has some negative findings and the director knows that the legislature is looking for any excuse right now to cut public welfare appropriations. If this thing comes out, it provides a wonderful excuse to cut back benefits to the poor. And so he wants to sit on it for a while, until the legislative session is over. Well, from noble motives, he wants to bury a good evaluation, you know, an accurate evaluation. Now . . .

Mike Patton: 'Cause he knows others will misuse it.

Defining Misuse

Carol Weiss: Well, yeah. I mean, there are all kinds of nuances of right and wrong motives and purity and impurity . . . And I find it very difficult to even conceive of some panel being able to reach consensus on what is appropriate or what is misutilization. I find the whole concept very troublesome. Because one person's misutilization is another person's sensible administrative practice.

Mike Patton: One person's freedom fighter is another person's terrorist.

Carol Weiss: That's right.

. . .

Mike Patton: It seems to me that what the groups' examples are leading us to is an approach that is not unlike what we've done with utilization. In effect, we haven't defined utilization, either, in the literature. But that hasn't kept us from talking about it. What definition there is has come from inductively finding out what definitions people out there use. Perhaps a better approach than having a group of experts sit around and decide what misutilization is would be to gather the perceptions of what people from the field themselves consider misutilization: How do they identify it? How do they think about it? What is the working knowledge of misutilization that exists in different practitioner groups? And come to understand the values that are brought to bear on it, and the relative priorities that people use, and the experiences they're having, with some notions of how often such experiences occur. I mean, we have a popular wisdom that internal evaluators are under lots of pressure. I find a lot of them who are struggling more with the problem of use than misuse; of getting attention rather than getting the thing manipulated. But I don't really think we know very much and that we need to go into the field and find out.

Jean King: It's going to be very tough to do that, though. The case study we did started getting to that, because we found cases where, in our professional judgment, there was inappropriate use. Things were happening that just shouldn't have been happening. But you go to the person who you knew, in your heart, was screwing around with the data, and that person said, Listen, you know, I believe in kids, and I am doing everything I can for kids, and what I've done here is take this informa-

tion and make it work for the program. I have done this for the good of
the children.

Mike Patton: That's all right. I mean, you record that.

Jean King: But that person's not going to say, Well, yeah, I misused
it. I come in—and this is the appropriateness question—I come in and
label that person villain, bad person. Whereas the person would say, and
maybe even the staff of this person would say, Well, geez, if this bad
information comes out, we're going to lose money. These kids are going
to be hurt and we can't let that happen.

Carol Weiss: Well, again, we come to this tension between truth and
utility. You know, is truth the ultimate good? Is taking the evaluation
report as reported and making it public, in this case, of higher value
than thinking ahead of what the consequences would be in making these
data available? And what would be sensible administrative and political
practice, in terms of whom to tell, when to tell, or whether to tell?

Mike Patton: It's a classic prior restraint applied to evaluation. I mean,
government uses prior restraint arguments all the time, and now we're
finding administrators and evaluators using such arguments.

Carol Weiss: But how much confidence—I think you'd probably be
the first to raise the question—How much confidence do we really have
that our data represent some ultimate truth? Evaluations are very situation-specific,[16] tentative approximations of a situation. And is it really
such a higher value to take them and run with them than to consider
what the effects on funding of programs for kids is going to be?

Milbrey McLaughlin: You raise a utility question, though, of a different nature; kind of two levels of utility questions. One is the administrative tension; you know, truth and utility at the administrative level.
What about utility issues that are inherent in the kind of embeddedness
that we were talking about yesterday; embedding evaluations in some
kind of theoretical and empirical tradition. What if, in fact, for a whole
bunch of administrative or social reasons, there are these great bubbles
or omissions in our evaluation literature, because of this local, situational tension?

16. *Alkin:*   It seems odd to find Weiss describing evaluation as a situation-specific
activity in light of discussion earlier in the book.

Carol Weiss: I would feel, because I'm not an administrator, that making the evaluation studies available in the literature is a given. I think all universities have that rule. You don't take on a study unless you're going to publish it.

Milbrey McLaughlin: I'm remembering something very specific. I'm remembering the response of a number of Harvard people right after the Jensen stuff came out. There's a whole lot of work that I know about that was never published, in the early 70s, that related to that.

Carol Weiss: By self-censorship.

Milbrey McLaughlin: Self . . . but it was addressing a different utility . . .

Carol Weiss: It was Alex's kind of self-censorship, where he doesn't think ethnic scores should be publicized.

Milbrey McLaughlin: Right. But somebody else coming along 15 years later, looking at the evaluation history, the social reporting of that period of time, will have a very skewed view of what was going on.

Carol Weiss: Oh, yeah. Oh, absolutely.

Milbrey McLaughlin: So that's a different kind of utility issue.

Carol Weiss: We don't always practice what we preach. I just think the whole thing needs very, very careful analysis before we even take the label of misutilization seriously as a usable concept. It seems to me it has so many problems. Validity problems . . . reliability problems. Can we ever agree? Can multiple observers ever agree on what is misutilization, except in the most blatant of extremes?

Jean King: One variable that we have to keep in mind is how much written information is available. Because if nothing is written down, then it's going to be real tough to find any misutilization.

Milbrey McLaughlin: It's a question of how far can you track data. To the extent that a person writes everything down, then there is something to examine; maybe this is what we want to argue for, that that's better, because then an external person can come in and say, I see what you did here, I see how this went. Although a user's not going to do the same thing . . .

Carol Weiss: Well, take an evaluation that shows some things are good and four things are not good. And the users do essentially what the evaluator recommends in the first case. They take seriously the negative findings, and do something very different from what the evaluator recommends in the second case. And they don't do anything at all in the third case. And in the fourth case, they ignore the evaluator and give more money to a program that doesn't seem to be worth it—and make what is a problem in the evaluator's view even larger. What's . . . what of that is misutilization?

Ernie House: I don't think it's misutilization.

Marv Alkin: I don't either.

Carol Weiss: None of that? Well then, what is misutilization?

Ernie House: You're right that we don't have a very good grasp on the concept of what it is, but some misutilization is a deliberate attempt to deceive and mislead, for example. I could talk about cases where that may be the case. That doesn't seem to me to be your example. There was no deliberate attempt to mislead people, to change the findings, or invoke findings that didn't exist.

Carol Weiss: No one tampered with the data.

Ernie House: What happens more often, rather than tampering with the data, although I guess that does happen in some places, is changing the conclusions, the wording of the conclusions. Administrators don't change the data, they say, "Change the conclusion."[17] You can write that conclusion differently, you know, jazz it up so you make a much more favorable conclusion than what the data will support. This is particularly likely to happen in internal evaluations. It gets a little tricky, because there's a certain judgment involved as to what the conclusions should say.

Mike Patton: Carol, where do your cautions and your concerns lead you in terms of next steps? Do you want to leave it alone?

Carol Weiss: Yeah. I think I want to leave it alone for the time being. Ernie gave an illustration of an evaluator who changed the conclusions under the pressure of program superiors and working colleagues. I can

17. *Hendricks:* I agree, and I'm watching the White House exert that sort of pressure right now on an evaluation I recently helped conduct. There are lots of ways to influence a report other than changing the data.

name, I think with no trouble, five or six evaluators whose conclusions are not substantiated by their data, who get either so enamored or so turned off by a program that they go way beyond the data in the way they write their conclusions. Is the evaluator misutilizing the study?[18] I just have so much trouble with the whole concept of misutilization. I don't even see how one could begin to study it, unless and until we have a clearer conceptualization of what it's all about.

Mike Patton: Where that leads me is to get to conceptualization from the field, to find out how people experience it, and how they're thinking about it, before we try to deal with it from our side, from the evaluator's side.

Milbrey McLaughlin: Mike, how have you dealt with the administrative tension? You must have sorted through a lot of those kinds of utility and use questions that are mediated by administrative imperatives.

Mike Patton: I come to the question late, because I've never had a personal experience with what I thought was misutilization, and I think it has to do with the negotiating process that goes on up front. We get clear about what's not going to happen and what is going to happen and what the evaluation can't speak to and what it can speak to. So the negotiating process, in clarifying utilization and the responsibility around it, reduces a lot of potential for misutilization.

Marv Alkin: And of course, you don't take on clients who appear to be high-risk users . . .

Mike Patton: Yeah, there's a selectivity there.

Carol Weiss: Well, and also you said that you are only responsible for the intended use by the intended user. So that frees you from responsibility from anything beyond that.[19]

. . .

Milbrey McLaughlin: That's right. You can think about categories of utilization. It's hard to think about categories of misutilization that aren't also intersected by so much in the way of judgment and values.

---

18. *Alkin:* I would call this "misevaluation" because writing the report is part of the evaluation.
19. *Ellett:* Just because Patton asserts he has no responsibility, it does not follow that he has no responsibility (not whether he asserts it).

Carol Weiss: Yes. Absolutely.

Marv Alkin: So now we're talking about misutilization of evaluation information by the evaluator, whereas before we were talking about misutilization of evaluation information by the users.

Carol Weiss: Because they're intermeshed.

Mike Patton: I'm not sure that the utilization thing is any cleaner in terms of values. It just seems to me we have more consensus on it. But there still is the question of a hierarchy of utilization, and whether certain kinds are more valuable than other kinds. You know: Is conceptual (changing the way that someone thinks about a program) use the same as instrumental use, and is intended use for intended users better than more important use that was unintended . . . Those are all value-laden questions.

Carol Weiss: We don't agree on the hierarchy, but we have good labels for types of use. And we all agree about what constitutes each type.

Mike Patton: That's because we studied it.

Carol Weiss: Well, yes, that's because we studied it. But I don't even know how you would, as you were hinting at just a few minutes ago, how you would go out and study misuse. I think if you interviewed four people in a setting—an evaluator, an immediate program director, somebody at a higher organizational level, and a director of a parallel program in another city or state—and asked about misuse of that evaluation, you would get total disagreement about what was use or misuse or appropriate practice or the evaluator's fault. I don't know, I just . . . I can't begin to see how you can get a handle on this. Maybe I'm wrong, and I hope I am. It's an interesting question . . .

Milbrey McLaughlin: It's just . . . I mean, Michael has talked about them as independent dimensions. Maybe the only way to resolve it, at least now, is to talk about more or less appropriate or situational aspects of use and nonuse.

Mike Patton: I don't know whether people can answer the question. When we did the interviewing in the federal health evaluations study, we never asked them about misutilization. We only asked them about utilization, and we built the whole interview structure around that. I don't know that one can't ask another set of questions about misutilization and have people respond to it, and content analyze it, and see indeed what the typologies are and what the prevalence is. I'm just feeling a need for the empirical piece now. In a sense, I think we're where we were with utilization when we started looking at it empirically. There was a lot of prescriptive literature about what to do about it, but the whole definitional thing started to change when we got out and started talking about the real world. And I suspect that there's a whole continuum of misutilization, just as there is for utilization. The blatant, deliberate changing of the data strikes me as the equivalent of the immediate, direct decision, where the evaluation has 100% of the impact. It is probably the endpoint in the continuum, and the mushiness is the rest of it.

Carol Weiss: I hope you go do this study, Michael. I'm behind you 100% . . . way behind you . . .

Mike Patton: Safely behind!

Carol Weiss: Part of my concern, I think, is triggered by something Jean said earlier. She went out and interviewed users, and in her heart, she saw what were obvious cases of misutilization, but the people involved did not describe them as such. To what extent are we reading in our own, or won't we almost inevitably be reading in our own preconceptions?

Marv Alkin: Well, anytime you go into a situation, Carol, and judge use, you bring in your own perceptions and values in judging the extent to which attitude change has taken place.

Carol Weiss: Well, we could test that.

Marv Alkin: And it would be a very difficult dimension of use for us to precisely categorize. And we would probably not all agree that, in fact, some instance of use had occurred and the extent of that use.

Carol Weiss: Well, I've done a study where we went back five years in a row and asked people the same attitudinal questions after a report came out, to see if people's attitudes had changed. I mean, we can measure them. And I think we're on much firmer ground on issues of that sort.

Mike Patton: It seems to me that the purpose of an empirically grounded theory kind of approach is to develop some distinctions and typologies, to sensitize us to some categories of misutilization. Whether or not we agree or disagree on the values that are involved, we need better, more systematic and detailed case data to sensitize evaluators to these dilemmas and to their own definitions, in the same way that the utilization literature has sensitized people to the different kinds and levels of use, and made that a part of their operating repertoire.

Carol Weiss: I think the cases exist. And maybe the research we need is to see if we could generate consensus among a set of researchers, about the extent to which these unwritten cases constitute misuse.

Mike Patton: Research on the value structure, then, of key operators . . .

Carol Weiss: No. I mean a group like us, sitting around, reviewing these case illustrations and seeing if we could agree on whether they represent misuse. One case leaps to mind: There was a study on the use of energy reports in the congressional debates during the Carter years. There was an energy report done by the Congressional Budget Office; there was an energy report done by the Congressional Research Service; there was a report done by the General Accounting Office; and there were two or three major university reports, all of which were available to the members of Congress. And all of which came to varying conclusions. And basically the story was about how different members of Congress selected those reports which were compatible with their own beliefs and constituent interests. And the debate on the floor and in committee was about which set of data were better data. But what the author was saying was that it was all a big smoke screen, because they weren't using the reports. They were using the reports as ammunition . . . or as bulwarks to hide behind. But the fact that they had the reports really made the debate much less useful than it would have been if they had honestly confronted their value differences, which they didn't do. They argued about coefficients of whatever . . . Now would we, looking in more detail at that instance, consider that misutilization?

Ernie House: No, I don't think that is misutilization. The context has so much to do with it. They're engaged in an adversarial process. There's a sense in which everybody's using his or her arguments to confront each other. It's like a courtroom. And so you present the best evidence for your side. Now within the setting, that's understood. That's different from an administrator taking an evaluation report and telling the evaluator, I'm changing the conclusions of this report. And then putting that out to the public. That's misuse.[20]

Carol Weiss: Well, all right. Let me just try one other case. There have been, over the years, a number of evaluations of the Women, Infants and Children's Nutrition Program, some of which were, in the early years particularly, quite favorable, and some of which, in the later years, were not so favorable. The president, in this current budget, is proposing to zero that program. He is not citing, so far as I know, the evaluations, but suppose he did. I mean, he's looking for places to cut and particularly social programs to cut. Suppose he sort of brandished the latest evaluations and said, "This shows the program isn't working, and therefore I am proposing to cut it out." Is that misuse?

Ernie House: No, I don't know that it is.

Carol Weiss: But if the president had picked out the three paragraphs of the evaluation that cast aspersion on the program, but on balance didn't represent the whole picture, I'd call that misuse.

Ernie House: Yeah. If you took this sentence out of here and this sentence out of there, then that's misrepresentation. Such as, when you see these movie reviews and it says, "Superb . . . " but what it really says is, "This was a superbly stupid movie."

Carol Weiss: I don't think you'll find many examples of that. I think you'll find a lot of these selective uses. There are seven studies and you pick the one you like.

Ernie House: Selected use in that sense is not misuse. But I disagree; I think we will find increasingly a lot of misuse because this stuff is being invoked for public purposes, for public policies. And I think it comes under great pressure. The more it's used, the more likely we'll find misuses. And I've been counting lots of misuses. They tend to come, it seems to me, when the evaluators are inside some larger organization to which they're responsible. That's where I'm finding most of them right now. Bureaucratic pressures are brought to bear upon the evaluators to alter their conclusions. Maybe it's not really a serious problem yet. I have encountered some instances.

---

20. *Hendricks:*   In a sense, isn't misutilization a compliment to the evaluation field? Would administrators make the effort to use evaluation findings for their own purposes if no one trusted or respected evaluations?

Carol Weiss: But that's not use. That's interference with the evaluation process itself. I mean, you haven't even gotten it to any potential user . . .

Ernie House: It's misuse . . .

Carol Weiss: It's distortion imposed on the evaluation by . .

Ernie House: It's misuse of evaluation, not misuse of evaluation findings.

Marv Alkin: That's a good point. And that's an important distinction.

Ernie House: Misuse of evaluation, rather than misuse of evaluation findings. Let me take an extreme case. If you hire somebody and you say—and this has happened—if you say to them, I'm hiring you, now here's what I want you to put in your report. Then the evaluator writes that up and that's published as an official evaluation report, then I think that's misuse of evaluation. It's misuse because it's deceiving the public or the audience for the evaluation as to what's going on.

Marv Alkin: Well, I wrote this article where I talked about the reasons for evaluation—one of which was as window dressing. How about misuse of the evaluation process, where you initiate a process in order to publicize the way that you are conducting evaluation, without any real concern for what the findings are. In other words, trying to provide a positive image to the program by the conduct of the evaluation process . . .[21]

Carol Weiss: I'm concerned that we don't muddy up the ethical and moral dilemma of evaluation with the use question, which it seems to me is external to the agency . . . to the evaluating agency or to the evaluating unit.

Ernie House: There is a conceptual distinction there between misusing an evaluation and misusing evaluation findings. There is a distinction to be made there.

Marv Alkin: Yes, but you see, there are two kinds of misusing evaluation: misusing evaluation in terms of a requirement for the anticipated findings and misusing evaluation in terms of the way in which the evaluation process is set up.

21. Alkin, M. C. (1975). Evaluation: Who needs it? Who cares? *Studies in Educational Evaluation, 1*(3).

. . .

Jean King: One thing I think we also need to bring up again is the notion of what people remember from evaluations. I mean, so far we're talking pretty close to the report or to the data. What do we do five years down the road when the superintendent remembers something and will act on that memory? It's pretty distressing, because they remember things wrong. Now is that misutilization? Well, sort of, but on the other hand, they're doing it with the right intentions and . . .

Carol Weiss: And we all remember things wrong.

Jean King: Yeah, right. People are fallible. So what do we do about it?

Susan Klein: Well, that's one advantage of having it written or documented in some way. You can go back and check.

Ernie House: I guess there is some point, as some people suggested, at which you have to give up some ownership responsibility for your findings. There will be cases where ten years later, people will remember findings contrariwise to what they were, and we have to give that up and not be responsible for that.[22]

Jean King: But is it possible that real misuse can happen that way?

Carol Weiss: Oh, I'm sure. I'm sure. I think the conclusion that the War on Poverty failed is a fairly common generalization about several hundred evaluation studies. It's probably wrong, or at least partially wrong. Some of the War on Poverty was good and some of it was not so good, but the going generalization is that the War on Poverty failed. It can be said, as Ernie has pointed out, that Charlie Murray's book has been used, in a large societal sense, to support Reagan's cutbacks in social programs. Is that misuse of evaluation?

Ernie House: Well, we know Reagan's going to use anything he can get his hands on. Its understood that politicians are going to do it because that's the way the game is.

Carol Weiss: Well, it's more than the politicians; it affected others as well. I think of the people who were hopeful and optimistic in the 60s,

---

22. *Hendricks:* I think Ernie is absolutely right. Surely we can't take responsibility for the entire future of humankind!

who became progressively disenchanted in the 70s, and who by the 80s said, Yeah, I guess maybe we have to go along with these cutbacks . . .

Ernie House: What bothers me more than the politicians using it is Coleman and Glazer saying that this is a brilliant study. That's what bothers me the most.

Review and Commentary

Part IV

In Part IV, we acknowledge the political context in which evaluations take place. The context constrains the actions of evaluators and the way in which they may conduct their evaluations. The context also imposes ethical dilemmas for evaluators; the context and actions of the evaluator also have implications for what will happen with evaluation reports and whether, and how, they get used.

The issues in Part IV are in many respects intertwined, but an attempt has been made to consider them under two general rubrics. In Chapter 12, various ethical issues affecting the evaluator are considered. In Chapter 13, we examine the general issue of misuse of evaluation reports and, by implication, the associated issues of use (and nonuse) and abuse.

Ethical Issues

Clearly, the full range of ethical issues is not considered within this seminar. Ethical issues were not the direct focus of the meeting and the topic emerged as a part of other discussion. Three issues, however, received attention: (a) ethical standards related to data that have been collected, (b) the ethical concern about the way in which the evaluation process will affect those providing data, and (c) the evaluator's ethical responsibility for guarding against potential misuse.

Occasionally during the course of an evaluation, evaluators will "find out things we never wanted to know and wish we didn't know after we found out." A number of seminar participants comment on such instances in their personal experiences. Alex Law describes a local program evaluated by the state that was found to have been quite successful, but that had not acted in accord with state guidelines. He questions whether the evaluator should "blow the whistle." His answer: No! Others address the same issue on a more individual basis. Suppose, for example, that the data collected related not to total program success (as in the Law example), but either to specific program characteristics or to actions of individuals. In such instances, what is the obligation of the evaluator to "blow the whistle"? Milbrey McLaughlin reframes the ethical dilemma by noting that such information could well have been gained in an interview situation based upon the development of a relationship of trust with the interviewee. Is such information to be considered "privileged" in the same way as information shared in an attorney-client relationship? McLaughlin concludes that such data would not be revealed "if it's not related directly to my sets of questions." Others indicate discomfort with the potential solutions and would like to have broadened the domain of situations in which the evaluator would reveal data. Carol Weiss, for example, comments on instances that constituted "direct programmatic weakening." For example, misappropriation of funds, although not directly related to the evaluator's set of questions, would be considered an action that weakens the program.

As I reflect upon my own experiences, I must say that I find few lively examples. In instances, however, where data relevant to the program come to light through the evaluation, it is my predilection not to reveal specific data sources or mention individuals, but instead to discuss the problem in general terms within the evaluation report. In this way, I feel that I have fulfilled my obligation related to the evaluation of the program—including meeting accountability purposes—and have maintained the confidentiality of sources as well.

The *second* ethical issue is dramatically presented by Michael Patton in his discussion about the conduct of interviews with farm families in northeastern Minnesota. He notes that the interviews introduced a painful topic that had, for the most part, been put aside by interviewees for a number of years. While no specific prescription is presented for evaluators, it is perfectly clear, as Patton notes, that evaluators cannot act as though "people are put on Earth, by God, for us to study." Evaluator sensitivity is a highly necessary prerequisite.

The *final* ethical issue considered within this chapter accounted for the greatest portion of the discussion. What is the evaluator's responsibility for guarding against misuse of evaluation information? Patton's point of view is one in which he assumes responsibility for intended users. In this assumption of responsibility, he presupposes that he will be able to establish a sufficiently strong relationship with his intended users and an appropriate situational responsiveness so that the evaluation will be "on target." By doing so, he believes, there will be little (or less) likelihood of the evaluation being misused by intended users. Patton acknowledges that a part of the evaluator's responsibility is to help assure that intended users do in fact use the evaluation information. Implied within that responsibility is the obligation of utilization-focused evaluators to be responsible for guarding against potential misuse by these intended users. Having acknowledged this position, Patton then indicates that he takes no responsibility for unintended use of the evaluation by unintended users. In essence, he maintains that the evaluator cannot possibly predict the unintended users and their possible unintended use, and therefore evaluators should stick to the responsibility that they are able to accomplish. Since he believes that he cannot control all of these unintended uses, he advocates working with the intended users in meeting their situational needs and then empowering them to "look after the unintended, and answer the distortions" as the best control.

Carol Weiss adds a caveat from a research perspective that an evaluator can better fulfill the responsibility related to unintended use by providing sound, well-documented, carefully conceptualized evaluations. Presumably she is recognizing that, from her perspective, evaluation reports get disseminated to a wide variety of individuals—many of whom might become users of the evaluation. Therefore, the best and perhaps the only defense against unintended use is to do a quality evaluation. Whether this is sufficient defense against unintended use (or, more appropriately, unintended misuse) is highly questionable.

The excitement in this chapter came from Ernest House's outrage at Patton's morality of attending to client concerns. He takes great offense at the evaluator's focusing his or her responsibility on the intended user. House argues that evaluators cannot limit their perspective in that way. To do so, he maintains, denies the broader society access to the evaluation. He states that this position is immoral; Patton counters that to do otherwise is improper.

Evaluation Misuse

As I have noted in Part I, there is substantial literature related to evaluation utilization. In this section of the book, we have examined another related concept—misuse. As Patton notes, use and misuse are separate dimensions. The use continuum has as its terminus "nonuse." In essence, this continuum defines the extent to which an evaluation is used. A more complex variant of this is presented by Hall, Loucks, Rutherford, and Newlove (1975) in their levels of use (LOU) matrix.

Misuse is a different, but related, concept. While nonuse is a measure of degree or magnitude, misuse is a measure of *manner* of use. On one end of this misuse continuum might be found something called "appropriate use." Misuse (or inappropriate use) represents the negatively loaded end of the continuum. Thus appropriate use/misuse depicts an ethical dimension.

Before engaging in further discussion on the topic of misuse, it is essential to examine a related matter. Seminar participants evidence a great deal of confusion in defining inappropriate actions by evaluators. Some want to define these as misuse, but this is not totally correct. It is important to distinguish between types of mis- (or inappropriate) evaluation. First, misevaluation, referring to the acts of the evaluator, may occur in a number of ways. Misevaluation may take place when the technical aspects of the evaluation have not been conducted adequately (e.g., data collection was done poorly or statistical analyses are incorrect). Misevaluation may also occur when the evaluator fails to understand the evaluation context properly and therefore misdirects the evaluation.

A third kind of misevaluation—and there are undoubtedly others—occurs when the evaluator fails to recognize properly his or her obligations for appropriate communication to potential users. Evaluation reporting is an essential element of the evaluator's responsibility. Whether the reporting is "dissemination" on the part of academic-oriented evaluators or the communication of results and the training of decision makers to be potential users on the part of consultative evaluators, reporting can be an area of potential misevaluation.

Each of these instances of misevaluation could be responsible for misuse. With reference to technical characteristics of an evaluation, Carol Weiss strongly argues that the evaluator's most important responsibility is the conduct of technically sound evaluation research studies. Moreover, she believes that the quality of the study reduces the potential likelihood of misuse. That is, she implies that well-done evaluations are less likely to be misused. In the second instance (understanding context), Michael Patton feels that an intensive focus on intended users develops a situational responsiveness that makes the evaluation results more relevant. He argues that relevant results, in combination with the rapport developed with intended users, reduces the likelihood of misuse by those users. He indicates that in his work he takes full responsibility for potential misuse by intended users.

With respect to the obligations of an evaluator for appropriate communication, several examples are provided. In my own work, I have documented instances of proper use of evaluation when the evaluator assumes a major responsibility for training decision makers in the appropriate ways to use evaluation information (see Alkin, Stecher, & Geiger, 1982). Milbrey McLaughlin, stimulated by the work of Dahrendorf (1971), notes the obligation of the researcher/evaluator to stem possible misuse by sketching potential abuses of the evaluation report and stipulating what the report does not say.

In addition to an evaluator doing "misevaluation," he or she also might engage more directly in misusing evaluation results. A more blatant misevaluation (and concomitant misuse) comes about when the evaluator accedes to decision-maker suggestions and modifies negative or controversial findings. Misuse by the evaluator also takes place, for example, in selective reporting to paint an inappropriate picture of the program. In this instance, the evaluator, having completed an evaluation report, selectively misuses the evaluation information. In many respects, it is difficult to differentiate these kinds of evaluator misuse from misevaluation because the reporting function, in whole or in part, is a major element of the evaluator's activities.

Thus, while some kinds of misevaluation might border on misuse, when the seminar participants refer to misuse, they are focusing on use by individuals other than the evaluator. These individuals might be clients or other intended users. The seminar participants generally acknowledge that misuse by such individuals is more easily controlled than misuse by unintended users. However, examples of misuse of this type are evident in the discussion.

Seminar participants express greater concern about misuse by a variety of individuals in the wider audience who may be viewed as recipients of the evaluation report, directly or indirectly. Patton, however, would have us make the distinction between intended users and unintended users. He then limits the evaluator's responsibility for misuse only to misuse by intended users.

A variety of situational examples are presented in the discussion of Part IV: Some may be viewed as misuse, others as misevaluation, and others defined as justified nonuse. A potpourri of issues are raised (and mostly not resolved). Is nonuse misuse if it is done on purpose? Is nonuse of a poorly done evaluation appropriate nonuse? If evaluations are not fully used is that misuse? What about partial use? What about distortions?

A number of fairly clear examples of misuse are presented, however. The most prominent of these involves a report having been rewritten by "agency people." Other examples are less clear-cut. Moreover, participants note that there are nuances of right and wrong, and "one person's misuse is another's sensible administrative practice." Seminar participants wonder about the tension between truth and utility and question whether people who modify or hold back data for the good of a program or for the good of the children in a program are in fact misusing evaluation. Carol Weiss notes, "After all . . . how much confidence do we have that our data represent some ultimate truth?"

Figure 1 presents a category system for misuse. The system consists of four dimensions that help to distinguish between potential misuse situations. These categories, or dimensions, are as follows: the client's purpose, the quality of the evaluation, users' intentions, and users' technical sophistication. Evaluation clients might commission an evaluation purely for symbolic reasons (for political gain, for publicity, to gain funding, to delay action, or to avoid taking responsibility). This kind of symbolic purpose constitutes misuse of evaluation.

In instances where evaluation was commissioned with an instrumental purpose in mind (a potential likelihood of use of evaluation information), the evaluation misuse model is further differentiated by whether the evaluation was done well or poorly. Clearly, nonuse of a poorly done evaluation is highly laudatory, as is use of a well-done evaluation. The other examples require further differentiation. The issue is whether nonuse of well-done evaluations is unintentional or intentional/blatant, the former of which I am willing to acknowledge as simple nonuse, with higher degrees of intentionality classified as misuse or abuse.

Likewise, informed users should know better than to rely on poorly done evaluations, and such instances I would categorize as misuse (as

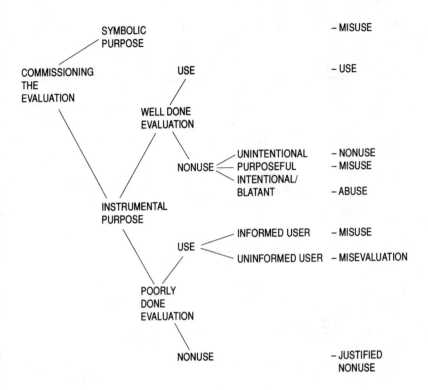

Figure 1. An Evaluation Misuse Category System
SOURCE: Adapted from Alkin & Coyle (1988).

well as misevaluation). An instance of a use of a poorly done evaluation by an uninformed user I simply call misevaluation.

References

Alkin, M. C., & Coyle, K. (1988). Thoughts on evaluation utilization, misutilization and non-utilization. *Studies in Educational Evaluation, 14,* 331-340.

Alkin, M. C., Stecher, B. M., & Geiger, F. L. (1982). *Title I evaluation: Utility and factors affecting use.* Northridge, CA: Educational Evaluation Associates.

Dahrendorf, R. (1971). *Homo sociologicus: Ein versuch zur geschicte, bedeutung und kritik der kategorie der sozialen rolle.* Opladen: Westdeutscher Verlag.

Hall, G. E., Loucks, S. F., Rutherford, W. L., & Newlove, B. W. (1975). Levels of the use of the innovation: A framework for analyzing innovation adoption. *Journal of Teacher Education, 26*(1), 52-56.

Hall, M. C., & Coyle, K. (1988). Thoughts on evaluation utilization, misutilization, and non-utilization. *Studies in Educational Evaluation, 14*, 331-340.

Closing

Michael Kean: I think the last day and a half has been very invigorating, for me at least. Now I don't know whether evaluation use is going to get improved as a result of this. I really don't know. But I'd like to see the possibility of some follow-up to this. I don't know how. I'd really like to think about the focus a bit more.

Mike Patton: I personally have gotten a lot of ideas about how to misuse evaluation.

[laughter and overtalk]

Mike Patton: I expect to be a lot better at that.

Michael Kean: I sort of feel like we've . . . you know, we've had the hors d'oeuvres, and maybe begun the first course, but there's an awful lot more to get ahold of . . .

Marv Alkin: I think this has really been a tremendously rewarding experience for me. It was my intention to get a group like this together in cordial surroundings, where people are likely to feel good about it and come up with great ideas. I wanted a small number of very high-quality people, so that it wouldn't be a standing in line to talk kind of thing or sitting in your seat listening to someone talk. I'm very pleased with the way I perceive that this meeting has worked. And I would welcome participation in something of this order again.

Susan Klein: Marv, there'll be opportunities for everybody to review what you've put together, comment, and expand some of their ideas, won't there? To some extent anyway?

Marv Alkin: To the extent to which I feel I can impose on people, I might ask for embellishments of some of the comments that were made here . . .

Mike Patton: And rights to delete?

Marv Alkin: And rights to delete . . .

Mike Patton: Accusations of a certain immorality on the parts of certain people we might want to leave out . . .

Marv Alkin: Right.

Mike Patton: Lest they be misused . . .

Ross Conner: It would be interesting if we could get comments from users. We have certainly some representatives . . . a principal or two.

Mike Patton: Well, I think of myself as a user now, because my position is actually program director. Marv was the external evaluator on the Caribbean project that I was directing.

Milbrey McLaughlin: I'm thinking about school principals . . .

[overtalk]

Ross Conner: . . . Just to ground us.

Mike Patton: Not stoned? Just grounded?

Marv Alkin: Okay, well, I think we'll call it quits. Or have we already?

Mike Patton: Well, thank you for bringing us together, sir.

Carol Weiss: Thank you, Marv. . .[1]

[applause]

[end of working meeting]

1. *Hendricks:* Excellent and very provocative discussion. A delight to read.

About the Participants
and Discussants

Participants

MARVIN C. ALKIN is a Professor and currently Chair of the Social Research Methodology Division of the Graduate School of Education at UCLA, and a former Director of UCLA's Center for the Study of Evaluation. He is especially known for his work in evaluation theory and evaluation utilization.

ROSS CONNER is a Professor in the Social Ecology Program at the University of California, Irvine. His writings have focused on evaluation methodology, the use of evaluation results in policymaking and decision making, and international evaluation. He is coeditor of the *Evaluation Studies Review Annual*, Volume 9.

ERNEST HOUSE is Director of the Laboratory for Policy Studies, School of Education, University of Colorado. He has authored several books on evaluation, and his most recent book is *Jesse Jackson and the Politics of Charisma* (1988).

MICHAEL H. KEAN is Director of Marketing at CTB/McGraw-Hill. Formerly, he was Executive Director of the Office of Research and Evaluation for the Philadelphia School District.

JEAN KING is Professor and Chair of Education at Tulane University, in New Orleans, Louisiana. Her research interests include the use of program evaluation, curriculum, and teacher education. She is the coauthor of *How to Assess Program Implementation* (1987).

SUSAN KLEIN is Senior Research Associate at the Office of Educational Research and Improvement, U.S. Department of Education. Her research and publication interests are in equity issues, evaluation, and dissemination.

ALEX LAW, now retired, was the Director of the Office of Program Evaluation and Research, California Department of Education. His research interests include program evaluation and the politics of evaluation.

MILBREY W. MCLAUGHLIN is Associate Professor, Stanford University School of Education. She was previously Senior Research Scientist with the Rand Corporation, Santa Monica, California. In that capacity she served as principal investigator of a number of studies, including a national evaluation of the ESEA Title IV consolidated program.

MICHAEL QUINN PATTON is on the national faculty of Union Graduate School, Union Institute, Cincinnati and a former Director of the Minnesota Center for Social Research. He is the author of several books on evaluation, including *Utilization-Focused Evaluation* (2nd ed., 1986) and *Practical Evaluation* (1983).

CAROL H. WEISS is Professor of Education, Graduate School of Education, Harvard University. She has written extensively on evaluation and the uses of evaluation. Her books include *Evaluation Research: Methods of Assessing Program Effectiveness* (1972), *Social Science Research and Decision Making* (1980), and *Reporting of Social Science in the National Media* (1988).

Discussants

FREDERICK S. ELLETT, JR., formerly Associate Professor of Philosophy of Education, Graduate School of Education, UCLA, is now Professor of Education at the University of Western Ontario. He is the author of articles that have appeared in *Educational Theory* and *Studies in Educational Evaluation.* His research interests include the theory of evaluation, human rationality, and theories of causation.

MICHAEL HENDRICKS is President of MH Associates, a Washington, D.C., consulting firm. He has consulted extensively at all levels of government—city, county, state, national, international—and with private and nonprofit agencies. Previously, he served for eight years as an evaluation official for the U.S. Department of Health and Human Services.

Appendix

Index to the Original Manuscript